Contemporary Perspectives on Research on Child Development Laboratory Schools in Early Childhood Education

A volume in
Contemporary Perspectives in Early Childhood Education
Olivia N. Saracho, *Series Editor*

Contemporary Perspectives on Research on Child Development Laboratory Schools in Early Childhood Education

edited by

Olivia N. Saracho

University of Maryland

INFORMATION AGE PUBLISHING, INC.
Charlotte, NC • www.infoagepub.com

Library of Congress Cataloging-in-Publication Data

A CIP record for this book is available from the Library of Congress
http://www.loc.gov

ISBN: 978-1-64113-635-8 (Paperback)
       978-1-64113-636-5 (Hardcover)
       978-1-64113-637-2 (ebook)

Printed in the United States of America

CONTENTS

PART III

FUNCTIONS OF CHILD DEVELOPMENT
LABORATORY SCHOOLS

PART IV

CONCLUSION

PART I

HISTORICAL PERSPECTIVE OF CHILD DEVELOPMENT LABORATORY SCHOOLS

CHAPTER 1

RESEARCH AND ISSUES ON CHILD DEVELOPMENT LABORATORY SCHOOLS

Olivia N. Saracho

Child development "laboratory schools are dedicated to research-based instruction and furthering innovation in education. Many of these schools are connected to universities, where students are able to benefit from university resources and best practices" (Khan, 2014, n.p.). They have been in existence on university campuses for centuries in the United States. The earliest colonial colleges (e.g., Harvard, Yale, William and Mary, University of Pennsylvania) administered Latin schools or departments to prepare students for college (Good & Teller, 1973). Rutgers Preparatory School was founded in 1768 and was linked to the university until the 1950s (Sperduto, 1967). During the course of time, the laboratory schools have changed to meet the needs of the teaching professionals and have frequently guided the instructional methods to improve the science and art of teaching (International Association of Laboratory Schools [IALS], 2018). They have also changed throughout the years from part-day, part-time programs (McBride, 1996; Myers & Palmer, 2017) to full-day care, some of which is inclusive of care offered through student service funds (Keyes, 1984; Shirah, 1988).

Contemporary Perspectives on Research on Child Development Laboratory Schools in Early Childhood Education, pages 3–14
Copyright © 2019 by Information Age Publishing

3

Traditionally, laboratory schools have been used to simultaneously support institutions in the preparation of teachers and provide high quality instructional programs for classroom children whose ages ranged from infancy through school-age. They were modeled after the teaching hospital as a laboratory for the preparation of medical professionals (National Council for the Accreditation of Teacher Education, 2001). Approximately, 75% of these child development laboratory schools have either been accredited or are in the process of getting their accreditation by the National Association for the Education of Young Children, which raises the quality of their early care and education programs (Carlson, 2003).

In the United States, more than half of the 4,000 higher education institutions offer early care and education programs (Carlson, 2003). Many laboratory schools are in operation in the United States and around the world. They were among the first preschools established in the United States. They are known by many names such as laboratory schools, demonstration schools, campus schools, model schools, university affiliated schools, child development schools, and so forth, and most have a connection to a college or university.

Universities, colleges, and other teacher education institutions administer and use them for the preparation of prospective teachers, educational experimentation, educational research, and professional development. The need for infant care (birth through age three) has prompted for infant rooms to become progressively prevalent laboratory preschool programs at colleges and universities in the United States (Myers & Palmer, 2017). Their enrollment may consist of either (a) only children of students, faculty, and staff or (b) children of parents from the surrounding community (Myers & Palmer, 2017). Children enrolled in the laboratory school range in ages from infant through school-age. However, some laboratory schools only have preschool or kindergarten children, although several focus on preschool through fifth or sixth grade, and some continue through high school. Such schools are associated with a college or university for explicit aims that go past the capacity of conventional public and private school settings (IALS, 2018).

Child development laboratories are used by a range of university majors, including speech pathology, audiology (Cook, 1984), medicine (Kourany, Humphreys, & Rabin, 1987; Puduano, 1978), teacher education, home economics, child development, family studies, and divisions in student, personnel service, or family housing, but the early childhood education and child development programs are the ones that used the laboratory schools to the maximum. Usually, programs require prospective teachers to engage in hands-on interactions with young children over the course of several weeks or an entire semester (Myers & Palmer, 2017). Numerous responsibilities are involved in the child development laboratory school's purpose, such as conducting research on (a) learning theory, (b) the children's growth and development, (c) on children, (d) the improvement of methodology and materials, and curriculum reform (Hendrick, 1980).

CHILD DEVELOPMENT LABORATORY SCHOOLS THREE-PART MISSION

The mission of the majority of child development laboratory schools consists of providing students with the opportunity to (a) experience and obtain a liberal education, (b) influence the world, (c) become socially responsible, and (d) become dependable citizens (Meacham, 2008). Thus, the child development laboratory schools at colleges and universities have established "a three-part mission: research (generating knowledge about child development), education (preparing teachers, therapists, and other child and family clinicians), and service (disseminating evidence-based information about child development and childrearing to parents and the general public)" (Elicker & Barbour, 2012, p. 139).

Conducting Research

From the beginning, university-based child development laboratory schools for preschool children have functioned as research sites where researchers conduct research to contribute to the knowledge base on child development and early childhood education. According to Osborn (1991), most of the research on child development was initiated in these laboratory schools. In 1883, Francis Wayland Parker, a pioneer of the progressive school movement in the United States, emphasized research on teaching (Campbell, 1965) at the Cook County Normal School of Chicago. In 1887, Nicholas Murray Butler (American philosopher, diplomat, educator, president of Columbia University) founded the Horace Mann School to serve as a coeducational experimental and developmental unit of Teachers College, Columbia University (Bauld & Kisslinger, 1987). In 1896, John Dewey created his well-known laboratory school at the University of Chicago. The school operated as a laboratory for experimentation with Dewey's philosophies concerning the child-centered curriculum. Dewey's work indicated his respect for relating inquiry to practice (Arnold-Grine, 2007; Barbour, 2003). Dewey believed that the laboratory schools were developed to test theory and enhance the knowledge of teaching and learning. Presently, there is an increased interest in the relationship between research and practice that helps develop educational concepts, test them, and replicate them in normal surroundings (Bonar, 1992; Provenzo, 1979).

Child development laboratory schools continue to provide opportunities to conduct research on different facets of child development and early childhood education, which has helped university faculty and students to relate theory, research, and practice. Faculty and students conduct research at child development laboratory schools to "generate and disseminate new knowledge and understanding of children, families, teachers, curriculum, and classroom processes" (McBride et al., 2012, p. 154).

Preparation of Teachers

Child development laboratory schools have considerably influenced the professional preparation of teachers, research, and progress in early childhood education (Barbour, 2003). They have distinctive assets for an early childhood educational environment, are usually located on the university grounds, and are used as a field experiences facility for preservice students who are pursuing a bachelor's degree in early childhood education. University professors provide theory and practice in their courses and use the laboratory school for preservice students to actually implement what they learned. The laboratory teachers assume several roles: (a) provide high quality instruction for the preschool children, and (b) demonstrate exemplary instructional methods for the preservice students who will become early childhood educators. As early as the 1820s, preservice students were practicing in schools and observing "model" instructional practices (Hendrick, 1980). The early childhood teacher preparation programs used the laboratory schools for research, teacher-training, teaching demonstration, teaching students about the young children's development (Osborn, 1991), experimentation of concepts, and testing theories.

THE VOLUME ON CHILD DEVELOPMENT
LABORATORY SCHOOLS

The present volume is composed of prominent researchers in child development laboratory schools who have contributed their academic work to this volume. The well-known researchers whose areas are in early childhood education, child development, and family and community studies, share their expertise in their manuscripts that anonymous reviewers accepted to be included in this volume. They describe the challenges that the child development laboratory schools have encountered and the progress of their movement. The volume is composed of four parts that include (a) the historical perspectives of child development laboratory schools, (b) models of child development laboratory schools, (c) roles of child development laboratory schools, and (d) concludes with insights and future research directions on child development laboratory schools. The first section provides background information on child development laboratory schools in early childhood education. In the first chapter titled, "Research and Issues on Child Development Laboratory Schools," Olivia N. Saracho discusses the importance of child development laboratory schools and provides an overview of the chapters in the volume. Then she identifies and describes several research strands and issues that were rooted in history.

HISTORICAL PERSPECTIVES

For more than two centuries, child development laboratory schools have been in existence as part of the university environment in Europe and America, although several documents indicate their beginnings were in the 1600s. Between 1850 and 1950, child development laboratory schools flourished (Hendrick, 1980). Through 1920, almost all foremost teacher preparation institutions in the country had a child development laboratory school on their college grounds. In addition, by the early 1920s, numerous universities had started to establish child development laboratory school programs (Osborn, 1991). These were basically laboratory schools for very young children. Although there is some disagreement about when and where the first child development laboratory school was established, it has been obvious for numerous centuries of their value in their use for guided, supervised student teaching; the demonstration of appropriate educational procedures (Lamb, 1962); conducting research on several facets of child development; and serving as model programs in early childhood education for the national and local educational communities (McBride, 1996). The first section describes historical perspectives. In the chapter titled, "Historical Development and Influences of Laboratory Schools," Olivia N. Saracho examines the historical development and influences of the child development laboratory schools. It begins with the origins of early childhood education and its early educational philosophers such as Comenius, Jean Jacques Rousseau, and Robert Owen. Then it describes the different institutions at that time including the primary school, "knitting school," infant school, kindergarten, child care centers including the different types of settings (such as center care; family day care; in-home, relative care; and no supplementary care), Head Start centers and nursery schools. Then it discusses the transformation of nursery schools to parent-cooperative nursery schools, works progress administration (WPA) emergency nursery schools, laboratory nursery schools, and child development laboratory schools. It also describes the origin and current status of the International Association of Laboratory Schools. It concludes with a summary of the historical perspectives and evolvement of the child development laboratory schools.

Child development laboratory (CDL) settings have had a century of venerable history. Originally conceptualized as venues for child study and knowledge generation to inform education and services for young children and families, CDLs have had to reexamine their purpose and place in the field of social sciences in tight economic times. Both the benefits and drawbacks of university based CDLs are explored. In this chapter titled, "A Consortium of University-Affiliated Child Development Laboratories for Applied Developmental Science: A Hypothetical Journey," Nancy Barbour, Andrew Stremmel, D. Reece Wilson, and Jennifer Kampmann consider the evolution of the CDL over the last 100 years and the potential for them to engage in research that corresponds with the principles of applied development science. They describe a hypothetical journey of three university laboratories that formed a consortium of CDLs to conduct cross-site research in the tradition of applied development science as a way of assisting CDLs to maximize their utility in the 21st century.

University-based CDL schools for infants, toddlers, and preschoolers have a long and rich history. Since their inception in the middle of the 1920s, they have assumed a vital role in adding to the ever expanding knowledge base on child development and early childhood education. In recent years, many laboratory school programs have shifted from providing traditional half-day, preschool classes to offering full-day child care programs, while at the same time maintaining the teacher training and research functions associated with the laboratory schools. Although offering full-day child care classes has expanded opportunities for laboratory schools to facilitate teacher training and research activities, it has also brought on many challenges not faced when working with half-day preschool classes. In the chapter titled, "Academics vs. Service in Child Development Laboratory Schools: Complementary and Competing Pressures," Brent A. McBride and Meghan Fisher provide an overview of these unique challenges and discuss possible strategies that laboratory school programs can implement in order to overcome such challenges.

MODELS OF CHILD DEVELOPMENT LABORATORY SCHOOLS

Child development laboratory schools have been essential adjuncts for most of the teacher education institutions. They vary in name and purpose. According to Perodin (1955),

From its earliest beginnings, a distinctive feature of teacher education has been the use of an actual school for children. Names given to these children's schools have varied according to their purposes. In the early days of teacher education in this country, they were named "model schools." Afterward, several were labeled "practice schools," then "training schools," and later, they were referred to as "laboratory schools," which has come into usage. (Perrodin, 1955, p. 1)

The original model or practice schools in the United States were privately owned and run like the teacher training institutions with which they were associated. For example, "Mother Seton's Teacher Training School," was established in 1808 and located in Emmitsburg, Maryland (Perrodin, 1955). The first laboratory schools were usually used as model schools, practice schools, or demonstration schools. Then both their purpose and title changed, such as "campus schools" or "laboratory schools." However, the beginning of the somewhat unrestricted, publicly sponsored normal schools in the United States failed to provide many of the novice teachers with the advantages of some professional education, including supervising their work with children. Specifically, after the Civil War, more normal schools were instituted and more teachers were needed. Therefore, laboratory schools became necessary. The normal schools initially opposed the scientific movement in education, but a small number of laboratory schools rapidly became remarkable contributors in educational research. John Dewey and Charles H. Judd at the University of Chicago and J. L. Meriam at the University of Missouri led the educational research movement that contributed to the development and progress of the laboratory schools (Lamb, 1962), which can be found in many of the present CDL schools. In the chapter titled, "An Innovative Early Childhood Laboratory School Contemporary Model," Elizabeth Schlesinger-Devlin and Megan L. Purcell discuss how one early childhood laboratory school serves as a pedagogical model for innovation within the field of early childhood education. Laboratory schools on university campuses often hold to the same three tenets of research, education, and service, as does the larger university community. These three "arms" serve as a basis for innovation. Elizabeth Schlesinger-Devlin and Megan L. Purcell describe how one early childhood laboratory school addresses the three arms in innovation. First, they provide a brief history of early childhood laboratory schools in general along with the history of the Ben and Maxine Miller Child Development Laboratory School (MCDLS) at Purdue University. Second, they include an in-depth discussion of current research occurring at the MCDLS. Finally, they present educational practices of the early childhood program along with university professional preparation programs and opportunities for service within the community and state. Throughout the chapter, Elizabeth

Schlesinger-Devlin and Megan L. Purcell discuss the benefits for teachers, children, families, university faculty, and MCDLS staff.

Laboratory schools for young children in colleges and universities have a long and rich history in Canada. Over this history, an understanding of the child has shifted. In the chapter titled, "From the Scientific Child to the Reconceptualized Child in Canadian University and College Early Childhood Laboratory Schools," Rachel Langford uses a critical analysis of the literature to examine the shift from a scientific view of the child associated with the child study and progressive education movements to a reconceptualized view of the child. The premise of her chapter is that different understandings of the child are entangled in the history of Canadian laboratory schools. Examining this shifting perspective is important because the paradigm or mindset that early childhood researchers and educators adopt to understand the child in a laboratory school communicates their research and pedagogical priorities and practices (Moss, 2014). For example, in the chapter titled, "Keeping Relevant in Changing Times: The Evolution of a University Laboratory School," Monica Miller Marsh, Martha Lash, Pam Hutchins, and Rochelle Hostler describe the Kent State University Child Development Center (CDC), which is considered an internationally known laboratory school that has evolved over time as it strives to stay relevant in a university setting that is constantly shifting and changing in response to social, economic, and political forces. They described how the Kent State University Child Development Center has become more closely aligned with the Early Childhood Education program by becoming an authorized International Baccalaureate Primary Years Program (IB PYP) world school. In addition, it has strengthened the children's program, moved the work of the CDC into the international realm, and aligned the CDC with the university's strategic plan. Simultaneously, the CDC continues to make an impact at the local level upholding and maintaining John Dewey's original purposes for laboratory schools. Monica Miller Marsh, Martha Lash, Pam Hutchins, and Rochelle Hostler document and analyze the effects of the changes with the introduction of the IB PYP to both the Center and the Kent State Early Childhood Education program.

ROLES OF CHILD DEVELOPMENT LABORATORY SCHOOLS

Traditionally, the role of CDL schools has been to train beginning teachers and model appropriate teaching techniques. Throughout time, their role has transformed. Most laboratory schools have developed into educational research centers and laboratories to validate educational theories (West & Gadsden, 1973). Still, the need for additional roles is becoming progressively more obvious. CDL schools need to provide a bridge between theory and practice. Other roles continue to emerge. For example, in the chapter titled, "The Role of the Child Development Laboratory School in a 21st Century Liberal Education," Sharon Carnahan addresses the function of the CDL school in a 21st century liberal education. She summarizes the historical context of laboratory schools and the parallel development of campus children's centers. Then she provides a discussion of the modern mission of the CDL school and how it has developed in a campus context as part of a strategic plan. The American Association of Colleges and Universities High Impact Practices are linked to laboratory school implementations. Next Sharon Carnahan discusses campus concerns about a CDL's mission and provides two plans for the liberal arts CDL schools of the future, which consist of (a) increasing interdisciplinary initiatives and (b) including cooperatives for applied developmental science and social entrepreneurship.

Laboratory preschools assume an important role in training teachers and disseminating appropriate practices for guiding children's social-emotional development. These guidance practices encompass the ways that teachers are expected to respond to the children's expression of ideas and display of emotions and support children's relationships with peers and adults (Gartrell, 2004). Laboratory preschools also generate knowledge about professional development for the early childhood education workforce. Social-emotional development and its associated guidance practices are a core focus in early childhood education theory, research, and practice. In the chapter titled, "The Role of Laboratory Preschools in the Promotion of High-Quality Social-Emotional Guidance Practices," Rebecca Swartz presents a review of the literature addressing adult-level, social-emotional factors that may influence social-emotional guidance practices. She uses the affective organization of parenting (Dix, 1991) and social convoy theory (Kahn & Antonucci, 1980) as theoretical frameworks to elucidate the variations in adult social-emotional resources among teachers that may influence their social-emotional guidance practices during daily routines and activities. These frameworks provide directions for the development of future research and practices related to social-emotional guidance. In addition, she discusses the role of laboratory preschools in (a) training teachers to use effective social-emotional guidance practices, (b) developing and disseminating teacher training pedagogy related to these practices, and (c) demonstrating these practices to their communities.

High-quality early childhood education is associated with a compelling range of immediate and long-term benefits for children, families, and society. Play-based early childhood education programs have been identified as the most conducive to achieving high-quality outcomes for children in the early years. However research continues to highlight the "schoolification" of the young children's earliest experiences, whereby child-led curricula and playful pedagogy are replaced by a focus on pre-academic skills, direct instruction, and standardized testing. Linked to the accountability agenda, this intensification of children's early years' experiences is leading to an emerging global quality crisis in early childhood education that unless disrupted has the potential to negatively impact children's learning and development. In the chapter titled, "Early Childhood Teacher-as-Researcher: An Imperative in the Age of 'Schoolification': Harnessing Dewey's Concept of the Laboratory School to Disrupt the Emerging Global Quality Crisis in Early Childhood Education," Emer Ring, Lisha O'Sullivan, and Marie Ryan suggest that situating the concept of the early childhood teacher as researcher within the framework of Dewey's laboratory school has the potential to support early childhood teachers in countering the threats to quality stemming from the schoolification movement. They assume that this concept provides the field with a much-needed remedy to prevent an emerging global quality crisis in early childhood education. Then Emer Ring, Lisha O'Sullivan, and Marie Ryan recommend possible scaffolds for developing the teacher-as-researcher role.

CONCLUSION

Throughout the previous century, college and university institutions have established CDL schools. In the early 1900s, they were initially considered to be sites for the recent discipline of child study but their purposes have progressed gradually. They also have assumed a fundamental function in promoting teaching, research, and service (such as outreach/engagement practice) in child development and early childhood education. However, a lot of them had to struggle for their survival when economic periods turned out to be problematic. Several extended operating programs were discontinued (Barbour & McBride, 2017). In the last chapter titled, "Child Development Laboratory Schools: Contemporary Research and Future Directions," Olivia N. Saracho reviews some research developments. She also describes the contributions of CDL schools including (a) their professional organization and international partnerships, (b) a proposal for the future, and (c) mission statements for contemporary universities. She proposes a theoretical framework for CDL schools and concludes with several recommendations for research and practice. Together, this collection of innovative papers emphasizes the importance of CDL schools. Although the volume has a wide representation of researchers and topics in CDL schools, it is assumed that there continues to be a void in the research literature. A wide-ranging scale of studies needs to be conducted to fill the gaps and offer insights about the CDL schools. However, the chapters in the volume can provide a better understanding on some areas on CDL schools.

REFERENCES

Arnold-Grine, L. (2007). *Laboratory schools: A critical link in facilitating and enhancing preschool teacher education.* (Unpublished doctoral dissertation). The Ohio State University, Columbus, Ohio.

Barbour, N. (2003). The early history of child development laboratory programs. In B. McBride & N. Barbour (Eds.), *Bridging the gap between theory, research and practice: The role of child development laboratory programs in early childhood education* (pp. 9–29). Kidlington, Oxford: Elsevier.

Barbour, N. E., & McBride, B. A. (2017). An Introduction to the future of child development laboratory settings—A consortium for applied. In N. E. Barbour & B. A. McBride (Eds.), The future of child development lab schools: Applied developmental science in action (pp. 1–3). New York, NY: Taylor and Francis.

Bauld, H. J., & Kisslinger, J. B. (1987). *Horace Mann-Barnard: The first hundred years.* New York, NY: Horace Mann.

Bonar, B. D. (1992). The role of laboratory schools in American education. *National Association of Laboratory Schools Journal, 17*(1), 42–53.

Campbell, J. K. (1965). *The children's crusader: Colonel Francis W. Parker.* New York, NY: Teachers College Press.

Carlson, D. (2003). Campus early care and education centers: A national description. St. Cloud, MN: National Coalition for Campus Children's Center.

Cook, R. (1984). University involvement: A key to campus child care survival. *Focus on Learning, 10*(1), 17–25.

Dix, T. (1991). The affective organization of parenting: Adaptive and maladaptative processes. *Psychological Bulletin, 110*(1), 3–25. doi:10.1037/0033-2909.110.1.3

Elicker, J., & Barbour, N. (2012). Introduction to the special issue on university laboratory preschools in the 21st century. *Early Education & Development, 23*(2), 139–142. doi:10.1080/10409289.2012.649665

Gartrell, D. (2004). *The power of guidance: Teaching social-emotional skills in early childhood classrooms.* Clifton Park, NY: Thomson/Delmar Learning.

Good, H. G., & Teller, J. D. (1973). *A history of education in America.* New York, NY: Macmillan.

Hendrick, I. G. (1980). University controlled laboratory schools in historical perspective. *UCLA Educator, 21*(2), 55–59.

International Association of Laboratory Schools. (2018). About Us. Retrieved from http://laboratoryschools.org/about-us/16-about-us

Kahn, R. L., & Antonucci, T. C. (1980).Convoys across the life course: Attachment, roles, and social support. In P. B. Baltes & O. Brim (Eds.), *Life span development and behavior* (Vol. 3, pp. 253–286). New York, NY: Academic Press.

Khan, S. (2014). *What is a lab school? Khan lab school.* Retrieved from https://khan-labschool.org/what-lab-school

Keyes, C. (1984). Campus child care centers: Diversity and changes. *Focus on Learning, 10*(1), 35–44.

Kourany, R., Humphreys, L., & Rabin, P. (1987). Observation of children in a child care program as a teaching aid for medical students. *Journal of Psychiatric Education, 11*(3), 171–177.

Lamb, P. M. (1962). The laboratory school: An historical perspective. *The Journal of Educational Research, 56*(2), 107–109.

McBride, B. (1996). University-based child development laboratory programs: Emerging issues and challenges. *Early Childhood Education Journal, 24*(1), 17–21.

McBride, B., Groves, M., Barbour, N., Horm, D., Stremmel, A., Lash, M., . . . Toussaint, S. (2012). Child development laboratory schools as generators of knowledge in early childhood education: New models and approaches. *Early Education & Development, 23*(2), 153–164. doi:10.1080/10409289.2012.651068

Meacham, J. (2008). What's the use of a mission statement? *Academe, 94*(1), 21–24.

Moss, P. (2014). *Transformative change and real utopias in early childhood education: A story of democracy, experimentation, and potentiality.* Abingdon, England: Routledge.

Myers, K. A., & Palmer, L. B. (2017). Impact of campus child care director leadership and activities on the internal success and integration of the campus center. *Journal of Early Childhood Research, 15*(1), 99–112. https://doi.org/10.1177/1476718X15577008

National Council for Accreditation of Teacher Education. (2001). *Teaching hospital model comes to schools of education: Can address quality and shortage issues.* Washington, DC: Author.

Osborn, D. K. (1991). Early childhood education in historical perspective (3rd ed.). Athens, GA: Education Associates.

Perrodin, A. F. (1955). *The development of laboratory schools in teacher education. Functions of laboratory schools in teacher education.* Lock Haven, PA: The Association for Student Teaching.

Provenzo, E. F. (1979). History as experiment: The role of the laboratory school in the development of John Dewey's philosophy of history. *History Teacher, 12*(3), 373–382.

Puduano, M. A. (1978). Bringing about learning in the college laboratory. *Journal of Nursing Education, 17*(6), 30–33.

Shirah, S. (1988). Campus child care: Meeting unique needs. *Journal of Instructional Psychology, 15*(4), 135–137.

Sperduto, F. F. (1967). *A history of Rutgers Preparatory School.* Somerset, NJ: Rutgers Preparatory School.

West, F., & Gadsden, T. (1973). A major role for laboratory schools. *Educational Leadership, 30*(5), 412–415.

CHAPTER 2

HISTORICAL DEVELOPMENT AND INFLUENCES OF LABORATORY SCHOOLS

Olivia N. Saracho

ABSTRACT

This chapter examines the historical development, issues, and influences of the child development laboratory schools. It begins with the origins of early childhood education, its early educational philosophers such as Comenius, Jean Jacques Rousseau, and Robert Owen. Then it describes the different institutions at that time including the primary school, "knitting school," infant school, kindergarten, child care centers (including the different types such as center care, family day care, in-home, relative care, and no supplementary care), Head Start centers and nursery schools. Then it discusses the transformation of nursery schools to parent-cooperative nursery schools, Works Progress Administration (WPA) emergency nursery schools, laboratory nursery schools, and child development laboratory schools. It also describes the origin and current status of the International Association of Laboratory Schools. It concludes with a summary of the historical perspective and evolvement of the child development laboratory schools.

Contemporary Perspectives on Research on Child Development Laboratory Schools in Early Childhood Education,
pages 15–45
15

THE ORIGINS OF EARLY CHILDHOOD EDUCATION

Early childhood education programs have existed in the United States since colonial eras. Although the number of children who attended primary schools has continued to be the same since World War II, the number of children in preprimary school (e.g., preschool, kindergarten) has increased. Several institutions in the United States have offered early childhood education programs, such as preschools, nursery schools, child care centers, Head Start programs, prekindergartens, kindergartens, and primary classes. These programs have several similar components, although they differ in institutional environments, children's ages, programs' foundations, programs' goals, and psychological theories.

The care and education of young children have taken place for centuries, but at a much later time were schools formed specifically for this purpose. However, families were responsible for informally educating and caring for young children. As far back as the ancient Greeks, educational philosophers were concerned for young children. For instance, Plato wrote at length about education. Even so, present education is more a result of contemporary educators and philosophers, than of ancient ones. It started when schools were particularly planned for young children and when institutions were established to care for groups of young children independent of their home.

Early Educational Philosophers

In 1628, Comenius wrote *School of Infancy* (published in 1896). It included his concept about the "school of the mother's lap," that is, children from birth to 6 years of age learned the basics of all knowledge (Osborn, 1991). Comenius' course of study included

> simple lessons in objects, [children were] taught to know stones, plants, and animals; the names and uses of the members of the body; to distinguish light and darkness and colors; the Geography of the cradle, the room, the farm, the street, and the field; trained in moderation, purity and obedience, and taught to say the Lord's Prayer. (Monroe, 1908, p. ix)

In 1658, Comenius published the first children's illustrated picture book, *Orbis Pictus* (Comenius, 1658), which was used as a textbook for children. It was originally published in Latin and German and has been translated into several other languages.

A century later Jean Jacques Rousseau wrote his classic book, *Emile* (1762/1911), which described the importance of early childhood education. Rousseau thought that education must start at birth and proceed until

25 years of age. He stressed the need to reinforce young children's actual growth rather than teaching them to socialize and getting them ready for life. He stated:

> Freedom, not power, is the greatest good. That man is truly free who desires what he is able to perform, and does what he desires. This is my fundamental maxim. Apply it to childhood, and all the rules of education spring from it. (Rousseau, 1762/1911, p. 48)

Rousseau believed that a sense perception was the basis for human knowledge. This belief is also integrated in Robert Owen's Infant School, Maria Montessori's *Casa Dei Bambini*, and current early childhood programs. The following section describes several institutions that were committed to the education and care of young children including those in America, Colonial periods, and European ancestries.

INSTITUTIONS FOR THE EDUCATION AND CARE OF YOUNG CHILDREN

In America, young children would begin primary school or what was referred to as *common school*. In this school, all of the children in the community were taught fundamental concepts. The majority of the children's education consisted of the common school; therefore, these children were unprepared to attend a secondary school or college. Some of the individuals who attended college skipped the common school, but in their early years they were taught at home. Spodek and Saracho (1994) provide the following descriptions of the institutions at that time: the primary school, the "knitting school," the infant school, the kindergarten, child care centers, Head Start centers, and nursery schools.

The Primary School

The purposes of modern primary education were based on those from colonial primary education. Particularly in the New England colonies, the focus was on a religious conviction that expected individuals to know how to read the scriptures in their specific language. This prompted the founding of primary schools under the administration of the neighborhood church. The reason for the schools was to teach reading that concentrated in spelling, grammar, and arithmetic, which was included soon after. The introduction to the Puritan School Law of 1647 offers confirmation of the religious backgrounds of colonial primary education. This confirmation is observed below:

> It being one chief point of that old deluder, Satan, to keep men from the knowledge of the Scriptures, as in former times, by keeping them in an unknown tongue, so in these latter times, by persuading from the use of tongues, that so at last the true sense and meaning of the original might be clouded by false glosses of saint-seeming deceivers, that learning might not be buried in the grave of our fathers in church and commonwealth, the Lord assisting our endeavors...It is therefore ordered that every township in this jurisdiction, after the Lord has increased them to the number of fifty householders, shall then forthwith appoint one within their own town to teach all such children as shall resort to him to write and read. (Nohle, 1898, pp. 24–25)

When the American colonies converted into a country after the revolutionary war, schools eliminated their religious value. Since the United States Constitution (a) did not endorse a specific religion, (b) was responsible for the separation of the church and state, (c) did not require the government to support religious schools, and (d) education was not referenced in the Constitution to be the federal government's obligation, the states became responsible for the schools. Therefore, the primary schools' function was to offer instruction in the basic subjects. At this level, reading, writing, and arithmetic were the main subject areas of learning and teaching. While other subject areas were part of the primary grades, they were not considered as important as the original subject areas.

The "Knitting School"

In 1767, Jean Frederick Oberlin developed the first school for young children. He was a Protestant minister who resided in Alsace, an eastern region in France. While Oberlin founded the school, his wife, Madame Madeleine Oberlin, did the teaching until her death in 1784. She was assisted by Sarah Banzet and Louise Scheppler, who also was the housekeeper in the Oberlin house. Children as young as 2 or 3 years of age attended the Oberlin school, which included teaching handicrafts, exercise, and play. The children would meet in a circle around Louise Scheppler, who would talk to them while she knitted. Soon older children assumed several of her tasks.

Before Oberlin's death, his "knitting school" extended to five neighboring village centers. Oberlin's procedures were usually rejected in other sections of France. In addition, the French Revolution and religious clerics considered them to be suspicious. Because Oberlin was a minister, French citizens were worried that his teaching would be both religious and counter revolutionary. Oberlin was esteemed both during and after the revolution, but his "knitting school" continued to be a detached phenomenon in France and the concept failed to spread out into Europe.

The Infant School

In 1816, Robert Owen, a social reformer, established in Britain the infant school, a type of primary education, in New Lanark, Scotland. The initial philosophies of infant education were

> that the children were to be out of doors as much as possible and to learn "when their curiosity induced them to ask questions," to dance and sing and not to be "annoyed with books." They were to be educated and trained without punishment or the fear of it, no unnecessary restraint was to be imposed on them and they were to be taught only "what they could understand." The teachers were told to think about such matters as forming good habits and helping the children to treat each other kindly. (Gardner, 1949, p. 6)

Pestalozzi and Rousseau inspired Robert Owen to create schools and a child care center for children of families who were working in his mill in New Lanark, Scotland. He prohibited very young children from working in his mill and restricted the number of working hours of children who were below 12 years old. They were only allowed to work 6 hours a day but children older than 12 years of age could work between 12 to 14 hours a day. During that period, the general practice was for children who were 6 years of age to work 12 hours daily without lunch break. They also did not receive any education (Osborn, 1991). Owen's school was formed as a portion of the extensive program on social reform. Owen's development of the infant school forestalled several of the modern educators' doubts.

The infant school helped the poor and working class children and extended beyond Owen's mill town. By 1825, there was a minimum of 55 infant schools in England, Scotland, Ireland, and several infant school societies. Owen's books were disseminated all over Continental Europe and the United States. By 1827, infant schools were being launched in Hartford, Connecticut; New York City; Philadelphia; Boston; and other American cities. Robert Owen arrived in the United States throughout this time and advocated at length around his latest beliefs of society and education. He bought from the Rappites, a religious order, the settlement of New Harmony in Indiana where he formed a communitarian society. In addition, he started an infant school. Both the school and the community had severe difficulties and after a few brief years, it failed. For approximately another decade, infant schools succeeded in New England and middle Atlantic communities. In the middle of the 1830s, the infant school movement had disappeared in America (Strickland, 1982).

The infant schools that developed represented the humanitarian origi-
nalities and principles of education that could be useful to the public primary schools. Social reformers supported the infant schools because they
perceived them to be a means of preventing the problems of urban life.
More important, it was anticipated that educating and socializing young
children from poor families in the infant schools would eliminate poverty forever. They offered a process for both moral and literary education
for the children of the urban poor whereas simultaneously released their
mothers to be able to work (May & Vinovskis, 1977). Less than a fourth of a
century after the end of the infant school movement, the Fröbelian kindergarten emerged in the United States.

The Kindergarten

The kindergarten is an exclusive educational institution that has its personal specific foundation. During the beginning of the 19th century, it was
created in Germany. The kindergarten curriculum was grounded on a spiritual religious philosophy involving the unity of nature, God, and humanity.
To represent these relationships, Friedrich Fröbel developed a sequence of
activities for 3- to 6-year-old children. The Fröbelian kindergarten was intended to utilize the *gifts*, the *occupations*, and the *mother's songs and plays* as
part of the activities. It would also assist young children to learn how to take
care of plants and animals. Eventually, the Fröbelian kindergarten started
to develop as an educational movement. The expansion of kindergarten
education required kindergarten teachers to be trained in that philosophy.
Before long kindergarten training institutions captured the interest of several young German women to become their students.

The wave of German migration in the middle of the 19th century at-
tracted numerous women who had kindergarten training to travel to the
United States. The wish to use the principles of the Fröbelian kindergarten with their individual children motivated them to set kindergartens in
their homes. Margarethe Schurz, a trained kindergarten teacher in Germany, invited her relatives' children to join her children at her home.
This became the original American kindergarten, founded in Watertown,
Wisconsin in 1856 (Swart, 1967). During the 1860s and 1870s, additional
German-speaking kindergartens were founded in several communities in
the United States.

Margarethe Schurz motivated Elizabeth Peabody to read about kindergarten education. In 1859, Elizabeth Peabody had a casual encounter
with Margaretha Schruz and became interested in kindergarten education. Mrs. Schruz gave her a booklet that had a portion of Fröbel's book
titled, *Education of Man* (Peabody, 1882). In 1860, Peabody opened the first

English-speaking kindergarten in Boston, Massachusetts based on Fröbel's philosophy (Snyder, 1972). In 1873, kindergartens were initiated into the public schools at St. Louis, Missouri. After 1890, the kindergartens expanded in greater numbers into the public school systems. In 1900, public-school kindergarten children were almost twice as many than private-school kindergarten children. But their complete presence in public education occurred around a century later. Private kindergartens were found in various cities throughout the interim, though they were supported by several associations, mothers' clubs, and philanthropic organizations. By 1914, all major cities in the United States had instituted public kindergartens (Ross, 1976). However, the curriculum had started to be modified and subject areas were presented. Although nature study, home and community life, literature, music, and art were at the basics, "each subject was determined by its ability to assist children in confirming and extending their daily life" (Weber, 1969, p. 96).

The kindergarten was considered to help the children of the poor in these early days. The quick increase of urban centers, the Europeans' immigration to America, and the expansion of huge city slums led to the creation of philanthropic kindergartens in numerous regions. Disputes helped to maintain kindergarten education for the underprivileged. For example, Fisher's (1908) *Report on the United States Commissioner of Education* (1867–1907) stated the following:

> Centering among, and concerning itself with, the children of the poor, and having for its aim the elevation of the home, it was natural that the kindergarten as a philanthropic movement should win great and early favor. The mere fact that the children of the slums were kept off the streets, and that they were made clean and happy by kind and motherly young women; that the child thus being cared for enabled the mother to go about her work in or outside the home—all this appealed to the heart of America, and America gave freely to make these kindergartens possible. Churches established kindergartens, individuals endowed kindergartens, and associations were organized for the spread and support of kindergartens in nearly every large city. (Fisher, 1908, as cited in Vanderwalker, 1908, pp. 19–20)

At the opening of the 20th century, an important disagreement surfaced in American kindergarten education. Conservative kindergarten educators thought that Fröbel had found the important components of education for young children that were pertinent to all children for all eras. A more liberal group considered that Fröbel's educational philosophy had a better meaning than the precise educational undertakings and the techniques resulting from it. Such liberal groups believed that, even though the initial kindergarten program was a movement in the right direction, detailed activities that are inadequate should to be removed. The appearance of the Child Study Movement, which began to create an experimental basis for knowledge about childhood, and the progressive education movement, which concentrated on autonomy and activity in the classroom, supported the liberal kindergartners.

The evolving philosophy of the reform kindergarten movement was perhaps best declared by Patty Smith Hill in the *Second Report of the Committee of Nineteen of the International Kindergarten Union* (International Kindergarten Union, Committee of Nineteen, 1913). She thought that the content of the kindergarten program must be connected to the children's current life instead of the life of children from a different culture and generation. They needed to be assisted to obtain the knowledge of the civilization through the children's individual experiences as a way to understand knowledge. Hill suggested actual child-oriented experiences and classroom play that were grounded on the normal activities of childhood. Children should be allowed to rebuild their own reality.

The reform movement attempted to preserve Fröbel's philosophy but deleting pointless formalism of the kindergarten method. Educators reinforced several components of the Fröbelian philosophy such as the following:

1. *The Concept of Development in Childhood.* Fröbel proposed that education for young children must vary in practice and content from that presented to older children. Although Fröbel's philosophy of child development differs from the current knowledge, the supposition that education should be developmentally pertinent continues to be valuable.

2. *Education as Self-Activity.* Education progresses as the human organism develops. The children's educational activity reinforces this developing procedure. Although child development has shifted from an approval of a "developing" progression, the notion of education as self-activity continues to be maintained in education.

3. *The Educational Value of Play.* Fröbel perceived play as an essential activity in assisting the children to grow and learn. During play, Fröbel viewed the children's symbolic replicas of adult activity. He tried to extract their important features and arrange them in an important sequence in his educational program. Presently, educators continue to advocate this conception of play in young children's education.

The kindergarten activists believed that several of the activities were inappropriate. As the play of American children varied from that of German children, various types of play activities must be promoted. Also, the activists believed that the children's present life must have a basis for learning.

Children's play had more autonomy and represented their life by including large blocks for building, dolls to represent families, and small housekeeping supplies.

The transformation of kindergarten education lasted throughout the 1920s and 1930s, directing the formation of the kindergarten that is found in our present society. Since the 1920s, several influences led to the expansion of kindergarten education. The shifting economy of the 1930s and 1940s reduced the quantity of public school kindergartens. Deficiencies in reserves and construction areas throughout this period led to the elimination of this education program from the public schools. Toward the end of the 1950s and the beginning of the 1960s, kindergarten education started to get a more encouraging interest and response. A fear for the children's intellectual development prompted a reevaluation of kindergarten curricula. Also, psychological theory indicated the value of early education and advocated to expand public assistance for kindergartens and the distribution of kindergarten education to huge quantities of children in various states.

Child Care Centers

Child care centers were the result of the Industrial Revolution. Previous to that time, women would work at home taking care of children (both theirs and others). The development of the factory structure that required the employment of huge amounts of women triggered the demand to take care of young children whose mothers were working throughout the whole work day. Throughout this time, the day nurseries helped the working class. Servants took care of the young children for middle and upper classes.

Child care centers (also known as day care centers or day nurseries) differed from the above institutions. They were initially intended to function as custodial instead of educational. The American day nursery was based on the French *crèche*, which means "crib." The earliest_*crèche* was founded in Paris in 1844 to relieve working mothers, prevent infant mortality, and provide instructions on hygiene. Then in 1854 the New York Nursery and Child's Hospital established the first American day nursery which began in New York City (Forest, 1927).

During the last half of the 19th century a large quantity of day nurseries were launched in the United States, frequently by settlement houses or philanthropic groups wanting to assist the children of immigrant and poor working women. Occasionally Fröbelian activities were offered to the children. Frequently, the single obligation of the caregiver was to maintain the children nourished, clean, and safe. Matriarchs cleaned and got meals ready as well as oversaw the care of a wide-ranging age of children (e.g., infants, toddlers, nursery-age children).

In the 1920s, nursery schools were introduced in the United States and day nurseries started to use educational programs. Throughout the next period, child care centers organized their age groups similar to the nursery schools including admitting only those children who were already toilet-trained. Nursery school teachers were prepared as educators and worked with caregivers who were informally trained.

All through World War II there was an extraordinary increase in child care centers in the United States. The Lanham Act of 1941 granted federal funds for child care on a matching basis to war-impacted communities. These were established to increase the number of women working during the war. Several of the Lanham Act centers were produced as emergency centers but were highly qualified programs. They offered staff training and satisfactory provision for materials and equipment. Various centers were opened 24 hours daily because there were three working shifts available for working mothers (Hymes, 1995).

In 1946, shortly after the end of the war, the Lanham Act was terminated and with it federal support for child care services. Where child care continued to be provided, it was much more limited. Often it was considered a child welfare service, a temporary aid to a family who had difficulty assuming traditional child-rearing responsibilities.

In the past 3 decades the demand has increased for child care as a normal service to families. Women from all social classes were seeking greater equality and finding that the lack of child care interfered with continual employment and promotion to positions of greater responsibility.

The history of child care centers had numerous phases of development and reconceptualization. Margaret O'Brien Steinfels (1973) described three phases in the history of the field. First, before 1920, child care centers were perceived to be an indispensable assistance to underprivileged working mothers. The accessibility of this assistance frequently permitted both fathers and mothers to work therefore accelerating the improvement of their social movement. Between 1920 to 1940, child care services were reduced and restricted, it was only available under circumstances of exclusive need. A stigma was attributed to them through the 1960s. Since the middle of the 1960s, child care amenities were once more considered to be indispensable to employed women, regardless of economic status. The assumption has extended this assistance to both mothers who (a) want to work and (b) need to work.

Numerous different reasons are attributed to the modification in attitudes concerning child care centers. Definitely the changing position of women in our society, the expansion in urbanization, and the change to a nuclear family are some reasons. In addition, the increasing body of knowledge that shows that a good-quality child care program has a positive outcome on young children and that day-to-day separation of mother from child throughout working hours is better than a complete separation (e.g., family breakup, death). Those who advocate and offer extended child care services need to be concerned about the quality of child care services (e.g., facilities, program, staff).

Various individuals and agencies offered several kinds of child care in different settings. Professional child care is mainly center care, while family day care might also have a professional element. Willer et al. (1991) identified and defined the following types of child care.

- *Center care:* Establishments where children are cared for in a group setting for all or part of the day. Centers can be categorized by their legal status and auspice [into] nonprofit centers, both sponsored and independent; and for-profit centers, both independent and members of a chain. Nonprofit, sponsored programs are further categorized by auspices, including those sponsored by Head Start, public schools, religious organizations, or other sponsors, such as employers or community agencies.
- *Family day care:* Care provided for a group of children in the caregiver's home. Often a family day care provider is a mother with children of her own at home. Family day care may be regulated or nonregulated. Nonregulated care includes providers who are not licenced or registered whether. . . .
- *In-home care:* Care provided by a nonrelative who comes into the home. Sometimes the provider brings her own children along into the home.
- *Relative care:* Care provided by a relative in the child's home or the relative's home.
- *No supplementary care:* Parents provide all care for their children or use nonparental arrangements only on an irregular basis. (p. 3).

Child care centers were eligible to obtain federal funds when they assisted low-income families who were entitled to receive cash assistance under Title XX of the Social Security Act. The state received funds (e.g., 75% of the cost of child care programs) according to the population that was entitled to Title XX assistance. Presently, more child care programs are accessible than they have been in previous decades, but there is variability in programs' support. Formerly, most of the child care programs served poor families and were supported by community and philanthropic agencies, although a small number of centers were privately owned, frequently by the individuals who managed them. Nowadays, the majority of the centers are run for profit, usually owned by a chain of companies or franchised centers. Children from every social strata are helped in these centers.

Head Start

Both the nursery school and the Montessori school were initially intended to help young children from poor families. When both of these programs were launched in the United States, they mainly assisted children from wealthy families, although several nursery schools and Montessori schools converted into a fraction of social service agencies helping the poor. Public funds did support such programs. All through the majority of American history it was assumed that it was best for parents to educate their young children. Such assumption had a radical transformation when the federal government established the Head Start program.

In 1965, President Lyndon B. Johnson announced a "war on poverty," designing Community Action Programs to assist poor communities. A community action program was Head Start, an all-embracing child development program to help children before they entered the public schools. The first Head Start program had 4- and 5-year-old children attend school during the summer for an 8 week period because during that period the majority of 5-year-old children were not able to attend kindergarten. Recognizing that the aims of the program were unrealistic because they could not be reached in 2 months, the program shortly functioned throughout the school year. Currently, Head Start is a program within the Administration for Children, Youth and Families (ACYF) in the Department of Health and Human Services. While the federal government supported the program, every community subsidizes its local program, which is overseen by a local community action agency or a public school system.

In 1975, performance standards were developed to make sure that each Head Start program provides the necessary services to achieve individually the constituent's goals:

1. *Education:* Head Start's educational program must meet each child's individual needs. It also addresses the needs as well as the ethnic and cultural characteristics of the community served.
2. *Health:* Head Start focuses on the importance of early identification of health problems. Since many low-income preschool children have not seen a doctor or dentist, a comprehensive health care program is provided for every child, including medical, dental, mental health, and nutritional services.
   a. *Medical and dental:* Children are given a complete physical examination, including vision and hearing tests, identification of handicapping conditions, immunizations, and a dental checkup. Follow-up care is provided for problems that are identified.
   b. *Nutrition:* Many children who enter Head Start may not have received nourishing meals at home. Children are provided with a

minimum of one hot meal and snack daily to meet at least one-third of their daily nutritional needs.

c. *Mental health:* The program is attentive to the mental health and psychological services that children of low-income families need.

3. *Parent Involvement:* Parents are considered to be most influential in the child's development. Parents are involved in parent education, program planning, and operating facilities. Many parents served on the Policy Councils and Committee to provide input on administrative and managerial decisions.

4. *Social Services:* Head Start assists families to assess their needs and then provides services, including community outreach, referrals, family needs assessments, providing information on available resources, recruitment and enrollment of children, and emergency assistance and/or crisis intervention.

5. *Service to Handicapped Children:* Following the 1972 Congressional mandate, at least 10% of its enrollment in each state must be available for handicapped children (Spodek & Saracho, 1994, p. 48).

Head Start has had a remarkable impact on (a) child development and child care services, (b) the improvement of state and local services for young children and their families, and (c) the preparation programs for individuals who work in early childhood programs. The program has helped many children. Since its initial stages, the funds for the program have expanded. However, the federal government's restricted financial plan has caused many young children who are qualified to be ineligible to attend the program.

The social situation in which Head Start operated during the 1980s made helping poor children more difficult. Family poverty, homelessness, and substance abuse has been greater than before. In addition, there was an increase in the quantity of families of young, single mothers. Between 1989 and 1990, more than 75% of Head Start families received an annual income of fewer than $9,000 and single mothers were heading most of these families (Children's Defense Fund, 1991). During the early years, approximately 700,000 children attended at a per-capita cost of $2,000 to $3,000. Through the early 1970s, the full-time program's enrollment plummeted below 400,000. In 2011, enrollment was near one million children (Armor & Sousa, 2018).

Early Head Start Program

In 1994, the Early Head Start (EHS) program was launched to help children from birth to age 3. Early Head Start programs deliver comparable services as preschool Head Start programs, but they are personalized to the exclusive needs of infants and toddlers. Based on the overall Head Start model, EHS programs assist parents, both mothers and fathers, in their function as leading caregivers and teachers of their children. Early Head Start programs offer family-centered services to low-income families with very young children. In addition, they provided rigorous, all-inclusive child development and family services to low-income infants and toddlers and their families, including pregnant women and their families. Early Head Start programs encourage the physical, cognitive, social, and emotional growth of infants and toddlers through safe and developmentally appropriate caregiving. This prepares these children for continued progress, development, and ultimate success in school and life.

EHS programs are intended to support the children's development and to allow their parents to achieve their responsibilities as parents and to progress to self-sufficiency. These programs also help families to attain their own individual purposes and become self-sufficient in an all-embracing assortment of areas, such as housing stability, continued education, and financial security. It is designed to develop healthful attachments between parent and child as well as child and caregiver. Amenities include the complete span of a family's needs from pregnancy through a child's third birthday. In addition, EHS programs organize the local community to deliver the resources and environment essential to guarantee a comprehensive, cohesive selection of services, and assistance for children and families (Early Childhood Learning & Knowledge Center, n.d.).

The Nursery School

The nursery school was formally founded in England in 1908 after the Board of Education disseminated an advertisement recommending the care of preschool children (Whipple, 1929). The nursery school movement arose from a cultural environment that differs from the one for kindergarten. In 1909, the McMillan sisters founded the original nursery school in London to care for the neglected children of poor parents (Whipple, 1929). Margaret McMillan, an English Christian Socialist, is considered the initiator of the nursery school idea. In cooperation with her sister Rachel, Margaret McMillan began an open-air nursery school in a poor section of London in 1913. The earliest nursery schools were single-story buildings with huge doorways or French windows that would open into gardens and big outdoor play areas. Children played both indoors and outdoors. The Macmillans' educational program had a social focus instead of a religious one like Fröbel's. It concentrated on facilitating the children's learning through observation instead of the symbolic system. Edward Seguin had more of an influence on the Macmillans than Friedrich Fröbel. This French educator had created numerous activities to develop the retarded children's sensory education. His impact is observed in existing special education programs.

Rachel and Margaret Macmillan used their experience in English health clinics for poor children. They established the nursery school as a protective measure for children's sicknesses, both mental and physical, that were so predominant in the slum areas. The fundamental philosophy of nursery education was one of *nurturance.* Nurturance was developed to focus on the whole child including the social, physical, emotional, and intellectual development. The duties of the initial nursery school consisted of bathing the children, dressing them in clean clothes, resting them, feeding them, making sure that they had enough fresh air, and educating them (Spodek & Saracho, 1994). Their first program consisted of both reinforcement of play and the planning of learning experiences and fundamental custodial care. They had baths for the children, clean clothes, and nutritious meals.

Nursery school for 3 and 4 year olds taught them how to take care (e.g., washing, tying shoelaces) of themselves. It was also essential for children to assume responsibility for watering plants, maintaining the animals, and keeping the school clean. Furthermore, they participated in explicit activities to cultivate the "senses," such as music and rhythmic activities, language activities, and art activities to learn form and color. Margaret Macmillan suggested activities that would promote reading and writing, mathematics, and science; whereas a different nursery school pioneer, Grace Owen opposed the instruction of the "Three R's" and curriculum lessons. Activities included free play activities, art construction, and working with water, sand, and other nonstructured materials.

The success of the Macmillans' efforts led to the Fisher Act of 1918, which permitted the formation of the nursery schools in local school systems all throughout England. Regrettably, the funds required to launch such programs were unavailable and the growth of nursery school education gradually developed.

In the 1920s, politicians and educationalists were becoming concerned about the young children's education. Also around that time, several London teachers who had worked with Margaret Macmillan and Grace Owen arrived in the United States to explain English nursery education. Nursery schools began at Teachers College, Columbia University, the Merrill Palmer School of Motherhood and Home Training, and numerous other institutions in the United States.

Throughout the following decades nursery schools dispersed gradually all over the United States. A study of nursery schools in 1931 recorded 203 in existence. Approximately half of these schools were associated with colleges and universities, a third of them were private schools, and a fifth of them were allied to child welfare agencies. This mixture of support, an ongoing feature of nursery schools, is comparable to their different purpose. All nursery schools were apprehensive about the children's education. Their function differed based on the support of the school. According to Davis (1933),

> A large number of colleges and universities use the nursery school as a laboratory for the preparation of teachers and for research. The schools sponsored by departments of home economics in college and universities act as laboratories and demonstration centers for preparental education and instruction on home management. Relief of parents from daytime care of their children is chiefly supported by nursery schools connected with day nurseries and conducted by family welfare or philanthropic organizations. (p. 31)

TRANSFORMATIONS IN NURSERY SCHOOLS

Over the years the nursery schools endured various transformations such as the parent-cooperative nursery schools, nursery schools for poor young children, Works Progress Administration (WPA) emergency nursery schools, laboratory nursery schools, and child development laboratory schools.

Parent-Cooperative Nursery Schools

The Chicago Cooperative Nursery School is an interesting version about the nursery schools. In 1915, a group of seven wives of faculty members from the University of Chicago coordinated a cooperative nursery school that would take care of their young children. Thus, the Chicago Cooperative Nursery School would allow young children to engage in play, mothers to have several hours of social relaxation without their children, and the possibility for mothers to learn about their individual children (Whipple, 1929).

In the 1950s, the parent-cooperative nursery schools expanded and continue to be in existence nowadays. The interest in high quality nursery school education at a realistic price and for an increase in parent education reinforced this development. Some parents may have owned the parent-cooperative nursery schools and may have also been involved in the children's program. The program usually included an education component, which consisted of adult classes or parent meetings about child development, child rearing practices, or other related areas (Taylor, 1968).

Nursery Schools for Poor Young Children

Nursery school education gradually progressed under its different support until the middle of the 1960s, when the federal government once more began to support preschool education for underprivileged children under the Economic Opportunity Act of 1964.[1] This Act initiated the Head Start program and represented a foremost transformation in American early childhood education.

Although nursery school education progressed through a succession of modifications, its progress did not provoke the profound theoretical struggle that described the progress of the kindergarten. In the first place, it was a more contemporary program. Furthermore, the earliest all-embracing method to nursery education was extensively sufficient to embrace change and diversity free of critical controversy. Spodek and Saracho (1994) identified the following fundamental modifications that surfaced in the nursery school concept:

1. *The change from nursery education as a program for the poor to one for the affluent.* The originators of nursery school conceived of their programs as an antidote for problems of poverty. In the United States, the nursery school became a source of information about children, a place for young women to practice for motherhood and home management, a place to "keep" children, as well as a place to educate middle-class children. This change was a consequence of the sponsorship of nursery schools in the United States. Without government support, most nursery schools outside of philanthropic agencies were supported by tuition payments. This limited opportunities for nursery education primarily to children of the affluent.

2. *A de-emphasis of the health aspects of nursery education.* Because the children served by American nursery schools had less need for the total care provided by the English nursery schools, programs were shortened to half-days or school hours. The responsibility for nutrition, health, and hygiene was omitted. Only in child care centers and Head Start programs do we see a manifestation of the original concept of nurturance.

3. *A shift from the emphasis on "training the senses" to a more broadly based education.* The same conditions that led to the reform movement in the kindergarten led to the shift in emphasis in nursery education. There was less concern for cognitive learning and more for emotional and social learning than in the kindergarten. With the current return to a concern for intellectual learning in young children, nursery educators have generally supported broad cognitive

skills and strategies rather than the too-specific learning tasks of the original nursery school (pp. 41–42).

WORKS PROGRESS ADMINISTRATION EMERGENCY NURSERY SCHOOLS[2]

The Great Depression of the 1930s affected the progress of nursery education. Low incomes and tax collections caused numerous school systems to decrease educational services and employment of teachers whose wages were no longer available. In 1933, the federal government, formerly under the Federal Emergency Relief Act (FERA) and later under the WPA, made money available to launch nursery schools to offer work to unemployed teachers (Spodek & Saracho, 1994). FERA, under the direction of Harry Hopkins, had the responsibility to provide for the unique needs of a number of individuals including unemployed teachers, nurses, service workers, and preschool children from underprivileged households (Hopkins, 1936).

Since FERA excluded the establishment of nursery, on September 6, 1933, Jacob Baker, assistant administrator of FERA, sent a letter to Grace Abbott, director of the Children's Bureau, calling attention to the relationship between the hardships of unemployed teachers and the consequences of the depression on young children. Baker pursued Abbott's assistance with FERA in creating emergency nursery schools. Hopkins sanctioned the founding of emergency nursery schools as part of the Federal Emergency Education program. On October 23, 1933, Hopkins informed State Emergency Relief administrators that

> the rules and regulations of the Federal Emergency Relief Administration may be interpreted to provide work relief wages for qualified and unemployed teachers and other workers on relief who are needed to organize and conduct nursery schools under the control of the public school systems. (National Advisory Committee, 1934, p. 8)

In the winter of 1933–1934, emergency nursery schools were opened under the sponsorship of FERA and in 1934 they were integrated into the WPA after FERA had ended. All together with the policy of protecting the "physical and mental well-being of preschool children from needy, underprivileged families," any child between the ages of two and five whose family was on relief was eligible to attend an emergency nursery school (National Advisory Committee, 1935, p. 16). The WPA nursery school program became a federally-funded early childhood education program in the United States, Puerto Rico, and the Virgin Islands (Burlbaw, 2009). Normal public school channels were used to run its nursery schools. Emergency teacher training programs were established to offer teachers of older children with the required skills to work with young children (Spodek & Saracho, 1994).

In a year, only a meager portion (between 44,000 and 72,000 children) of the 10 million preschoolers with unemployed fathers was helped. In addition, there was a range of 6,000 to 8,000 individuals working at the emergency nursery schools, which consisted of nearly 51% teachers, 12% nurses, 17% nutritionists and cooks, and the rest were janitors, clerks, maids, and other service workers. The emergency nursery schools were arranged and opened by local governments and usually were run under the combined sponsorships of state departments of education and local public school systems (Cahan, 1989). Although the main motive for launching these nursery schools was to generate jobs for the unemployed, Hopkins did recognize that "the educational and health programs of nursery schools can aid as nothing else in combating the physical and mental handicaps being imposed upon these young children in the homes of needy and unemployed parents" (Langdon, 1938, p. 472). The teamwork of early childhood educators, social workers, physicians, and public health officials aimed to alleviate part of the despair involving children throughout the depression by offering thousands of them with the "opportunity for wholesome development, for better living" (Department of Education, 1936, p. 34). Still, the schools were neither day nurseries for children of the working poor nor progressive nursery schools. Instead, they were "poverty track institutions designed to safeguard the health and welfare of impoverished preschool children during very hard times" (Tank, 1980, p. 359).

Numerous communities ran WPA nursery schools. These gave security to unemployed teachers and a worthwhile educational experience to children. Federally supported schools were run in the majority of states in the United States and extended into the thousands, considerably surpassing the quantity of nursery schools that had prevailed in this country at that point (Spodek & Saracho, 1994).

The termination of the depression and the embarking of World War II indicated that a demand to give unemployed teachers a job was no longer a problem, which triggered the termination of the WPA nursery school. The growing economy and the manpower requirements of the armed services and the defense industry demanded adding to the labor force. Since women were employed for war labor, institutions were required to take care of their children. Under the Lanham Act, the federal government founded child care centers in the majority of war manufacturing centers. These offered care and education to the children of mothers who were working in war-related businesses. Soon after World War II was over, funding for such programs was removed right away. In various circumstances, though, because the necessity for child care continued, the centers persisted to function in the support of local governments or philanthropic organizations (Spodek & Saracho, 1994).

VARIATIONS OF LABORATORY SCHOOLS

Usually the laboratory schools' responsibility has been to help prepare teachers and simultaneously provide high quality teaching programs for classroom children. Such laboratory schools are typically associated with a college or university for particular purposes. Throughout the years, the laboratory schools have been modified to manifest the different university needs of the teaching professional and have frequently guided the means to conduct research that contributes to knowledge (International Association of Laboratory Schools, 2018). The following sections describe the different variations of laboratory schools.

Earliest University-Administered Schools

Schools that are associated with the university have a prolonged history in the United States. Such history goes back to the original colonial colleges (e.g., Harvard, Yale, William and Mary, University of Pennsylvania) that oversaw Latin schools or departments to get students ready for college (Good & Teller, 1973). Rutgers Preparatory School, which was established in 1768, is the oldest of these schools, and sustained its associations to the university up until the 1950s (Sperduto, 1967). Similar to the majority of preparatory schools, it was a private school that offered its students with a properly exclusive educational experience. The growing accessibility of high-quality high school education contributed to the slow disappearance of these schools. Simultaneously, many universities started to consider the "laboratory school" concept (Cucchiara, 2010).

"A laboratory school is a school largely or entirely under the control of the college, located on or near the college campus, and organized for the purpose of preparing teachers" (Perrodin, 1955, p. xi). The expression laboratory experience was applied from the initiation of the Normal school movement in teacher education and many of the Normal schools had a laboratory school connected to them. The phrase laboratory experiences, conversely, differed with Dewey's meaning of the term.

Initially, laboratory schools usually meant "practice schools" because their purpose was to offer practice for preservice teachers in an explicit way of teaching (Johnson, 1968). Approximately during the middle of the 19th century, when the initial Normal schools were being established in the United States, laboratory schools were usually called "model schools," because they were intended to exemplify model teaching processes through demonstration and observation (Blair, Curtis, & Moon, 1958).

Laboratory schools have been essential additions of most teacher education institutions. Their difference in names suggests their main purpose. Perrodin (1955) states,

> From its earliest beginnings, a distinctive feature of teacher education has been the use of an actual school for children. Names given to these children's schools have varied according to their purposes. In the early days of teacher education in this country, they were named "model schools." Later, some were designated as "practice schools," then "training schools," and more recently, the term "laboratory schools" has come into usage." (p. 1)

Laboratory schools were used to provide inservice teachers with experiences and teaching demonstrations. According to Williams (1942), in the year 1600 Franciscan Friars in New Mexico required preservice teachers to have student teaching experiences. In 1774 a member of the Pietists' religious order established a school at Dessau, Germany, to train teachers who were required to work directly with children. Later, Pestalozzi, a Swiss educator, was influential in the formation of two schools for teachers to observe and educate children. The first school was introduced at Burgdorf, Switzerland, and was replaced by the well-known school at Yverdon, which Pestalozzi ran from 1805 to 1825 (Williams, 1942). Other schools followed such as when Johann Friedrich Herbart, a German philosopher and psychologist, met Pestalozzi while he was tutoring in Switzerland. In 1809, he joined the University of Königsberg where he started a practice school. In 1843, one of his pupils, Karl Volkmar Stoy, began his own seminary and practice school at Jena, a German university city. Then Professor Wilhelm Rein, a German educational theorist, was in charge of the school using Herbartian principles. In 1857, a seminary and practice school was founded in Leipzig, Germany. Professor Zuller, one of Herbart's supporters, ran this school until 1883 (Hall, 1899).

Herbart, Pestalozzi, and others had a complete impact on laboratory schools in American teacher education. According to Good (1956),

> It will not be denied that the normal school was an academy with reviews of the common branches and a few professional studies and skills added. It would have been purely American if it had not incorporated Pestalozzi's theory and practice into its professional work. (p. 12)

Herbart's impact on teacher education in the United States, especially on laboratory schools, was evident in the work of Colonel Frances W. Parker and the association that is currently known as the National Society for the Study of Education (Good, 1956). The National Society for the Study of

Education (NSSE) was created in 1901 and a year later began publishing its annual *Yearbook* on topics that were of interest to educators from multifarious views.

The Pestalozzian movement of the 19th century gave prominence to an extremely structured approach grounded on object instruction, which had an intense effect on Normal schools, particularly on the Oswego Normal School. This movement reformed the concentration of laboratory schools to the training of preservice teachers in distinctive techniques of teaching, laboratory schools changed its term to "training schools" (Johnson, 1968). The impact of the Herbartian movement at the beginning of the 20th century modified the term to "demonstration schools," which was based on Herbartian concentration on meticulously organized lessons. The demonstration school teachers organized and demonstrated such well devised lessons for novice preservice teachers to observe and replicate (Blair et al., 1958).

The thought of the laboratory school as a place to train preservice teachers was extended close to the turn of the century. In 1883, Colonel Frances W. Parker directed the Cook County Normal School of Chicago to focus on research and the study of teaching. Before long the Horace Mann School at Teachers College in New York City was founded for the similar purpose (Anderson, 1992; Bonar, 1992; Page & Page, 1981). Colonel Parker, G. Stanley Hall, and John Dewey led the development for further scientific study of children and experimenting with their theories in schools (Whipple, 1929).

During the 19th century, numerous universities and normal schools (teacher training institutions) launched "laboratory schools." In contrast to college-preparatory schools, laboratory schools were specifically connected to the research or teacher-training purposes of the universities. Throughout the years such schools had various purposes including teacher preparation, demonstration, and research (Cucchiara, 2010). In 1904, Dewey wrote an article on the connection between educational theory to practice. In this article, he differentiated between professional laboratory experiences and apprenticeships based on the history of laboratory schools. He perceived the object of preservice laboratory experiences in relation to intellectual analysis, critical reflection, and investigation rather than practice to develop their teaching skills. Although Dewey's 1904 article is considered a crucial influence to the literature about preservice teacher education, it failed to have an impact on laboratory experiences (Nolan, 1982).

Lastly, the societal circumstances of the 1930s led to a different view on the purpose of the laboratory schools. Inspired by Dewey and others, teachers were considered to be skilled technicians instead of educational policy makers. Again the term for laboratory schools was modified to "experimental schools" because it was used for teachers to test and improve innovative educational concepts (Blair et al., 1958). "Experimentation was basic, and the accepted and standard methods and approaches were constantly challenged through scientifically designed studies" (Blair et al., 1958, p. 7). The different terms were confusing. Andrews (1964) commented:

> From its beginning, this field has suffered because of confused and inade-
> quate set of names for its personnel and their relationships. Accurate commu-
> nication is difficult. Several of the well-accepted terms have unfortunate con-
> notations and the efficiency of many people suffers from a misunderstanding
> of their roles and duties. (p. 8)

To reduce the misinterpretation about the function of laboratory experiences, in 1973, the Association of Teacher Educators (ATE) published the
Guidelines to Clinical Experiences in Teacher Education and provided a basic
term that separated clinical experiences into laboratory experiences and
practicums. "Laboratory experiences are direct and simulated experiences
which foster the analytical study of teaching and critical investigation of the
responsibilities of teachers and schools, and practicums are related to the
development of teaching skills" (ATE, 1973, p. 10). This distinction supported Dewey's concept because it adopted and confirmed the need for
pre-student teaching experiences to cultivate an environment of analysis
and investigation that would frame the complete preservice preparation
program (Nolan, 1982).

Child Development Laboratory Schools

Child development laboratory schools replaced nursery schools to serve
as research centers in a variety of ways (e.g., teachers observe the children's
development, public health nurses find out about the children's physical
development). The shift of nursery schools to child development laboratory schools offered the opportunity to observe and experiment with young
children in a natural environment. They provide an impartial arena to
conduct research in a range of disciplines such as education, psychology,
medicine, nutrition, and sociology. Investigation with methods of research
is essential to study how young children behave as natural as possible. John
Dewey, the American philosopher of education identified the laboratory
school as a facility for methodical inquiry. Between 1894–1904, he was head
of the Department of Education and Philosophy at the University of Chicago where he established a laboratory school (Page & Page, 1981). Dewey's
purpose for the laboratory school disregarded its use to train teachers. Instead he considered the laboratory school to be a model situation to conduct educational research. He believed that the laboratory school provided
the opportunity to experiment with theories and contribute knowledge to
teaching and learning. Dewey aspired to generate a science of education

in a laboratory where innovative educational concepts might be created, verified, and duplicated in natural environments (Bonar, 1992; Provenzo, 1979).

In 1894, John Dewey began the progressive education movement at the University of Chicago Laboratory School. He wanted to use this school to create theories of child development and education. At the same time, organizations like the Child Study Association were established to study child growth and development. Such comparable concerns merged into the 1920s after private beneficiaries (e.g., Rockefeller Foundation) joined with universities to establish several child development laboratory schools on university campuses. They were usually in psychology or home economics departments. They were used for research, service, and training purposes associated with children and families (Barbour, 2003). Presently, this three-way undertaking continues to guide university-based child development laboratory programs (Wilcox-Herzog & McLaren, 2012). The increase of laboratory schools throughout the first half of the 20th century made it possible to conduct many rigorous educational studies that have added to the knowledge on child development such as John Flavell's theory of mind (Wilcox-Herzog & McLaren, 2012). In 1942, Edward I. F. Williams used a pre-World War II study of laboratory school purposes to declare that a campus school ought to be used as a laboratory for observation, participation, and class demonstrations as well as preliminary classroom teaching with minor concentration on investigation (Williams, 1942). In the beginning of the 1950s the main intention had shifted from research to the preservice field experiences related to college training previous to student teaching. Conversely, diminishing school populations in the 1960s and registrations in colleges of education prompted the laboratory schools to conduct research to justify their need (Bonar, 1992).

Child development research stimulated the development of preschool laboratories. Lawrence Frank, who from 1923 to 1929 was the director of the Laura Spelman Rockefeller Memorial, influenced university-based research in early childhood education. He directed the child-development program in the Rockefeller Foundation from 1929 to 1933 and became a member of the General Education Board in 1933. Through the Laura Spelman Rockefeller Memorial, he donated a million dollars a year that had been selected to assist children (Braun & Edwards, 1972). Frank gathered pertinent research from child care centers to raise consciousness of the meaning of the children's early childhood development (Davis, 1964).

University and colleges have established child development laboratory schools in Europe and America for a minimum of two centuries, although various records indicate that they were initiated during the 1600s. Throughout the 1820s, normal schools in the United States were offering controlled teaching environments to their preservice teachers to experience teaching opportunities. Europe, America, and even Japan included child development laboratory schools. According to Hayo (1993), in Japan they were known as "attached schools." Between 1850 and 1950, laboratory schools flourished. In 1874 the U.S. Commissioner of Education stated that 47 of the nation's 67 state normal schools had laboratory or training schools for their teacher education programs (Hendrick, 1980). In 1920, almost all of the leading teacher education institutions in the country had a child development laboratory school.

An International Network

The increase of early childhood programs needed a way to share concepts and experiences with those who were in similar situations. After the founding of the initial nursery school in 1915, many Child Development Laboratories throughout the country had been established to offer public assistance. Nevertheless, the absence of a professional organization for administrators of Child Development Laboratories made several directors feel isolated and without knowledge or information about other laboratory programs. There was a need for a national network that could help laboratory administrators and teachers to communicate with each other to learn about national advances and practices of Child Development Laboratories (Anderson, 1992). In 1983, the National Organization of Child Development Laboratory Schools (NOCDLS) was formed and set the following goal:

> supporting child development laboratory schools in their endeavors to provide a pragmatic approach for integrating early childhood theory and practice and to form a national supportive system/network among individuals associated with these schools. (NOCDLS By-Laws, 1983, cited in Anderson, 1992, p. 2)

The NOCDLS Steering Committee established a national profile of laboratory schools to attain this goal and up-to-date knowledge about theory and practice that can be accessible to individuals who are working in laboratory schools (Anderson, 1992).

In an increasingly international environment, laboratory schools all over the world have started to create contacts with each other. The majority are presently associated with the International Association of Laboratory and University Affiliated Schools (IALS). The IALS is an international association of laboratory and university associated schools involved in practices of teacher training, curriculum development, research, professional development, and educational experimentation to support the members' institution and advocate the support for all of the children's learning. It was originally called the National Association of Laboratory Schools (NALS). After more than 5 decades, the NALS, the International Association of Laboratory, University Affiliated Schools,[3] and the association's board of directors agreed to replace its name with the International Association of Laboratory Schools (IALS). This new name represents their present worldwide membership and goals for the upcoming development of knowledge. It also helps take the far-reaching meaning of "laboratory schools" to involve a variety of diverse university relationships including campus-based schools, charter schools, professional development schools, child study institutes, research and development schools, and others (IALS, 2018). In addition, IALS has a broad definition for laboratory school to appropriately meet a wide range of structures, which differ substantially based on the situations in which the schools were established. For example, the laboratory school may be an institution officially merged into a university department, such as the one originated by John Dewey. Such is the situation for most of North American and Japanese laboratory schools, like the Shinwa Kindergarten School of Kobe Shinwa Women's University, lately joined IALS (Cucchiara, 2010). Historically, NALS made important contributions. Therefore, many of its documents use that name including its newsletter and publications (IALS, 2018).

CONCLUSION

Based on the contributions of European educational pioneers (e.g., Pestalozzi, Fröbel) the concept of Early Childhood Laboratories historically was established by researchers who examined child development and who intended to research and test their groundbreaking concepts on education and teaching (e.g., G. Stanley Hall, Dewey). Various terms including laboratory, laboratory school, campus child care, and university-based schools were used based on their different responsibilities (Loizou, 2013). Child development laboratory schools have been present since the 1830s and have served an important function in the child development movement throughout the beginning half of the twentieth century. They (a) were used to study the young children's development and learning of children and (b) supported teacher education programs with their preparation of teachers and demonstrations of appropriate practice (Cucchiara, 2010). Teacher-training institutions ran the original laboratory schools. They function as "model schools" for preservice teachers to observe professional teaching methods, practice them using the up-to-date equipment, and refine their personal teaching abilities. This kind of laboratory school initially was launched in New England in the 1820s and by the 1860s extended remotely to the west such as Minnesota (Loizou, 2013).

Prominent early educational pioneers in Europe inspired the development of nursery schools in the United States and science of child psychology in the United States (Braun & Edwards, 1972). Some of the initial nursery schools in the United States emerged throughout the beginning of the 1900s. Not many of these pioneers were acquainted with each other and differed in their educational backgrounds and interests in preschool children, but they influenced very distinctive programs, which provided the foundation for the nursery schools (Whipple, 1929).

During the 20th century, all laboratory schools multiplied into other directly related purposes including both those that concentrated on Dewey's experimental research and those that focused on practice teaching in the initial schools. Laboratory schools fluctuated between providing opportunities for research, student teaching, curriculum development and dissemination, inservice education, preservice observation, and classroom participation. The main purposes were based on usefulness. If the country had a shortage of teachers, laboratory schools emphasized practice teaching, whereas if the demand for teachers dropped, these professional schools concentrated on other alternatives (Bonar, 1992).

Beginning in the 1920s, numerous universities likewise started to establish child development laboratory programs or centers (Osborn, 1991), which were basically laboratory schools for very young children. Similarly these previous laboratory schools or centers function as a facility (a) to train preservice and in-service teachers in early childhood education and child development, (b) to conduct research on several facets of child development, and (c) to set up model programs in early childhood education at the national and local educational levels (McBride, 1996). Several of them also functioned as child care centers for university students and faculty. Important research appeared from these child development centers, such as norms for child development (Gesell at Yale), intelligence tests (Kuhlman at Minnesota), and studies of child play (Parten at Minnesota). Oddly, teacher educators had limited studies and applications in early childhood classroom (Cassidy & Sanders, 2001).

NOTES

1. The Economic Opportunity Act of 1964 (United States Public Law 88-452) sanctioned the creation of local Community Action Agencies as element of the War on Poverty. The federal government managed such agencies. It stated, "It is the purpose of The Economic Opportunity Act to strengthen, supplement, and coordinate efforts in furtherance of that policy" (United States Government, 2011).

2. This nursery school program had its name changed several times: Emergency Nursery School program (1933–1943), WPA nursery school and parent education program (1937–1938), WPA family life program (1938–1942), and WPA Child Protection program (1942–1943). Toward the end of spring and

early summer in 1935, FERA's name changed to "WPA nursery school" (Arboleda, 2018).

3. The International Association of Laboratory Schools (IALS) is an international association of laboratory and university affiliated schools.

REFERENCES

Andrews, L. O. (1964). *Student teaching*. New York, NY: Center for Applied Research in Education.

Anderson, O. A. (1992). A national profile of child development laboratory schools (Master's thesis). Utah State University, Logan, Utah. *All Graduate Theses and Dissertations*. Paper 2355.

Armor, D. J., & Sousa, S. (2018). The dubious promise of universal preschool. *National Affairs and the Public Interest, 36*. Retrieved from https://www.nationalaffairs.com/publications/detail/the-dubious-promise-of-universal-preschool

Association of Teacher Educators. (1973). *Guidelines to clinical experiences in teacher education*. Washington, DC: American Association of Teacher Education.

Barbour, N. (2003). The early history of child development laboratory programs. In B. McBride & N. Barbour (Eds.), *Bridging the gap between theory, research and practice: The role of child development laboratory programs in early childhood education* (pp. 9–29). Kidlington, Oxford: Elsevier.

Blair, L. C., Curtis, D. K., & Moon, A. C. (1958). *The purposes, functions and uniqueness of the college controlled laboratory school.* Lock Haven, PA: Association for Student Teaching.

Bonar, B. D. (1992). The role of laboratory schools in American education. *National Association of Laboratory Schools Journal, 17*(1), 42–53.

Braun, S. J., & Edwards, E. P. (1972). *History and theory of early childhood education*. Belmont, CA: Wadsworth.

Burlbaw, L. M. (2009). An early start: WPA emergency nursery schools in Texas, 1934–1943. *American Educational History Journal, 36*(2), 269–298.

Cahan, E. D. (1989). *Past caring: A history of U.S. preschool care and education for the poor, 1820–1965*. New York, NY: National Center for Children in Poverty.

Cassidy, J., & Sanders, J. (2001). A university lab school for the 21st century: The early childhood development center. In J. Cassidy & S. D. Garrett (Eds.), *Early childhood literacy: Programs and strategies to develop cultural, linguistic, scientific and healthcare literacy for very young children and their families, 2001 yearbook* (pp. 1–19). Corpus Christi, TX: Center for Educational Development, Evaluation, and Research. Retrieved from https://files.eric.ed.gov/fulltext/ED468858.pdf

Children's Defense Funds. (1991). *The State of America's Children, 1991*. Washington, DC: Author.

Comenius, J. A. (1658). *Orbis Pictus*. Syracuse, NY: C. W. Bardeen.

Comenius, J. A. (1896). *Comenius' school of infancy: An Essay on the education of youth during the first six years* (Will S. Monroe, Ed.). Boston, MA: D. C. Heath.

Cucchiara, M. (2010). New goals, familiar challenges? A brief history of university-run schools. *Penn GSE Perspectives on Urban Education, 7*(1), 96–108.

Davis, M. D. (1933). *Nursery schools: Their development and current practices in the United States.* Washington, DC: U.S. Government Printing Office.

Davis, M. D. (1964). How NANE began. *Young Children, 20,* 106–109.

Department of Education, Commonwealth of Kentucky. (1936). *Educational Bulletin, 4.* Frankfort, KY: Author.

Dewey, J. (1904). The relation of theory to practice in education. In C. A. McMurry (Ed.), *The third yearbook of the National Society for the Scientific Study of Education, Part I.* (pp. 9–30). Chicago, IL: The University of Chicago Press.

Early Childhood Learning & Knowledge Center. (n.d.). *About the Early Head Start Program.* Retrieved from https://eclkc.ohs.acf.hhs.gov/programs/article/about-early-head-start-program

Fisher, L. (1908). Report on the United States Commissioner of Education (1867–1907), *Bulletin 1909,* number 7, whole number 407. Washington, DC: Government Printing Office.

Forest, I. (1927). *Preschool education: An historical and critical study.* New York, NY: Macmillan.

Gardner, D. E. M. (1949). *Education under eight.* London, England: Longmans, Green.

Good, H. G. (1956). *A history of American education.* New York, NY: The MacMillan Company.

Good, H. G., & Teller, J. D. (1973). *A history of education in America.* New York, NY: Macmillan.

Hall, J. W. (1899). Professor Rein's practice school at Jena, Germany. In *National Education Association, Journal of Addresses and Proceedings* (pp. 882–884). Chicago, IL: University of Chicago Press.

Hayo, M. (1993). Clinical education and the role of attached schools in preservice teacher education. *Peabody Journal of Education, 68,* 53–57.

Hendricks, I. G. (1980). University controlled laboratory schools in historical perspective. *UCLA Educator, 21*(2), 55–59.

Hopkins, H. (1936). *Spending to save.* Seattle, WA: University of Washington Press.

Hymes, J. L., Jr. (1995). The Kaiser Child Service Centers—50 years later. *Journal of Education, 177*(3), 23–38. doi:10.1177/002205749517700303

International Association of Laboratory Schools. (2018). *About us.* Retrieved from http://laboratoryschools.org/about-us/16-about-us

International Kindergarten Union, Committee of Nineteen. (1913). *The kindergarten; reports of the Committee of nineteen on the theory and practice of the kindergarten.* New York, NY: Houghton Mifflin.

Johnson, J. A. (1968). *A brief history of student teaching.* DeKalb, IL: Creative Educational Materials.

Langdon, G. (1938). Works Progress Administration emergency nursery school. *Progressive Education, 15,* 472–484.

Loizou, E. (2013). An early childhood research laboratory framework: Necessity the mother of invention. *European Early Childhood Education Research Journal, 21*(4), 581–595. doi:10.1080/1350293X.2013.845445

May, D., & Vinovskis, M. A. (1977). A ray of millennial light: Early education and social reform in the infant school movement in Massachusetts, 1826–1840. In

T. Harevan (Ed.), *Family and kin in urban communities, 1700–1930* (pp. 62–99). New York, NY: New Viewpoints.

McBride, B. (1996). University-based child development laboratory programs: Emerging issues and challenges. *Early Childhood Education Journal, 24*(1), 17–21.

Monroe, W. S. (Ed.). (1908). *Comenius school of infancy.* Boston, MA: Heath.

National Advisory Committee on Emergency Nursery Schools. (1934). *Emergency nursery schools during the first year.* Washington, DC: Author.

National Advisory Committee on Emergency Nursery Schools. (1935). *Emergency nursery schools during the second year.* Washington, DC: Author.

Nohle, E. (June 30, 1898). Report on the United States Commissioner of Education (1897–1898), Vol I, 24–25. Washington, DC: U. S. Department of the Interior, Bureau of Education. Bulletins of the Bureau of Education, Government Printing Office.

Nolan, J. F. (1982). Professional laboratory experiences: The missing link in teacher education. *Journal of Teacher Education, 33*(4), 49–53. doi:10.1177/0022487 18203300412

Osborn, D. K. (1991). *Early childhood education in historical perspective* (3rd ed.). Athens, GA: Education Associates.

Page, F., & Page, J. A. (1981). *Laboratory schools: Updated or outdated?* Retrieved from ERIC database. (ED213672)

Peabody, E. P. (1882). The origin and growth of the kindergarten. *Education, 2*, 507–527.

Perrodin, A. F. (1955). The development of laboratory schools in teacher education. *Functions of laboratory schools in teacher education.* Lock Haven, PA: The Association for Student Teaching.

Provenzo, E. F. (1979). History as experiment: The role of the laboratory school in the development of John Dewey's philosophy of history. *History Teacher, 12*(3), 373–382.

Ross, E. D. (1976). *The kindergarten crusade: The establishment of preschool education in the United States.* Athens, OH: Ohio University Press.

Rousseau, J. J. (1911). *Emile* (Barbara Foxley, Trans.). London, England: J. M. Dent. (Originally published in 1762)

Snyder, A. (1972). *Dauntless women in childhood education.* Washington, DC: Association for Childhood Education International.

Sperduto, F. F. (1967). *A history of Rutgers Preparatory School.* Somerset, NJ: Rutgers Preparatory School.

Spodek, B., & Saracho, O. N. (1994). *Right from the start: Teaching children ages three to eight.* Boston, MA: Allyn & Bacon.

Steinfels, M. O. (1973). *Who's minding the children? The history and politics of day care in America.* New York, NY: Simon & Schuster.

Strickland, C. E. (1982). Paths not taken: Seminal models of early childhood education in Jacksonian America. In B. Spodek (Ed.), *Handbook of research in early childhood education* (pp. 321–340). New York, NY: Free Press.

Swart, H. W. (1867). *Magarethe Meyer Schurz: A biography.* Watertown, WI: Watertown Historical Society.

Tank, R. M. (1980). *Young children, families, and society in America since the 1820s: The evolution of health, education, and child care programs for preschool children* (Doctoral dissertation). University of Michigan, Ann Arbor. Retrieved from University Microfilms International (No. 8106233).

Taylor, C. W. (1968). *Parents and children learn together.* New York, NY: Teachers College Press.

United States Government. (2011). Economic Opportunity Act of 1964 explained. Retrieved from http://everything.explained.today/Economic_Opportunity _Act_of_1964/#Ref-1

Vanderwalker, N. (1908). *The kindergarten in American education.* New York, NY: Macmillan.

Weber, E. (1969). *The kindergarten: Its encounter with educational thought in America.* New York, NY: Teachers College Press.

Whipple, G. M. (Ed.). (1929). History of the movement in preschool and parental education. In *Twenty-eighth Yearbook of the National Society for the Study of Education.* Bloomington, IL: Public School.

Wilcox-Herzog, A. S., & McLaren, M. S. (2012). Lessons learned: Building a better laboratory school. *National Association of Laboratory Schools Journal, 4*(1), Article 3. Retrieved from http://digitalcommons.ric.edu/nals/vol4/iss1/3

Willer, B., Hofferth, S. L., Kisker, E. E., Divine-Hawkins, P., Farquhar, E., & Glantz, F, B. (1991). *The demand and supply of child care in 1990.* Washington, DC: National Association for the Education of Young Children.

Williams, E. I. F. (1942). *The actual and potential use of laboratory schools in state normal schools and teacher colleges.* New York, NY: Teachers College, Columbia University.

CHAPTER 3

A CONSORTIUM OF UNIVERSITY-AFFILIATED CHILD DEVELOPMENT LABORATORIES FOR APPLIED DEVELOPMENTAL SCIENCE

A Hypothetical Journey

Nancy Barbour, Andrew Stremmel, D. Reece Wilson, and Jennifer Kampmann[1]

ABSTRACT

Child Development Laboratory (CDL) settings have had a century of venerable history. Originally conceptualized as venues for child study and knowledge generation to inform education and services for young children and families, CDLs have had to reexamine their purpose and place in the field of social sciences in tight economic times. Both the benefits and drawbacks of university based CDLs are explored. In this chapter, the authors consider the evolution of the CDL over the last 100 years and the potential for them to engage in research that fits with the principles of applied development science. A hy-

Contemporary Perspectives on Research on Child Development Laboratory Schools in Early Childhood Education, pages 47–62

pothetical journey of three university labs engaged in a consortium of CDLs doing cross-site research in the tradition of applied development science is described as a way to help CDLs maximize their utility in the 21st century.

INTRODUCTION

Imagine, if you will, that policy makers rely on a consortium of university-affiliated CDL settings for information relevant to the development of policies affecting the lives of young children and their families. This fictional consortium of university-affiliated child development laboratories for applied developmental science, or the lab consortium for short, issues both quarterly reports of research done by their members as well as commissioned reports for various policy entities. These reports are issued as policy briefs intended for action. Imagine the power and resonance that multi-site, multi-methods inquiry might bring to the child and family policy world.

In this chapter, we take a hypothetical journey to explore how a consortium such as this might look. This journey is couched in the context of applied developmental science (ADS) guiding the research agenda and rationale for laboratory programs. After providing a brief description of an ADS framework, we examine the original intent of CDL programs, the changing contexts of labs, and the current challenges facing university-based laboratory programs. Conjuring up three very different, hypothetical CDL settings, we illustrate how a consortium approach can meet the principles of ADS and provide the necessary data for policies to improve the lives of children and families. Finally, we explore the timeliness and relevance of CDLs engaged in such a scenario.

WHAT IS APPLIED DEVELOPMENTAL SCIENCE?

In their 2005 overview of ADS, Lerner, Wertlieb, and Jacobs focus on the potential of ADS to address the real social problems affecting families and children (see also McBride et al., 2012 for a cogent analysis of ADS). Lerner et al. (2005) describe ADS as having historical roots in the work of G. Stanley Hall as he developed "descriptions of children in their natural contexts in order to fully illuminate both development and the impact of context and the necessary connection between science and practice" (p. 5). In the early 1990s, a national task force on ADS brought together the organizations engaged in the "application of developmental psychology knowledge base to societal problems" to develop definitions and guidelines for professional preparation of ADS scientists, and, eventually, for the parameters of a new journal dedicated to ADS (Lerner et al., 2005, p. 6). The three essential components of ADS are described as:

Applied: Direct implications for what individuals, families, practitioners, and policymakers do.

Developmental: Systematic and successive changes within human systems that occur across the life span.

Science: Grounded in a range of research methods designed to collect reliable and objective information systematically that can be used to test the validity of theory and application (Lerner et al., 2005, pp. 6–7).

The emphasis woven throughout the definitions and explications of ADS is on the relationship between individuals and their contexts over time. These definitions clearly describe science that acknowledges historical changes over time, positive interventions that inform science, and science that informs interventions. It is strengths-based and collaborative not just among scientific disciplines but between the community and the researchers. Unlike the early years of child study where scientists strove to identify universals of development, ADS "is devoted to discovering diverse developmental patterns by examining the dynamic relations between individuals within multiple embedded contexts" (Lerner et al., 2005, p. 12). The authors call this research work "outreach scholarship." We believe that ADS is a useful framework for contemplating the future of CDLs and the implications of creating a lab school research consortium.

EARLY HISTORY OF CHILD DEVELOPMENT LABORATORY SETTINGS

Early in the 20th century, there was a quest for knowledge about how children developed, learned, and thrived. One of the first university laboratory schools, begun by John Dewey in the late 1800's at the University of Chicago, was a demonstration site for the application of psychological principles and methods based on a belief that children were active, curious, and motivated to explore and understand their world (Dewey, 1899). Though offering a slightly different focus (childhood education rather than child development), it heralded the beginning of the scientific study of the education of young children in context as well as the development of theories related to child development.

While Dewey's laboratory school was a venue for him to enact and document the innovative ideas he had for education, other universities were engaged in documenting the process of child development. Lawrence K.

Frank, the forward thinking economist employed by the Laura Spelman Rockefeller Memorial Foundation (LSRM), helped to establish a handful of research institutes for the study of child development. With the support of the Rockefeller Memorial Foundation, these institutes were housed at nine universities, including Yale, Iowa State, Columbia, and Michigan (Elicker & Barbour, 2014; Barbour, 2003). Frank's work, and the work of other institutions like the Merrill-Palmer Institute and the Bureau of Educational Experiments, later known as Bank Street College, began the age of the child development lab school (CDL), now over 100 years old.

By 1929, the list of CDL settings was growing. The National Society for the Study of Education (NSSE) 1929 yearbook (Whipple, 1929) reported on preschool and parent education and the work being done to document child development. The research emerging from these sites was helping to build the evolving field of child study. Milton Senn, a former director of the Yale Child Study Center, described this period as having an "auspicious climate for the start of the child development movement... [and the] high hope that scientists also could point the way to improved care of the nation's children" (Senn, 1975, p. 11). With Lawrence Frank's focus on the development of the CDLs, rich research opportunities were being developed. Lomax (1977) saw Frank as a "visionary who believed developmental research was essential to social progress" (p. 284). Frank envisioned these university sites as interdisciplinary; independent of department affiliation; engaging in research, training, and service; and focusing their agendas on child welfare (McBride et al., 2012). Frank's involvement was deep in both the child welfare issues and in the ways researchers chose to study them (Schlossman, 1986). Lawrence K. Frank, in many ways, was ahead of his time. He saw the necessity of doing research that could make a difference in the lives of young children. He understood the necessity of disciplines like medicine, psychology, sociology, and anthropology taking part in the research endeavor (Barbour, 2003). Most importantly, he understood the necessity of disseminating new knowledge to those who could make change happen—policy makers. What might policy makers see today when they examine CDLs?

CHILD DEVELOPMENT LABORATORIES TODAY

Today, CDLs possess the following high quality elements:

> a clearly defined mission that connects with the greater good of the community; a mix of both "soft" and "hard" funding sources; collaboration across disciplines; strong personnel; ongoing professional development; and balance across the three components of labs schools—research, service, and professional preparation. (Barbour & McBride, 2017, p. 2)

Depending on the mission of the university setting, the expectations for faculty scholarship, and the particular focus of the CDL, these quality elements might look quite different from one CDL to another.

We offer here some hypothetical examples of how CDLs operate. One CDL operating on University A campus is a land grant, research intensive institution and may function as a setting for faculty research from many different departments on campus, generating knowledge in a number of different areas. Consequently, the CDL does not guide the research focus, but provides an optimal research laboratory for other researchers. On the other hand, University B has a long-established CDL that engages in research described as teacher research but also has developed applied scholarship focused on translation of their teacher research to community-based programs. Lastly, University C does not have an on-campus CDL but does have a fully engaged Early Childhood Institute contracted to do research and evaluation of innovative community-based programs like Head Start and the Boys and Girls Club.

Over the past 100 years, much has changed for CDLs and for higher education in general. Kostelnik (2017) offers an expansive view of the recent trends in higher education and the impact of these on the CDLs. As very special entities on university campuses, she sees great promise in the shifting landscape of CDLs. Kostelnik (2017) explains, "Addressing this tri-part mission of research, teaching, and engagement has defined CDLs since the time of John Dewey. It is also what sets them apart from early childhood service programs on campus and in the community" (p. 95).

THE FUTURE OF CHILD DEVELOPMENT LAB SCHOOLS

Most CDLs see the tri-part mission of research, service, and professional preparation as central to their work. However, the degree to which programs participate in each of these missions of teacher preparation, research, and service vary (McBride et al., 2012). In order to remain relevant, it is imperative for traditional CDL programs to address current issues and trends in education and society as a whole. Kostelnik (2017) has examined CDLs and the ways they are engaging with these issues and trends by looking at programs through the lens of a rich ecosystem. Drawing on Bronfenbrenner's ecological systems theory, she places CDLs at the center of the ecosystem, and explores how they are influenced by various systems levels. She explains,

> To do their work well, CDLs must be in tune with the ecosystem in which they function. Of course, that involves a complex mesosystem of their home colleges and departments; affiliated administrators, students, and faculty; as

well as the children and families served. However, higher education is the overarching exosystem in which CDLs are embedded and to which they must respond effectively if they are to provide value to the institutions and professions they serve. (Kostelnik, 2017, p. 96)

Current issues and trends in higher education that affect CDLs and how they operate include: economic realities of post-graduation employment, niche programs, and collaboration. A brief explanation of each follows.

Post-Graduation Employment

As tuition rises at institutions of higher education, due in part to the drastic drop in state support, parents and students are carefully examining what majors will allow them to earn a living salary. Unfortunately, early education/elementary education positions are some of the lowest paying majors (Carnevale, Cheah, & Hanson, 2015). Similarly, many child care settings struggle to offer their teachers a living wage. Whitebook, McLean, and Austin (2016) tell us, Across all states, child care workers made less than two-thirds of the median wage for all occupations in the state. In a few states, the median wage for preschool teachers approached or exceeded the state median wage for all occupations, but in nearly half of the states, preschool teacher wages ranged from about 60 to 75 percent of the overall median wage. (p. 19) Preparation that occurs in the context of a CDL with an ADS focus may offer graduates skills in applied research, experience in authentic community issues, and connections with community service agencies. It would also prepare them to be teacher researchers.

Niche Programs

The curricula of programs in higher education look very much alike. There are similar looking programs offering common courses (Kostelnik, 2017). This is true with early education programs, as well, making it difficult for prospective students and their parents to differentiate one program of study from another. In order to make their programs stand out, some institutions are examining ways to position themselves as unique. One way to accomplish this is to create niche programs.

Possible niche programs in early education could have tracts or courses of study that give students the knowledge, skills, and dispositions to excel in a specialized area. Examples of these areas could include poverty studies, social justice, and technology. For instance, a CDL that is focused on social justice and poverty might have field experiences that extend into the community, giving student interns experience in programs such as Head Start or other income-based programs and a deeper understanding of critical social issues.

Collaboration

As budgets shrink and institutions, both public and private, struggle to find ways to do more with less, professional collaborations are becoming more common. For example, Barbour, Wilson, and Ryan Newton (2017) describe several partnerships and collaborations between public institutions. In particular, a partnership between a local school division and a CDL has created the opportunity for the addition of a preschool classroom to serve students of all economic levels. The local school division did not have space for more classrooms, but through a partnership with the local CDL, a classroom was added that also allowed for greater diversity.

With this collaboration of university CDL and a community in need, the students were able to make connections with the local school division and have authentic experience with a population experiencing poverty in their community.

Ecosystems and the CDL Consortium

As noted, Kostelnik (2017) describes the ecosystem of CDLs as thoroughly embedded within the community at the mesosystem level (e.g., home, school, family, home college), the exosystem level (e.g., college, university, stakeholders), and the macrosystem level (e.g., economics, culture, public policy). With the notion of collaboration via the CDL consortium, she sees great potential for the boundaries between the systems to become more permeable and flexible. Kostelnik also sees great potential for a CDL consortium that is embedded in these various and nested systems over time. The collaborative relationships among the universities engaged in a CDL consortium expands the range of the ecosystem exponentially.

CDL HISTORY, CHALLENGES, AND ADS COME TOGETHER

The three-part mission of CDLs is, perhaps, the key to connecting as sites for ADS. Over the long history of lab schools, these three functions have been quite fluid for many CDLs. The fluidity fluctuates based on institutional priorities, political will, faculty interests, and community needs. With ADS as a goal, the overlay of ADS essential elements (applied, developmental, and science) onto the traditional CDL missions (research, service, and professional preparation) becomes both a challenge and a goal. In the case of a consortium, there is the option to choose a particular research focus that guides the collaborative relationship across the consortium members. One approach might be for each CDL to define what component of a certain phenomenon to study and ways it will engage the context and the individuals. Alternatively, the consortium members may decide to study the same research question using different methodologies with different populations. The power of the consortium lies in access to diverse communities and populations, engagement of different theoretical approaches, and the availability of multiplicative points of view. The process is best conceptualized by developing a hypothetical consortium research project, which we attempt to do shortly.

The long-ago voice of Lawrence K. Frank seems to be present in this description of ADS. Likewise, the establishment, almost 100 years ago, of the early child development sites at places like Yale, University of California–Berkley, and University of Iowa, was intended to facilitate the knowledge development that would inform policies affecting families and children. The one enduring characteristic (and criticism) of these early laboratories has been their isolation from the contexts of individuals so clearly defined in ADS. How, then, can we (CDL settings) make the leap from isolation to embeddedness in the quest to engage in ADS? What would it take to push CDLs to this reciprocal, contextual way of engaging in research? Do CDLs offer the opportunity to study real problems within an individual's context, using rigorous methodology that will illuminate developmental principles over the life span (Barbour & McBride, 2017)? The "outreach scholarship" is the one sticking point in conceptualizing the CDL as a site for ADS. How do CDLs move from isolated and contrived settings to those having relevance to human ecology (Lerner et al., 2005)?

A HYPOTHETICAL JOURNEY OF THREE UNIVERSITY LAB SCHOOLS

After much deliberation among a charter group of ten university CDL representatives, a proposal was developed and submitted to the Imaginary Foundation for Child Study, requesting startup costs for the lab consortium. The funds cover the housing and salary of a consortium coordinator on University A campus, including physical space, computers and other technology, administrative assistance, meeting and training room access, and some travel funds. The coordinator is responsible for communicating with the ten consortium member institutions, arranging virtual meetings, coordinating institutional review board procedures, and managing the consortium budget. They keep track of funding RFPs, comb resources for foundation funding, and communicate the information to the consortium chair (CDL director at the home institution). The coordinator also manages the dissemination of policy briefs and research reports.

The Three University Partners Study

At one of its meetings, there is much discussion on how CDLs can address current issues in early childhood education using an ADS model, while demonstrating to their home institutions the relevance and value of CDLs in the generation and application of new knowledge. Partners in this consortium understand that, from a university standpoint, the most important contribution of a CDL is its contribution to the progress of educational thinking, whether it is the testing of psychological principles on child-centered pedagogy or the building and sustaining of community partnerships to enhance learning. Working together allows the partners to address meaningful problems more coherently across institutions and geographic regions using a transdisciplinary and integrative perspective (Kostelnik, 2017).

There is discussion of a collaboration among three of the consortium members, each with vibrant research agendas focused on the development of early childhood teachers. A multi-site, multi-method study is proposed to address innovative ways to prepare students studying to be teachers and provide ongoing professional development for practitioners who need further support and assistance in their roles, so that they might better meet the learning needs of all children. Each university CDL defines which component to study and how they will engage the context and the individuals involved based on a discussion of their respective strengths and established niches.

All three of these sites have a common goal to engage in research that might inform policy makers and practitioners working with children. Engaging in a collaborative effort across multiple sites increases the potential size and diversity of the study participants and allows for different conceptual, methodological, and geographical perspectives. Together, these programs can address real problems using a multimodal and collaborative approach.

University Case 1, located in the central Midwest, has a CDL that engages in traditional research on children's learning and development, using quantitative methods. Most of the research is faculty led by those within the department of child development or by faculty outside of the department who regularly use the CDL as subject pools for their research. Typically, faculty from diverse disciplines have studied issues like children's nutrition and wellness, music and movement, the design of optimum indoor and outdoor learning environments, and children's abilities to form friendships and resolve conflicts, to name a few. Thus, at University Case 1's CDL, research and discovery lead to the generation of new knowledge in multiple disciplines, but it has not been coordinated to address any common, overarching questions. Faculty and students from many different departments use the facility to observe and document children's thinking, learning strategies, and social interactions in order to expand the work of practitioners from a wide variety of disciplines. In particular, undergraduate and graduate students from a variety of disciplines are able to learn about child development based on an outlook of human nature that views children as active, curious, and motivated to explore and understand their world.

The CDL at University Case 2, located in the Eastern region of the United States, is known for its efforts to develop learning communities in which students and teachers engage together in the intellectual and ethical pursuit of teaching and learning, and in so doing, view themselves as researchers who generate, not simply consume, knowledge. More specifically, the vision of the CDL at University Case 2 is to create and nurture a learning community in which students and faculty see themselves as teacher–researchers, change agents, activists, and reflective thinkers, who study teaching practices and the experiences of children in systematic ways in order to solve daily classroom problems and improve educational processes within the classroom.

What does such a lab school look like? Classrooms are inherently social places wherein teachers and children negotiate the curriculum together. There is no prescribed curriculum to follow. In essence, the classroom is a teaching and learning laboratory in which children, students, and teachers are given opportunities to make decisions, pursue authentic questions and concerns, connect what is known to the unknown, and be successful as they explore, test ideas, and discover through play, informal learning activities, and projects.

Prospective teachers learn that to take seriously the complexity of teaching, they must have a voice and an active role in the process of finding the answers to the many problems and dilemmas of teaching practice. Teachers systematically and intentionally collect data about their teaching and children's learning, analyze and interpret it, and use their findings to make better teaching decisions. As this CDL demonstrates, lab schools can have an important influence on practice in teacher education, where there often is a disconnection between theory, research, and practice. When CDL teachers model a teacher as researcher stance and engage prospective teachers in classroom research, lab schools become centers of critical inquiry in which teachers produce knowledge as they interact with children in complex and challenging teaching–learning situations.

University Case 3, located in the upper plains, does not have an on campus CDL, but it does have a well-established Early Childhood Institute that has been putting stronger emphasis on community collaborations to achieve increasingly complex academic challenges, particularly challenges related to limited resources needed to sustain research and provide outreach efforts. The program is committed to engaging in research and evaluating community-based programs and organizations like Head Start, the

Boys and Girls Club and, more recently, activities that occur at the state children's museum that is located in the university town.

Partnering with community agencies allows University Case 3 to extend their missions of teaching, research, and outreach beyond the university confines. Community partners provide spaces in which faculty, preservice teachers, public school teachers, children, families, and industry workers come together to explore different ways of engaging children in solving problems of purpose. The problems are derived from a variety of sources including children's wonderings, teacher questions, and community issues. For example, after several visits to the museum to explore and wonder about each of the interactive exhibits, children's questions and insights, along with teachers' understanding of integrated subject matter and learning standards form the basis of a problem at the children's museum. The outdoor stream is in need of repair to sustain healthy aquatic life. Together, museum staff, teachers and their classes of children, university faculty and their students engage in solving the problem using the scientific method. Through this community collaboration utilizing problem-based learning, children engage in authentic learning experiences, teacher candidates have enriched field-based experiences that allow for critical reflection of their teaching and learning experiences, community partners learn how they can become involved in children's learning, and everyone reaps the benefits of community engagement and research in solving real world problems.

In this example preservice teachers, from freshman to seniors, are involved in some way with the delivery of curriculum, management of classrooms, and communication with families and colleagues. They are using reflective practice to make connections between their content learning and their community-based field experiences with an emphasis on seeing value in learning in context. Faculty from the Early Childhood Institute are in residence at the community partnership sites to serve as clinical mentors and to engage in research. This role connects theory to practice and allows faculty to provide professional development for classroom teachers and community partners, supervise and mentor undergraduate students, and collect data on the effectiveness of community problem-based learning and inquiry. Building on close observation and assessment of children's learning, paying close attention to their questions, interests, and ways of understanding, while nurturing their curiosity, imagination, and creative thinking, students and teachers together foster holistic development and inquiry-based learning.

The identified goal of the proposed research among these three consortium partners is consistent with contemporary ADS. Specifically, the goal is to prepare practitioners with a broader vision of how to apply theory and method to inform practice in the real world of communities and society, where a priority has been placed on developing teachers who can be better equipped to help all children learn and be successful. University Case 1's lab school is a demonstration site for the application of our most advanced and tested ideas related to child development and early childhood education. Research there might best help students and prospective teachers (at all levels, not just early childhood) develop a better understanding of principles of human development, including how children from diverse backgrounds and languages interact, communicate, think, and learn when given opportunities to explore through play and informal learning opportunities. For example, in our proposed study, University Case 1's focus might be on questions like, "How do children learn and how does development in context influence learning?" "What strategies do children use to help them be successful?"

University Case 2's CDL is a demonstration site for teacher research, where teachers learn to become researchers of their own educational practice. The aim of teacher education is the study of teaching and learning, by teachers themselves, and it is viewed as essential to building a grounded theory of what teaching actually is, what it involves, how it is learned, and what it means. This CDL might address questions like, "Who am I becoming as a teacher?" "What motivates me as a teacher in the classroom?" "How does my motivation affect children's learning?" and "What does it mean to teach young children in an age of standardization and accountability testing?"

The research conducted by University Case 3 might help us gain a better understanding of the role of community and even industry in the education process, and how together with universities and schools the CDL can partner to redesign educational curriculum to emphasize scientific inquiry and increase interest and aptitude in STEM disciplines. This research might examine how teacher education programs prepare new teachers to be deeply engaged with children in authentic problem-based learning. It might provide insights into more meaningful and sustained professional development aimed at helping practicing teachers to plan, design, assess curriculum, and teach using inquiry. Questions such as, "How do community-based partnerships aid teachers in better preparing children to learn 21st Century skills?" and "How does problem-based learning better prepare children for career, college, and life skills?" could be addressed.

The value of an ADS Consortium is to bring together multi-disciplinary partners across several CDLs, each with their own mission priorities and strengths. In this section, we created a fictitious example of how three universities might collaborate to address an important issue—the professional preparation and development of teachers to be not only sound practitioners, but also theorists, researchers, and community partners, with the aim of providing promising practices that will enable all children to learn. Together, they address different aspects of this issue enabling coherence and convergence of our current knowledge on development, learning, and practice across programs and geographic settings (Kostelnik, 2017). Each university demonstrates that, although they are structurally and functionally diverse, they can serve as places for the generation of new knowledge and inquiry that employs the characteristics of ADS; namely, a commitment to engage in applied, developmental research using a variety of methods in a variety of community contexts. Together, they can contribute to a growing database that is informed by the voices of practitioners, researchers, and community partners engaged in a robust and meaningful research agenda that challenges conventional ideas about field experiences, tests the impact of different curricular models on children's learning, and evaluates the benefits of partnerships among various partners in educating children and improving the well-being of communities. As such, it can inform future research, practice, and policy.

CAN WE GET THERE?

What would it take to make the idea of an ADS consortium a reality? As in any collaboration, there must be buy in from faculty and administration, funding to support and sustain collaboration and cross-site research and professional development, and a commitment to engage in reciprocal, contextual, and embedded research. These are just a few of the things that would need thoughtful discussion among those seeking to develop a consortium.

CDL program directors often have enough difficulty convincing their university administrators of the centrality of lab schools in the generation of new knowledge and outreach to the community, and they struggle to justify their existence in times of limited resources. Opportunities to enhance research activity and grant funding through participation in a consortium may be just the ticket for strengthening the value of lab schools on university campuses, especially as they develop robust joint and reciprocal research and teacher development agendas. Bringing CDLs together has advantages conceptually but managing and sustaining a collaboration of several programs has challenges practically. This will require resources to support regular communication among member institutions through opportunities for essential face-to-face dialogue. Using multiple sites for a single research study raises such questions as how data collected across settings will be stored and shared and who will manage the database and oversee research protocol. McBride (2017) offers a foundation for what a database management system might look like within a consortium model. He suggests that "a core infrastructure component would be creating systems within each participating member of the consortium for gathering, organizing, managing, and sharing data as part of consortium efforts" (p. 8).

Further, McBride (2017) discusses the development of an advisory committee to represent the various stakeholders (CDL directors, teachers, children, faculty researchers, etc.) that would be involved in consortium projects. This group would be charged with creating a shared vision, core commitments, and goals for the consortium, and overseeing the progress of its activities. Having a web presence would enable investigators and teachers from the consortium to be in regular communication about research proposals and information sharing, including research questions and methodologies, and generated reports on how to provide professional development or engage community partners in collaborations locally. In particular, the consortium web site could provide evidence-based information on how to work meaningfully with community-based programs to support data collection, analysis, and interpretation of research results for making program decisions.

Horm (2017) also offers some useful insights into what it might take to develop an ADS lab school consortium in her cogent discussion of Educare as a model of multi-site, collaborative and policy relevant research. Educare is a high quality comprehensive child and family development program designed for children and families living in poverty. Educare and quality lab schools share similar features that embrace the principles of ADS, including the delivery of high quality programs informed by sound research questions and methods aimed at addressing meaningful problems of practice that can direct future research and provide relevant information to practitioners and policymakers (Horm, 2017). Among her list of important considerations for the development of a lab school consortium are (a) the need for strategic decision-making about including lab schools that can address the needs of varied populations, (b) an articulated research agenda and theoretical framework that can address the gaps in the literature on early childhood teacher professional development and help educators make sense of the findings, (c) ongoing communication and professional development to maintain proper momentum and expertise in the conduct of ADS, (d) funding to support collaboration and infrastructure, (e) and continued involvement of practitioners and policymakers in research and dissemination efforts.

We, along with our colleagues McBride (2017) and Horm (2017), believe that there is hope for the realization of an ADS lab school consortium. This multi-site collaborative might enhance and support the role of lab schools in their missions to generate new knowledge through robust collaborative research that addresses the unanswered research questions in early childhood teacher education, better prepare early childhood teachers to use and conduct research in their classrooms to improve teaching and learning, and provide new insights into the kinds of research needed to inform practice and policy.

NOTE

1. The authors would like to acknowledge Dr. Brent McBride, University of Illinois, Urbana–Champaign for his leadership in bringing together a group of child development laboratory advocates to brainstorm the concept of a CDL consortium.

REFERENCES

{REF}Barbour, N. E. (2003). The early history of child development laboratory programs. In B. A. McBride & N. E. Barbour (Eds.), *Bridging the gap between theory, research, and practice: The role of child development laboratory programs in early childhood education* (pp. 9–30). New York, NY: Elsevier.

Barbour, N. E., & McBride, B. A. (2017). Introduction: The future of child development laboratory schools. In N. E. Barbour & B. A. McBride (Eds.), *The future of child development lab schools: Applied developmental science in action* (pp. 1–4). New York, NY: Routledge.

Barbour, N. E., Wilson, R., & Ryan Newton, J. (2017). Making the shift from preschool to laboratory school; A case example. In N. E. Barbour & B. A. McBride (Eds.), *The future of child development lab schools: Applied developmental science in action* (pp. 71–82). New York, NY: Routledge.

Carnevale, A. P., Cheah, B., & Hanson, A. R. (2015). *The economic value of college majors.* Washington, DC: Georgetown University, Center on Education and the Workforce. Retrieved from https://1gyhoq479ufd3yna29x7ubjn-wpengine .netdna-ssl.com/wp-content/uploads/The-Economic-Value-of-College -Majors-Full-Report-web-FINAL.pdf

Dewey, J. (1899). *The school and society.* Chicago, IL: University of Chicago Press.

Elicker, J., & Barbour, N. (Eds.). (2014). *University laboratory schools.* New York, NY: Taylor and Francis.

Horm, D. (2017). Educare as a model of multi-site, collaborative, policy-relevant research. In N. E. Barbour & B. A. McBride (Eds.), *The future of child development lab schools: Applied developmental science in action* (pp. 83–94). New York, NY: Routledge.

Kostelnik, M. (2017). What child development laboratories need to do to thrive: An administrator's perspective. In N. E. Barbour & B. A. McBride (Eds.), *The future of child development lab schools: Applied developmental science in action* (pp. 95–112). New York, NY: Routledge.

Lerner, R. M., Wertlieb, D., & Jacobs, F. (2005). Historical and theoretical bases of applied developmental science. In R. M. Lerner, F. Jacobs, & D. Wertlieb (Eds.), *Applied developmental science: An advanced textbook* (pp. 1–29). Thousand Oaks, CA: SAGE.

Lomax, E. (1977). The Laura Spelman Rockefeller memorial: Some of its contributions to early research in child development. *Journal of the History of the Behavioral Sciences, 13,* 283–293.

McBride, B. A. (2017). Data and infrastructure supports: Critical components for the future of child development laboratory schools. In N. E. Barbour & B. A.

McBride (Eds.), *The future of child development lab schools: Applied developmental science in action* (pp. 5–21). New York, NY: Routledge.

McBride, B. A., Groves, M., Barbour, N., Horm, D., Stremmel, A., Lash, M., ... Toussaint, S. (2012). Child development laboratory schools as generators of knowledge in early childhood education: New models and approaches. *Early Education and Development, 23*(2), 153–164.

Schlossman, S. L. (1986). Perils of popularization: The founding of Parents Magazine. *Monographs of the society for research and child development, 50*(4/5), 65–77.

Senn, M. J. E. (1975). Insights on the child development movement in the United States. *Monographs of the Society for Research in Child Development, 40*(3/4 Serial No. 161), 1–107.

Whipple, G. M. (Ed.). (1929). *Twenty-eighth yearbook of the National Society for the Study of Education: Pre-school and parental education.* Bloomington, IL: Public School.

Whitebook, M., McLean, C., & Austin, L. J. E. (2016). Early childhood workforce index–2016. *Center for the Study of Child Care Employment.* University of California, Berkeley.

CHAPTER 4

ACADEMICS VERSUS SERVICE IN CHILD DEVELOPMENT LABORATORY SCHOOLS

Complementary and Competing Pressures[1]

Brent A. McBride and Meghan Fisher

ABSTRACT

University-based child development laboratory schools for infants, toddlers, and preschoolers have a long and rich history. Since their inception in the mid-1920s they have played a vital role in adding to our ever expanding knowledge base on child development and early childhood education. In recent years, many lab school programs have shifted from providing traditional half-day preschool classes to offering full-day child care programs, while at the same time maintaining the teacher training and research functions associated with lab schools. Although offering full-day child care classes has expanded opportunities for lab schools to facilitate teacher training and research activities, it has also brought on many challenges not faced when working with half-day preschool classes. The purpose of this chapter is to provide an overview

Contemporary Perspectives on Research on Child Development Laboratory Schools in Early Childhood Education,
pages 63–77
Copyright © 2019 by Information Age Publishing

of these unique challenges, as well as a discussion of possible strategies which lab school programs can implement in order to overcome such challenges.

Child development laboratory (CDL) schools began to emerge on college and university campuses during the 1920s as part of the child study movement. Although these early laboratory school programs took on many different forms and existed within a variety of institutional formats (e.g., large Research I universities, small private institutions of higher education), they all addressed in one form or another the tripartite mission of engagement in research, teaching, and outreach/engagement activities that served as the foundation for laboratory schools (Barbour & McBride, 2017). Over time laboratory school programs varied in terms of the emphasis they placed on each part of their tripartite mission (McBride & Baumgartner, 2003). In spite of this variation, laboratory schools have played, and continue to play a central role in the generation of new knowledge that informs the child development and early childhood education fields (McBride et al., 2012).

Providing high quality early care and education services for enrolled children and their families has always been a central role played by CDL schools. Although important, this service mission cannot be the sole reason for laboratory schools to exist on college and university campuses. As outlined by Kostelnik (2017), laboratory schools encompass the total academic enterprise—that is, conducting research on child development and early education; preparing the next generation of early childhood professionals; and engaging with the community to improve the lives of individuals, families, and communities. Unfortunately, in recent years many laboratory schools have been struggling for continued existence due to the shrinking support base available on many college and university campuses (McBride et al., 2012). Laboratory schools require significant financial, personnel and facility investments, and it has become increasingly difficult to justify these investments. One strategy employed in recent years by many laboratory schools to address this challenge has been to move away from traditional half-day preschool programming on a part-day, 9-month basis that has been common in such programs, to full-day, year-round programming (McBride et al., 2012). Although such shifts can be effective in addressing many of the financial challenges confronting laboratory schools, many have been reluctant to make such transitions due to the perceived movement in emphasis away from an academic mission to one of a service only mission to the university community—that is, campus child care (McBride & Baumgartner, 2003). Service and academic missions, by design, are not mutually exclusive endeavors and should be viewed as complementary processes underlying university-based early care and education programs—that is, service activities can inform the teaching and research initiatives taking place, while the research and teaching activities can form the foundation of the early childhood programming being provided for enrolled children and their families.

The failure of laboratory schools to implement full-day programming models due to this perceived dichotomy between service and academic missions leads to several unintended consequences. For example, offering half-day programming for enrolled children on a nine-month basis, with an optional short-term, half-day summer experience for a small group of children was a very traditional model that was prevalent in both university-based laboratory school programs and community-based preschool programs in the 1940s, 50s, 60s, and 70s (Barbour, 2003). Such traditional 9-month, half-day preschool programming does not reflect the nature of early care and education programs that dominate the early childhood landscape in 2017 (Barbour, Wilson, & Newton, 2017). Although important, half-day preschool experiences on a 9-month basis do not meet the early care and education needs for a majority of families in the United States, especially for those children from low-income and high-risk backgrounds. This disconnect limits the ability of laboratory schools that maintain a traditional half-day preschool program model to generate new knowledge that can inform the current early care and education fields.

The emphasis on half-day programming also limits the diversity in the children being served by laboratory schools. With an emphasis on traditional preschool programming, children attending laboratory schools using such models tend to come from well-resourced families that have the ability to have one parent at home to provide care for the child during days/times when they are not receiving the preschool programming, or they have the financial resources to manage multiple care arrangements (e.g., nannies) and dedicated individuals to transport the child between settings and during the summer months. Additionally, in maintaining a traditional preschool programming model, laboratory schools will fall short in meeting their teacher training missions. The program model and child populations in such programs do not match what university students conducting practicum and internship placements will find when they assume leadership roles within community based settings such as Head Start programs, state funded Pre-K programs, and community-based early care and education programs (Kostelnik, 2017). Similarly, the populations served by laboratory schools that maintain a half-day preschool program model are not attractive to researchers desiring to gather data from children and families. The limited SES and developmental diversity reflected in such programs introduces potential bias in any data being gathered with this population, and limits the generalizability of findings to only children who come from well-resourced family backgrounds comparable to those of children at the laboratory schools. Additionally, bias will be inherent in any data gathered from teachers and the teaching strategies they employ within the UNIQUE environments found in such laboratory schools that maintain a traditional half-day preschool program model. As a result, researchers are less likely to see the laboratory schools as viable options for their work.

Finally, one of the hallmarks of the outreach/engagement mission of CDL schools is to serve as a "model" program for the local, state, national, and international early childhood communities. In serving in this model program capacity, laboratory schools are able to share their knowledge base and collective expertise beyond their institutional boundaries, and to ultimately impact the types of services being offered in community based settings. Given that the traditional half-day preschool model used by many laboratory schools is not reflective of early care and education programs across the United States, these programs are unable to fill their model program role for the field.

Taken together, these unintended consequences experienced by laboratory schools that are reluctant to move towards full-day programming due to the perceived dichotomy between service and academic missions severely limits the ability of such programs to effectively address the teaching, research, and outreach/engagement missions commonly associated with laboratory schools. As mentioned earlier, service and academic missions, by design, are not mutually exclusive endeavors. The CDL program on the University of Illinois at Urbana–Champaign (UIUC) campus has been in existence since 1942. For the past 25+ years this NAEYC-accredited program has had a history of providing high quality, full-day early care and education services for enrolled children and their families, while at the same time being integral to teaching, research, and outreach activities of faculty and students from across campus. What follows in this chapter is a summary of the many lessons we have learned during this time period that have allowed for the CDL program to successfully balance both service and academic missions to the UIUC community.

HISTORICAL CONTEXT OF THE CDL PROGRAM

The CDL program has a rich 75-year history of facilitating and supporting teaching, research, and outreach activities of faculty, staff, and students on the UIUC campus. Begun in 1942 as part of what was then known as the School of Home Economics, this program has evolved over the years in terms of its configuration, children served, program models implemented, and academic oversight. Prior to 1990 a traditional half-day, 9-month preschool model was used to provide programming for children ages 3 to 5. Beginning in 1990 a move was made to expand the services being provided to include both full-day, year round early care and education programming, as well as traditional half-day, nine-month preschool programming. In 2003 a new facility was built that greatly expanded the services being provided for enrolled children and families, with an emphasis on full-day, year-round programming for children from birth to 5 years of age. Currently the CDL program serves 160 children ages birth to 5 years in 12 full-day, 12-month early care and education classrooms. As the CDL program moved towards a full-day program model, several protocols, procedures infrastructure supports were put in place to allow the program to successfully balance service and academic activities as a laboratory school. A glance at our most recent *Annual Report* (CDL, 2017) provides evidence of how this balance has led to the CDL program being fully integrated into the teaching, research and outreach/engagement activities of the UIUC community. As highlighted in the activities outlined in this report, CDL teachers and staff play an instrumental role in connecting theory and research being presented in University courses to practice for the UIUC community. In facilitating 4,187 student observations, 1,272 student class projects, 16 research projects, and 77 student internship/practicum placements, the CDL program was integrated into the teaching, research, and outreach/engagement activities of faculty, staff, and students from six of the colleges on the UIUC campus (i.e., Agricultural, Consumer and Environmental Sciences; Applied Health Sciences; Education; Fine & Applied Arts; Liberal Arts & Sciences; Media) and the School of Social Work, as well as faculty and students from five departments at other Universities. This ability to successfully balance the demands of a heavy service and academic mission on the campus of a Research I university has allowed the CDL program to emerge as a leader in university-based laboratory schools. In the sections that is an overview of the most important factors that have allowed the CDL to successfully maintain its commitment to the three-part mission of laboratory schools while providing high quality full-day, early care and education services for enrolled children and their families.

CRITICAL FACTORS FOR SUCCESSFULLY BALANCING SERVICE AND ACADEMIC MISSIONS

Physical Facilities That Support Laboratory School Activities

During the design phase of the new CDL building in 2003, visits were made to several CDL schools at other universities to gain a sense of what was, and was not, working at other institutions. Based on these visits it became apparent that when observation booths, research rooms, university classrooms, storage space, and so forth, were not created or in place to support these programs, lab school activities were not occurring. The physical setting needed for a program with a primarily service mission (i.e., campus childcare) differs greatly from that required for laboratory schools fulfilling both a service and academic mission. The creation of physical space to support teaching and research objectives is critical for enabling laboratory schools to successfully balance service and academic activities. This insight led to the final design of the new CDL facility that included a university classroom on the second floor of the building to encourage professors to utilize the facilities for class observations. Observation booths were built between each of the children's classrooms with one-way mirrors and five-way zoned sound systems that allow observers to clearly hear any sound within the classroom. Two pull-out research rooms were created within the building to support the work of university researchers. Staff offices were built upstairs to allow teachers to conduct clinical supervision meetings, meetings with researchers, and other functions related to laboratory school activities. Finally, recognizing the large number of students and faculty as well as parents, teachers, and children that would be utilizing the building, traffic flow and security considerations were taken into account. All entrances in the building were designed to be locked to visitors except for the front entrance where guests sign in and can check out observation equipment at the staffed front desk. This system enabled easy access for observations to take place, yet maintained the security of the program. By creating the physical space that acknowledges both the service and academic activities taking place within the program, the CDL is able to effectively balance and mitigate what is often the competing pressures on the physical facilities of such programs.

Faculty Member in Leadership Role

One of the most integral factors in sustaining the CDL's commitment to lab school missions has been the positioning of a tenured faculty member in a leadership role at the CDL. As both program director and a professor of human development, the faculty director has been able to serve as a liaison between the department, college, campus, and laboratory school; advocating the importance of supporting teaching and research to the classroom teachers, and advocating the needs of the children and teachers to the researchers and instructors who wish to use the facility. Without a faculty member in this position, there is a risk of a disconnect developing between the laboratory school staff and the university faculty and researchers due to different priorities and/or a failure to see the importance of the others' objectives (Clawson, 2003; Stremmel, Hill, & Fu, 2003). Placing a faculty member in this role enables laboratory school activities to become integral parts of departmental and campus activities while still maintaining the integrity and quality of the early care and education service dimension of the program.

Financial Support for Academic Activities

Supporting the teaching, research, and outreach functions of laboratory schools while balancing these academic activities with the service mission of early care and education requires investments of time and money. In the case of the CDL, competitive salaries and benefits must be offered to find and retain qualified master-level teachers who are dedicated to participating in the academic functions of the program such as providing assistance to researchers, training student workers, and contributing to community outreach efforts. Time must be created for teachers to complete these tasks through office hours, and additional staff must be hired to cover these office hours while the teachers are out of the classrooms. Funding to support these and other academic activities which are not directly related to the service mission of providing high quality early and education services for enrolled children should not come from the tuition paid by parents (McBride & Baumgartner, 2003). In developing an operational plan for the CDL, cost models were developed that carefully distinguished between academic expenses and costs directly related to the care of children at every level of the operation. This ensures that parents are not paying for expenses that are not related to the actual care of their children. The CDL has been fortunate in its ability to receive funds to support activities related to the academic mission from departmental, college, and campus resources. These revenue streams are used to support teachers' office hours both directly and indirectly—directly, through funding received to support staffing needs during teacher office hours, and indirectly, through contributions made by the university to fund one full-time kitchen employee at the CDL, which permitted revenues that ordinarily would have been directed towards kitchen support to be spent on master teacher office hours. Finally, the university provides support for graduate research assistants to orient and work with researchers, data collectors, and classes using the facility to support teaching and research related activities. This university support for the financial costs associated with academic activities allows the CDL program to effectively balance the demands of maintaining a service and academic mission.

Clearly Articulated Priority of the Academic Mission

Another critical factor for successfully balancing academic and service activities within a laboratory school environment is ensuring there is clarity in how teaching, research, and outreach activities are identified as being a high priority with laboratory schools. As articulated by Kostelnik (2017), although important, this service mission cannot be the sole reason for laboratory schools to exist on college and university campuses. In order to remain viable, laboratory schools must have a strong commitment to fulfilling its academic mission by being able to actively support and facilitate teaching, research, and outreach activities. In expanding to a full-day, full-year program model, the academic mission has been kept on the forefront of CDL teachers' minds through messages in the staff handbook, as well as communication with the director, assistant director, master teachers, and other teachers during daily interactions and staff meetings. The administration at the CDL has also conveyed the importance of the academic missions to staff through their actions by providing teacher office hours to support lab school activities. While the provision of high quality early care and education services is always the main impetus behind decision making, teachers at all levels are encouraged to make these decisions within the framework of supporting teaching, research, and outreach. For example, as teachers are rearranging classroom furniture and toys, they need to consider whether their new arrangements might obstruct observers' views of the children from the observation booths, and avoid doing so whenever possible. When the importance of academic missions are continually reinforced for teachers through program literature, daily conversations with other staff members, and supportive administrative actions, laboratory schools can better ensure that academic activities will continue to play a central role in program functioning while balancing such activities with the service aspects of the program.

Placement of Qualified Staff in Critical Positions

In order to successfully balance service and academic activities in laboratory school settings, it is crucial that positions of leadership are filled by qualified staff members who are dedicated to supporting the three-part mission of such programs. At the CDL, careful consideration is taken when selecting individuals to fill key program roles such as the associate director, program coordinator, master teacher, and head teacher positions. Individuals in these positions must demonstrate an ongoing commitment to the teaching, research, and outreach missions associated with the laboratory school, and use this commitment to establish an atmosphere that is conducive to balancing service and academic activities. The administrative team sets expectations for teacher roles, provides support to allow teachers to engage in lab school activities, communicates the philosophy of the lab school to the staff, and oversees the implementation of lab school activities. Likewise, master teachers and head teachers instill commitment to the three-part mission in the staff members and students they work with through staff supervision, training, and classroom programming. Such committed staff play a crucial role maintain the balance of service and academic activities in laboratory school programs.

Establishing Protocols for Working With Vulnerable Populations

While addressing academic activities is important, the well-being of the children is critical as laboratory schools strive to maintain a balance between academic and service functions. To protect the interests of children and maintain the quality of classroom programming, a careful screening process is needed to filter proposals from researchers, instructors, and students. For example, research and teaching activities implemented at the CDL program that work in the infant and toddler classrooms must pass a selective screening process and undergo fine-tuning in order to ensure that the activities will not detract from the young children's classroom experiences. At all age levels, no more than one researcher is allowed in a classroom at a time, and researchers are required to spend time building rapport with any children that they involve in their research. In addition, student placements in classrooms are carefully considered according to students' experience with children, the ages of children they have worked with, and so forth. Having such protocols in place allows laboratory schools to negotiate the demands of facilitating academic related activities with the desire to maintain high quality service activities for enrolled children.

In retrospect, a combination of several critical factors has allowed the CDL to successfully maintain its commitment to teaching, research, and outreach activities while balancing the service related demands associated with full-day programming: designing the physical space to support lab school activities, placing a tenured faculty member in a leadership role to bridge academic and childcare needs and perspectives, obtaining university support to fund the academic and operating costs of the program, clearly articulating the CDL's commitment to academic missions to staff members, placing highly qualified and dedicated individuals in key administrative and teaching positions to reinforce commitment to the three-part mission, and, finally, creating sensitive screening protocols and procedures for research and teaching proposals to protect the interests of the children in the program and maintain high quality classroom programming. It is important to emphasize, however, that while the success of the CDL's ability to balance service and academic related activities associated with laboratory schools is commendable, this balancing act has not evolved without problems or setbacks. In the following section, we will discuss some of the struggles we have encountered and the lessons we have learned over the years as we continually focus on the delicate balance between service and activities in laboratory school settings.

LESSONS LEARNED WHILE ATTEMPTING TO BALANCE SERVICE AND ACADEMIC ACTIVITIES

At the CDL one of the most difficult aspects of moving to full-day expanded early care and education services within a laboratory school framework has been the difficulty of transitioning staff from functioning within a "childcare framework" to a "lab school framework." Here, a lab school framework is conceptualized as one within which teachers engage in reflective thought, actively connect research and theory with practice, serve as role models to student interns and observers, and provide support for laboratory school activities. This framework contains expectations for teachers that go well beyond those typically encountered in an ordinary childcare setting. It requires teachers to actively be aware of why they do what they do with children, how the classroom programming they create contributes to children's development, and how such programming fits within the philosophy of the program and the missions of the lab school. Administrators and teachers at the CDL have experienced several learning opportunities over the years as they struggled to balance service and academic related activities.

Individualizing Staff Training

When utilizing a master teacher model that is commonly found in laboratory schools, employees range from recent high school graduates to teachers with master's degrees and extensive experience in laboratory school environments. Consequently, it is unrealistic to expect all staff members to be at the same point in their adjustment to the lab school setting initially. With the expansion of the CDL program on the UIUC campus, 32 new staff members who were hired at the opening of the new facility. Although most of these teachers had considerable childcare experience, very few had ever worked in a laboratory school setting. In recognition of this fact, a slower, more gradual approach was adopted in supporting and facilitating staff during this crucial transition to a laboratory school environment.

Defining the philosophy of the CDL and its commitment to balancing service and academic missions collaboratively with staff members, encouraging reflective practices, and emphasizing the importance of the connection of research and theory with practice, were instrumental in this processes. In retrospect, we found that it was important to start wherever each employee was within her or his understanding of the laboratory school model and provide training from there, rather than using one method to train all personnel. It is important to note that it was not always the case that employees with the least education needed the most guidance in adjusting to the laboratory school framework. For example, despite having received her bachelor's degree and having considerable experience working with children, one newly hired lead teacher had difficulty using her knowledge of child development to inform/guide her planning and practice in the classroom. This teacher's previous childcare experiences had not required her to engage in reflective thought or to actively apply her knowledge of theory and research. Through intensive mentorship from the age-level master teacher and paid time spent auditing an early childhood development course, this teacher was gradually able to improve in her ability to work within the laboratory school model, and was able to begin connecting theory and research to her practice. Supporting teachers' professional growth needs at all levels within the master teacher model is crucial. Such support includes an emphasis on how the transition to a full-day lab school framework requires staff to have the requisite skills needed to successfully balance service and academic activities within laboratory school settings.

Defining the Role of the Master Teacher

While the use of a master teacher model is widely discussed within laboratory school settings, the "right way" to implement this model is not yet known. The career ladder model is most appropriate for large laboratory school programs where the massive amount of academic and service tasks required by teachers necessitates the division of responsibility across levels of teachers. Under this career ladder model, lead teachers use release time from the classroom floor to assume responsibility for the clinical supervision of student teachers, internship and practicum students, in addition to working with researchers and instructors implementing projects in the program. Assistant teachers provide continuity for classroom programming when lead teachers are performing these duties outside of the classroom. Accordingly, it was not until the expansion of the CDL program that it seemed necessary to shift to this staffing model. Defining the role of the master teacher has been an ongoing challenge within the expanded program, and the role is continually being redefined as we gain more experience using this model. In addition to providing mentorship, professional feedback, and staff supervision to other age-level teachers, master teachers at the ECDL are also required to lead their own classrooms, train student interns and workers, participate in the hiring of new staff members, and work with researchers and instructors as needed—all critical functions necessary for balancing the service and academic missions of laboratory schools. Developing a functional and appropriate master teacher staffing model is critical for achieving success in balancing service and academic activities in laboratory school settings.

Scheduling Meetings

Scheduling time for staff to engage in meetings and complete lab school activities is another critical component of successfully balancing service and academic activities. Student workers must be available in order for teachers to leave their classrooms, and student coverage is often difficult to find, particularly during school breaks, midterms, and finals (McBride & Baumgartner, 2003). In addition, too many integral teachers cannot be absent from one classroom at a time, and this interferes with the program's ability to provide time for master teachers to hold supervision meetings with staff and classroom teams. Due to these challenges, teachers sometimes need to meet before or after work hours to talk; a solution with which staff is dissatisfied. Efforts must be made to accommodate the scheduling needs of staff using strategies such as identifying dependable student workers and permanent floating substitute teachers that can be utilized as needed. Scheduling time for office hours, staff meetings, and master teacher meetings is essential to the success of a lab school program. If teachers are not able to talk with one another and engage in reflective practice and program planning, if they are not able to take time to meet with researchers/instructors, and if they are not able to take time to engage in outreach efforts, the program will struggle as they are confronted with the challenges of balancing service and academic activities in laboratory school settings.

Staff Turnover

Historically, most laboratory schools, including the CDL, have experienced relatively low turnover rates due to the presence of highly committed and qualified staff. Some employees at the CDL have been working in their positions for as long as 15–20 years. With the movement to full-day, full-year programming and the introduction of a career ladder model, however, rates of turnover have increased. Such increases in staff turnover have also been evident in laboratory school programs across the country (Stremmel et al., 2003). This increase is due to several contributing factors. The master teacher model draws from employees who tend to be at very different points in their life courses both personally and professionally (i.e., employees include recent high school graduates, undergraduate students preparing for graduate school, established teachers in the early childhood community, etc.). As a result, turnover due to differing life course needs such as moving on to graduate school, seeking a new job, or retiring are not uncommon and are even to be expected. In addition, some employees may choose to leave if they find that they prefer working in a more typical childcare setting over working within the lab school framework. Related to this, employees may be asked to leave if they are unable to meet the expectations associated with working in a lab school setting. The departure of a familiar staff member and the training of new staff members can be potentially disruptive for children as well as classroom teams of teachers. The key to minimizing the potential negative impact is for programs to have a plan in place to ease such transition periods. Incorporating standardized training procedures for new staff members (i.e., checklists of training information to be covered by new staff, immersion into the laboratory school model, specific training topics to be covered by different staff and administrators, etc.). Creating effective ways to prepare for and respond to turnover will not only allow laboratory schools to reduce the strain caused by staff transitions in their own programs, but will also allow them to inform the turnover practices of other laboratory schools and community-based programs through dissemination and outreach efforts. Advanced preparation for dealing with staff turnover will also allow laboratory school programs to maintain the balance between service and academic activities as they experience such transitions.

CONCLUSION

An increasing number of CDL schools are moving towards full-day programming and expanded services in order to cope with budget cuts and greater demands for campus childcare (McBride & Baumgartner, 2003). Full-day programming often decreases lab school activities when the emphasis is shifted to a service mission priority. However, this type of programming also holds the possibility of increasing opportunities for laboratory school activities, particularly when critical issues involved in the transition to full-day programming are foreseen and managed. The expansion to full-day childcare and doubled enrollment at the CDL at the University of Illinois provides an example of one program which, while still evolving, has already established a working model for balancing the demands associated with a heavy service mission (i.e., early care and education services for 160 enrolled children and their families) with the competing, and often conflicting demands associated with being an actively engaged laboratory school that is fully integrated into the teaching, research, and outreach missions of the UIUC community. Many of the issues raised in this chapter will need to be explored and addressed as other laboratory schools across the country explore moving towards the provision of full-day, year-long programming for enrolled children and their families while still actively supporting the teaching, research, and outreach initiatives of their host institutions.

NOTE

1. The content of this manuscript was presented at the 2017 National Association for the Education of Young Children Professional Learning Institute in San Francisco, CA. Portions of the manuscript were previously published in the *Journal of Early Childhood Teacher Education* Vol. 25, 2005.

REFERENCES

Barbour, N. E. (2003). The early history of child development laboratory programs. In B. A. McBride & N. E. Barbour (Eds.), *Bridging the gap between theory, research, and practice: The role of child development laboratory programs in early childhood education* (pp. 9–29). Oxford, England: Elsevier.

Barbour, N. E., & McBride, B. A. (2017). Introduction: The future of child development laboratory schools. In N. E. Barbour & B. A. McBride (Eds.), *The future of child development lab schools: Applied developmental science in action* (pp. 1–4). New York, NY: Taylor & Francis..

Barbour, N. E., Wilson, R., & Newton, J.R. (2017). Making the shift from preschool to laboratory school: A case example. In N. Barbour & B. A. McBride (Eds.), *The future of child development laboratory schools: Applied developmental science in action* (pp. 71–82). New York, NY: Taylor & Francis.

Child Development Laboratory. (2017). *2016–2017 Child Development Laboratory Annual Report.* Retrieved from https://cdl.illinois.edu/annual-report/

Clawson, M. A. (2003). The dilemma of linking theory and research with practice and innovation in child development laboratory programs. In B. A. McBride & N. E. Barbour (Eds.), *Bridging the gap between theory, research, and practice: The role of child development laboratory programs in early childhood education* (pp. 51–87). Oxford, England: Elsevier.

Kostelnik, M. (2017). What child development laboratories need to do to thrive. In N. Barbour & B. McBride (Eds.), *The future of child development laboratory schools: Applied developmental science in action* (pp. 95–112). New York, NY: Taylor & Francis.

McBride, B. A., & Baumgartner, J. (2003). The changing profile of teaching, research, and outreach activities in lab school programs. In B. A. McBride & N. E. Barbour (Eds.), *Bridging the gap between theory, research, and practice: The role of child development laboratory programs in early childhood education* (pp. 181–199). Oxford, England: Elsevier.

McBride, B. A., Groves, M., Barbour, N., Horm, D., Stremmel, A., Lash, M., . . . Toussaint, S. (2012). Child development laboratory schools as generators of knowledge in early childhood education: New models and approaches. *Early Education and Development, 23,* 153–164.

Stremmel, A. J., Hill, L. T., & Fu, V. R. (2003). An inside perspective of paradigm shifts in child development laboratory programs: Bridging theory and professional preparation. In B. McBride & N. Barbour (Eds.), *Bridging the gap between theory, research, and practice: The role of child development laboratory programs in early childhood education* (pp. 89–111). Oxford, England: Elsevier.

PART II

MODELS OF CHILD DEVELOPMENT
LABORATORY SCHOOLS

CHAPTER 5

AN INNOVATIVE EARLY CHILDHOOD LABORATORY SCHOOL CONTEMPORARY MODEL

Elizabeth Schlesinger-Devlin and Megan L. Purcell

ABSTRACT

This manuscript discusses how one early childhood laboratory school serves as a pedagogical model for innovation within the field of the early childhood education. Laboratory schools on university campuses often hold to the same three tenets of research, education, and service, as does the larger university community. These three "arms" serve as a basis for innovation. This manuscript highlights how one early childhood laboratory school addresses the three arms in innovation through, first, providing a brief history of early childhood laboratory schools in general along with the history of the Ben and Maxine Miller Child Development Laboratory School (MCDLS) at Purdue University. Secondly, an in depth discussion of current research occurring at the MCDLS is included. Finally, educational practices of the early childhood program along with university professional preparation programs and opportunities for service within the community and state is presented. Importantly,

Contemporary Perspectives on Research on Child Development Laboratory Schools in Early Childhood Education, pages 81–100

an exploration of the benefits for teachers, children, families, university faculty, and MCDLS staff is included throughout the topics of this manuscript.

The study of young children has a long history with deep pedagogical roots. Early childhood programs have been in existence as far back as John Locke's (1632–1704) philosophical concept called educational experiences through play. Johann Pestalozzi (1746–1827) established the first preschool in 1801 as a child-centered program, and the first nurseries in the United States originated in Boston in the 1840s (Beatty, 1995). This history demonstrates the importance of focused interest and investment in young children's progression and advancement. The list of influential philosophers and theorists such as Rousseau, Itard, Froebel, Vygotsky, Piaget, Montessori, Erickson, Gerber, and others each played a vital role in the establishment of the field in early childhood education. The information on the early childhood field is expansive but, for the purpose of this manuscript, the field of knowledge will specifically focus on early childhood laboratory schools, and even more specifically on one early childhood laboratory school that is integrated into an academic department at a mid-west research university.

HISTORY OF EARLY CHILDHOOD LABORATORY SCHOOLS

A brief history of early childhood laboratory schools in the United States begins with the work of John Dewey. The oldest laboratory school was founded in 1894 at Chicago University with the vision of Dewey and support from Chicago University President William R. Harper (Barbour, 2003; Monroe, 2009). Dewey noted the focus in creating the early childhood laboratory school was addressing two fundamental pieces: (a) creating a rich environment where young children were active participants of their growth and development, and (b) the intentional collaboration of interdisciplinary professionals working together conducting research establishing best practices (Tanner, 1997). Another early childhood laboratory school with a historical past includes Bank Street, established in 1916 by Lucy Sprague Mitchell and Harriet Johnson. Dewey was influential to Mitchell and Johnson who shared his ideology of children needing meaningful learning experiences (Boegehold, Cuffaro, Hooks, & Klopf, 1977; Bank Street School for Children, n.d.; Johnson, 2006). Bank Street School for Children included training teachers and others on how to create environments where children thrived in their development and growth (Bank Street School for Children, n.d.). More early childhood laboratory schools were emerging around the same period with related beliefs and visions for the value of child-directed, play rich environments and included the aspect of research and teacher education. Examples of early childhood laboratory schools include:

- The Horace Mann Laboratory School was founded in 1887 as a program focused on "experimentation, training of teachers, and demonstration of the best educational practices" (Johnson, 2006, p. 31) and later became a demonstration school.
- The University of Missouri laboratory school was established in 1904 and is another example of a common perspective in the early childhood field that included bridging research with the education of young children (Johnson, 2006).
- The Iowa State University early childhood laboratory school, established in 1924, documents the first research in a laboratory school beginning in 1926 (Iowa State University, n.d.). Lawrence Frank, an economist with the Laura Spelman Rockefeller Memorial Fund, supported the early childhood laboratory school at Iowa State.
- The University of Minnesota laboratory school, known today as Shirley G. Moore Lab School, was established in 1925. This program echoed Dewey's views because it was created to provide a "living laboratory, where the Institute's research is put into practice" (University of Minnesota, n.d.).
- Purdue University's early childhood laboratory school, established in 1926, was originally named Purdue Nursery School, renamed Purdue Child Care Program, and, is now, named the Ben and Maxine Miller Child Development Laboratory School (MCDLS). The MCDLS was first established "in order to give practice for senior students taking the course in Child Care and Management" (Purdue University, n.d.).
- The University of Berkley in California founded the Institute of Child Welfare in 1927, which provided care for young children (Harms & Tracy, 2006). This was another program established with the support of Lawrence Frank, and the resources from the Laura Spelman Rockefeller Memorial Fund. (Barbour, 2003; Elicker & Barbour, 2015; Monroe 2009). The program at Berkley also became the "one of the first such sites in the country, some of the most famous and innovative longitudinal studies in childhood development originated here" (University of California–Berkley, n.d.).

The trend of early childhood laboratory schools established throughout 1900–1950s echoed Dewey's ideology of providing quality early childhood education and the infrastructure to support and conduct research. Programs also incorporated the vision from Bank Street in fostering teacher education. Over the years, early childhood laboratory schools were challenged to demonstrate and define their value. Programs have adjusted to the needs of the community while some have had to close their doors due to lack of funding while other programs integrated service for providing high-quality early childhood care. The changing needs in early childhood education have sometimes caused laboratory schools to struggle to maintain the core of the vision and mission (File, 2012).

A GLIMPSE OF THE CONTEMPORARY EARLY CHILDHOOD LABORATORY SCHOOLS

Today, early childhood programs associated with universities that are defined as laboratory schools typically include three arms, similar to those of the university as a whole: research, education, and service (Elicker & Barbour, 2015). The levels of research vary within each program as well as the type of educational experiences and support provided for the students attending the university. The structure and services of programs range in enrollment services that can include infants to preschool age children within full day or part day schedules on a university campus.

The contemporary definition of early childhood laboratory schools begins where all laboratory schools started—the idea of creating an environment where play is integral to the growth and development of children. The curriculum focusing on the education of young children begins with "young children" (Tanner, 1997). There is value to incorporating the opportunity for research of young children with collaboration of experts in the field. Research provides the avenue for learning and gaining wisdom, which translates to the opportunity to understand and implement best practices within the early childhood setting. Laboratory schools also create the atmosphere to train professionals in and for the early childhood field and influence other programs to incorporate best practices.

Additionally, early childhood laboratory schools have had to begin to address service as a reality of its constraints. As laboratory schools were first established, they were not intended to provide full-time care for children. However, it is now common for an average child to spend 10 to 12 hours a day, 5 days a week, 50 weeks a year, in the care of a nonrelative. Even with these changing statistics and need for high quality early childhood education and care, the modern day early childhood laboratory school continues to incorporate research, and a child centered, open environment, and more recently service through the scope of collaboration and engagement or service. The strength of the modern lab school is its consistency to the integrity of these original founding ideas of environment, research, and teacher education.

The intent of this manuscript is to share how the pedagogy of a specific early childhood laboratory school at Purdue University maintains the original mission of a lab school in contemporary ways while demonstrating the three arms of research, education, and service. The MCDLS at Purdue University is the oldest laboratory school in the state of Indiana. The MCDLS is a strong, contemporary example of building upon the theory and ideas of Dewey's and Bank Street's foundational perspectives for a new era. Children need hands-on and meaningful experiences in learning within an environment that is intentional about collaboration with a link to teacher education and training. "Dewey's mind was not compartmentalized; in fact, he tried to bring relevant fields together and link them with practical concerns" (Tanner, 1997, p. 16).

RESEARCH, EDUCATION, AND SERVICE IN EARLY CHILDHOOD LABORATORY SCHOOLS

Laboratory Schools across the country have unique responsibilities and dynamics in how each program participates in supporting the research of faculty, students, and staff at a university or college. Each has a distinctive infrastructure for research within their programs as early childhood laboratory schools are the ideal environment for collaboration and innovation. Those who engage in research in an early childhood laboratory school include partnerships with children, parents, teachers, undergraduate and graduate students, faculty, and staff. Laboratory schools within the early childhood field are a melting pot for ideas and connections conducted through research within the context of a supportive and safe setting.

The vital role early childhood laboratory schools play in research is crucial. Authors Nancy Barbour and Brent McBride (2016, p. ix) in *The Future of Child Development Laboratory Schools: Applied Developmental Science in Action* state: "These programs often play a central role in supporting teaching, research, and outreach/engagement activities in the fields of child development and early childhood education." In this light, we can see that early childhood laboratory schools are the ideal locations for creative ideas and flourishing concepts and theories.

Benefits of an early childhood laboratory school include teamwork between teachers in creating developmentally appropriate lesson plans, classroom design, and engaging activities with young children (Scales, Perry, & Tracy, 2012). The atmosphere within a laboratory school lends itself by creating more opportunities for teachers to explore, take risks, and try new things while maintaining the importance of a developmentally responsive and rich environment for the children and families they work with. Because teachers are open to try new and exciting ideas, they are supported as they embrace unique opportunities and experiences with researchers.

Additionally, research within early childhood laboratory schools creates an atmosphere in which exploration, testing, piloting, and developing theories, methodology, and best practices within the early childhood field occur. Special attention is made to maintain the careful balance of the community to explore the process of research while supporting and nurturing the growth and development of the children and families in the program (Johnson, 2006).

The research that occurs within a laboratory school setting often lends itself to the learning, and application of best practice. This new knowledge supports the "education" that occurs both within the program as well as for those who engage with the laboratory school from outside the program (Harms & Tracy, 2006). In field experiences and connected to coursework, Zeichner (2009) states that the experiences the university students have can be more heavily guided by program staff and university faculty and these experiences are insured to be of high quality.

The final "arm" of service may take many forms from a laboratory school. As stated above, Elicker and Barbour (2015) note that there is an increased demand for high quality care from families in the workforce. Logically, the laboratory school can fill that gap as a service to the community. As well, service may be perceived as the laboratory school being a demonstration site for research and high quality educational programming. McBride et al. (2012) state that the dissemination of research and knowledge is essential in the current context of laboratory schools. Building capacity across the community for high quality early childhood education then becomes a service role for the laboratory school.

This manuscript will highlight work that is occurring at MCDLS that demonstrates the three arms of research, education, and service. The authors will share multiple present-day research projects occurring within the early childhood laboratory school at the MCDLS that demonstrate the benefits of research in a laboratory setting with the perspective of fostering exploration and inquiry. Next, the authors will discuss how education is building the knowledge base of current and future professionals in the field of early childhood education as well as other professions. Lastly, the perspective of service from MCDLS is shared. Service, in this perspective, is seen not only as filling the need for high quality early childhood education for university and local families but also as a demonstration site for the research and education that will be described in this manuscript.

Research at MCDLS

The mission at MCDLS states: "The Ben & Maxine Miller Child Development Laboratory School at Purdue University is a place where young children and families learn and grow. Actively engaging the world around them, each day children, teachers, parents, researchers, and university students play and work together, creating a safe, loving community of discovery" (Purdue University, n.d.). The laboratory school is an environment where it is important to cultivate ideas and stimulate innovative ways to approach research through collaboration with children, families, early childhood teachers, faculty, staff, students, and researchers. The laboratory school is an ideal environment to brainstorm, flesh out methodology, implement thoughts into practice, and provide an environment where ideas grow and develop through processes of co-constructing knowledge.

The origination of any research topic varies within the laboratory school; the focus can be the award of a grant, a dissertation thesis, a class project or assignment, or a special interest to an individual researcher that can include faculty, students, and/or staff. Regardless how the research topic is initiated, the laboratory school's mission is to facilitate bringing everything and everyone together within an environment designed to conduct research. The following section shares research in different phases, the first studies of pilot research conducted at MCDLS and, the second, shares on-going research and projects at MCDLS.

Pilot Studies at MCDLS

The MCDLS functions as an environment where pilot research occurs that builds into larger more expanding research. The idea of piloting studies is the basic nature of exploring, changing, fixing, and growing as concepts evolve and become concrete. As Dewey noted the "it (laboratory schools) has but one purpose: to make discoveries about the education of the child by putting theory into practice in an experimental setting and modifying theory by what is learned" (Tanner, 1997 p. 19).

Mathematics pilot study. An example of this was the pilot study from graduate student, Sue Ellen Richardson; her project began as a thesis to her dissertation. The pilot study titled: *Through their eyes: Early childhood teachers as learners and teachers of mathematics.* Early childhood teachers were interviewed about their mathematical teaching, beliefs, and understanding of children's learning (Richardson & Bofferding, 2015). Several early childhood teachers from the lab school gave Richardson feedback on the interview questions and participated in data collection which included taking pictures of children engaged in mathematical activities. The pilot study allowed her to develop the framework for her dissertation research.

The MCDLS teachers were given the time to reflect on their own knowledge and experiences with math which was a benefit. The reflections created dialogue with one another about the important concepts of teaching math and ways to implement math instruction in the classroom. The natural conversation that developed grew to emphasize professional development training for the entire laboratory staff. Richardson built the foundation of her study in the lab school where she later implemented the framework to conduct research for her dissertation. Future implications of the study will likely focus on teacher perception for teaching math skills to young children, and the importance for preservice programs to address teacher's self-confidence in mathematical instruction.

Early engineering skills pilot study.   Another pilot study, that later published titled: *Children's Social Competence, Physical Activity, and Early Engineering Thinking in the Imagination Playground™, Traditional Playground, and Dramatic Play Area* was conducted in Head Start programs and at MCDLS (Elicker, Anderson, Choi, Schlesinger-Devlin, & Gold, 2013). The study began with the need to develop an assessment tool piloted at MCDLS. The research team began by developing an evaluation instrument to determine early engineering skills, to describe and classify large motor movement, and observe social interaction of preschool children. Several cycles of observations were conducted to finalize the assessment tool and then establish reliability and validity with the research team.

Further extension of this study included a parent workshop focusing on teaching parents the importance of block play with their children. The Block Party was rolled out through the support and participation of Purdue University Extension. A short video clip was created to share the information about the Block Party (PU Extension, 2013). Parents participated in the Block Party with their children; stations were set up with different types of blocks for the children to play with. As the children played with the blocks the parents received information about the importance of block play and the skills their children were learning. The research from the initial study extended into another aspect of research by the publication: *Preschoolers' engineering play behaviors: Differences in gender and play context* (Gold, Elicker, Anderson, Choi, & Brophy, 2015). This one study began as a pilot to create an assessment tool, using the assessment tool with a research project, extended the knowledge gained from the study to parent education, than to another focus of block play with children which expanded to professional development for teachers (Gold, Elicker, & Beaulieu, 2017).

Air quality pilot study.   Another ongoing research project that began as a pilot study was an air quality study conducted by a civil engineering professor and a team of graduate students. Professor Brandon Boor and graduate students Bara AlArfaj, Kun Huang, and Tianren Wu began an indoor air quality research study to evaluate the airborne pollutants young children are exposed to and potentially improve the indoor air quality for child care facilities. A Wideband Integrated Bioaerosol Sensor (WIBS) was placed on the floor in the infant/toddler classroom with children 6 weeks to 24 months. The machine collected air samples while the children participated in their daily routine. The initial pilot study lasted 5 days to explore the ability of the machine to collect data from a lower surface; typically air quality studies collect air samples from the height of an average adult and rarely collects samples from a floor setting (Boor, Wu, 2018).

As the study developed, an additional pilot phase began with the introduction of children and staff wearing a small Actigraph watch which records movement, at the same time the classroom was recorded using a video camera to code the types of movement the Actigraph watch sensed. The phases of these pilots all were conducted within the infant/toddler classroom. The study expanded in to include all the children in the program ranging from 6 weeks to 5 years of age (Boor, Wu, 2018).

A valuable collaboration from the research conducted by Boor and his team included a professional development opportunity for the early childhood teachers. Boor and Wu presented the data collected while in the infant/toddler room to the laboratory teachers. The presentation allowed for the laboratory teachers to ask questions, reflect on possible implications of the information gathered and facilitate conversation to share with the potential families participating in the next phase of the study.

As of this writing, the pilot study continues to collect data within the early childhood laboratory school. The intent for the pilot study is to create a framework for research methodology to be rolled out to early childhood child care programs throughout the state. Questions of the study include possible correlations to upper respiratory infections or breathing problems such as asthma. Understanding more of the air quality systems within early childhood programs could have implications on the type of air filtrations implemented within centers. (Boor, Wu, 2018).

Ongoing Projects at MCDLS

Pilot research conducted at MCDLS demonstrates the inclusive environment for collaboration and intentional reciprocation of ideas and concept which is the exact foundation of Dewey's vision created over 100 years ago. Two ongoing research projects that this manuscript highlights will articulate the evolution of collaborative work that was established in MCDLS prior to additional participants for collaboration. The first was gardening with the children enrolled at MCDLS, and the second was implementing a teacher designed science, technology, engineering, and math (STEM) curriculum within one of the preschool classrooms. Both serve as models to the organic development of research collaboration in an interdisciplinary field. Additionally, both exhibit the notion that early childhood laboratory schools are an environment for cultivating ideas and informing the body of knowledge in early childhood education.

Gardening with young children.   Gardening with the children in the laboratory school was something MCDLS had already been doing on a small scale, planting tomatoes and cucumbers in several pots and spots in the playground around the spring and summer months. The gardening was initiated by the teachers with children in their classrooms; the challenge was to look at creating a larger understanding of the importance of sustainability and connecting the food we grow to the food we eat in our meals and snacks. The trend of growing food locally in such projects as Farm-to-Table which includes a preschool perspective for gardening in *Getting Started With Farm to Early Care and Education* from the National Farm to School Network. The importance of gardening and sustainability was something the MCDLS community wanted to explore. Participating in a garden develops children's scientific knowledge and understanding of the environment, the importance of exposing young children to active gardening (Nimmo & Hallett, 2008; Miller, 2007).

The meals are catered at MCDLS through the Department of Hospitality, Tourism, and Management (HTM), which also is a laboratory school for culinary arts; both laboratory schools are housed within the college of Health and Human Sciences. The relationship between HTM and MCDLS grew to include the opportunity to share in gardening. The Marriott building houses HTM and has a dedicated garden space with ten plots down the street from the Fowler house where MCDLS is housed, which is a reasonable walk for the children and staff. Collaborating with the chef at HTM and other supporters the children weeded the garden plots, cultivated the soil, planted herbs and vegetables, watered and weeded the plots, and harvested the food. All the children in the program participated in the gardens including children from 6 weeks to 5 years in age. The seven laboratory classrooms visited the garden weekly and everyone participated in the maintenance of the garden.

Several opportunities developed from the relationship with HTM; the children taste tested several types of tomatoes, they made pizza with the basil and tomatoes, and they learned how to make gazpacho with undergraduate students from HTM in the demonstration kitchen. The children learned that the rabbits liked the strawberries, which meant they harvested very few strawberries for snack. Children learned the differences between weeds and the vegetables. The children with the support of the laboratory school teachers became scientists and researchers through action research. The children measured the growth of the plants, learned to water the root of the plants rather than the leaves, and documented the changes in their growth through photography, journaling, and drawings.

This small-scale project later extended into other opportunities. The gardening project began in spring, 2014. As it continues to sustain participation from year to year it gains momentum in research. Sara Schmitt (n.d.), a faculty in the department of Human Development and Family Studies, who was working on a study titled *Developing On-Site Food Gardens at Early Childhood Education Centers* asked the preschool laboratory teachers to review curriculum she was developing to integrate self-regulation with gardening. The laboratory school teachers implemented the lessons with their children, accessing the gardening experiences they had with their children and provided feedback for the activities. The laboratory school teachers were able to draw on their experiences with the collaborative gardening project at HTM and provided guidance and feedback to Schmitt. The input provided by the real world experience of the gardening with young children created an avenue for collaboration for lesson plans that then were implemented in larger community based early childhood programs. The goal of this particular research is to publish early childhood activities to assist in developing self-regulation in young children. It is an example of how the laboratory school environment lends itself to creating opportunities and experiences for young children that lead to larger implications and supports later emerging research. The benefits for the laboratory school teachers was the exposure to activities children could participate in to foster and develop self-regulation. Laboratory school teachers were able to implement the self-regulation activities within other contexts of the daily routine for children. The teachers also noted their ability to recognize signs more quickly from children when they were needing additional assistance in managing their choices.

Another development from the gardening with young children was the publication of *Personal Gardens: Who Is Growing Their Own in the U.S.?* (Bir, Widmar, & Schlesinger-Devlin, 2018), a collaboration with Professor Nicole Olynk Widmar in agriculture and economics and a Purdue student. The gardening experience organically developed at the MCDLS because of the interest to build on best practices, and later emerged links to curriculum development and research. This is an example of how the laboratory school is an environment where research is cultivated. The unique environment of the laboratory school is the possibility for a wide range of research to occur over a long period of time which lends itself to growing into other facets of research that are yet to be thought of.

Teacher designed STEM curriculum.   Science, technology, engineering, and math (STEM) are other areas of development and interest in the early childhood field. As an early childhood laboratory school, the topic of STEM was explored at MCDLS in teacher certification, demonstration classrooms as well as curriculum development in STEM with children as young as age two. The relationship between the College of Engineering and MCDLS has been long lived; it provides a site for research, which included studies such as air quality, adaptive wheelchairs, designs in child-resistant medicine bottles, and providing a demonstration exhibit for engineering students.

A recent collaboration has developed with the goal of developing new curricula. The incubation for this began with collaboration with faculty members from the Human Development and Family Studies Department and the Department of Engineering Education. Together the faculty invited a laboratory school teacher to a training focusing on STEM plus C (science, technology, engineering, and math plus computation). The engineering faculty participants were from the Research Institute for Pre-College Engineering (INSPIRE) through Purdue University.

The teacher education focused on the stages of engineering design. The prompt to the training included a demonstration for participants to see engineering concepts which could be included with literacy. A children's book was read to the group, which had a problem to solve. In the story the character was working to keep their vegetables growing in the garden from the rabbits that were eating them. (Fleming & Karas, 2002). The dilemma in the story created an opportunity to create a solution to the problem using engineering design. Through the process of using a children's literature classroom teachers could build upon the collection of books they already had to incorporate STEM. In addition to the literature example, classroom teachers participated in training where they learned how to incorporate and teach the stages of engineering.

A unit plan was shared with the teachers, which included the phases of engineering design through STEM: brainstorming, planning, design, testing, and application for children enrolled in kindergarten through second grade. The 3-day-long training offered elementary school teachers a STEM unit plan they were able to share the activities in the classroom. Materials and resources from INSPIRE were also provided to the teachers. The goal of the laboratory schoolteacher's participation was to implement and adapt the unit plan, which had been designed for the kindergarten classroom and apply it to a preschool classroom. The training and cooperation this provided prompted two objectives by the teachers first to implement the unit plan with a preschool age group. The second to create a list of children's literature books and provide a guideline or lesson plan for implementing the stages of engineering design.

The teachers gathered and created a list of books including: *The Little Mouse, The Red Ripe Strawberry, and The Big Hungry Bear* by Don and Audrey Wood (1984), *The Little Red Hen* by Paul Galdone (1973), and *I Need a Lunch Box* written by Jeanette Caines (1988). The task was to pilot the stories with children in the preschool classroom at MCDLS using the stages of engineering design.

The first objective began with a pilot activity using a preschool book titled: *I Need a Lunch Box* and developing it into a STEM activity. The story was about two siblings, one who was starting kindergarten and the other who was too young to start school. The older sibling needed to choose a lunch box. The story explores a variety of lunch box designs; some for packing favorite toys, others for packing favorite animals. At the end of the story, the older child chooses a lunch box they can take to school and the younger sibling gets a lunch box to pack their favorite toys in. The introductory activity helped the laboratory school teacher understand where the children were developmentally. The result was the creation of a lesson plan using literacy within the classroom and demonstrating how a classroom teacher could expand the story into a STEM lesson.

The teacher read the story, which had a problem for the children to solve: What type of lunch box would they design? The children experimented with creating a design for the lunch box. They testing several mediums like watercolors on a piece of copy paper, cardboard, tissue paper, and wax paper. The children reflected at each design stage; the observations they made while painting the different materials. The group collaborated at the end of the experiments to determine the best type of median to use in creating a lunch box design. The weeklong activity was documented by videotaping the conversations and noting key observations made during the pilot of both the children and the teacher.

The pilot allowed for a better understanding of the language preschoolers used in describing their observations. A preschooler who was responding to the teacher's question—"Which worked better the cardboard piece or the tissue paper?"—said, "The cardboard is better because it won't fly away." The concept of durability and strength was articulated in a practical and developmentally appropriate context through the language context available to the preschooler.

The next phase of this ongoing project is to put into application the additional children's literature books from the teacher list, as well as implementing the kindergarten unit in the preschool classroom.

Benefits of Research at MCDLS

Research is a key component to early childhood laboratory schools; it is one of the aspects to an innovative and contemporary program. Table 5.1 includes a summary of a range of research conducted at MCDLS. Dewey set out to have children engaged in active learning. The children at MCDLS participate in a balance of child directed learning and teacher directed activities. The ability to document a portion of these aspects falls into research. Children's everyday play documented in ways that provide insight and knowledge. The additional responsibility as a laboratory school is providing opportunities for preservice teachers.

The benefits of conducting research within an early childhood laboratory school support maintaining high quality early childhood programs. Research demonstrates the value of highly qualified early childhood teachers which has a direct correlation to the benefits of children's development (Berk, 1986; Phillips, 1986). In addition to the benefits of highly qualified teachers it is important to have continuing professional development

TABLE 5.1   Summary of Research Conducted at MCDLS

Title of Study	Investigator	Subjects	Purpose
Gait Characteristic of Infants Carrying Toys	Dr. Laura J. Claxton, research assistant: Amanda J. Arnold, Department of Health and Kinesiology	Newly walking infants (13–14 months of age) and toddlers (23.5–24.5 months of age) who are experienced walkers	Investigate how carrying a toy or not carrying a toy impacts walking stability in newly walking infants and experienced walking toddlers.
Towards a Mechanistic Understanding of Biological Particle Resuspension in Infant and Toddler Near-Surface Microenvironments	Professor Brandon Boor and Tianren Wu, PhD Student, Civil Engineering	Infants	Evaluate the airborne pollutants young children are exposed to and improve the indoor air quality.
Multi-Modal Data Collection for 0–9 Months	Dr. Stephen Elliott Technology, Leadership, and Innova Co PI – Kevin O'Connor, Zach Moore, Kevin Chan, Jeff Chudik, Ben Osborne, Wes McHaren, Torrey Hutchinson	0–9 month olds	Examine the performance of biometric devices, such as fingerprint seniors you may see on your mobile phone, over time for a distinct population of 0–9 month olds
Child and Parental Perceptions of Technology	Dr. Deborah Nichols Linebarger, PhD Human Development and Family Studies, and Graduate: Yemimah King, Undergraduates: Emma Curdes, Candace Harsh.	4–8 year olds	How young children and families think about and use different technologies including television, computers, tablets, smartphones, video games, and books

(continued)

TABLE 5.1   Summary of Research Conducted at MCDLS (continued)

Title of Study	Investigator	Subjects	Purpose
Effects of Variable Priming on Young Children's Grammatical Morpheme Use	Laurence B. Leonard, Ph.D. and Windi C. Krok, M.S. CCC-SLP	2½–3½ year olds; native English Speaking Children	Examine how children's lering of –ing verbs (e.g., is walking, is playing, is eating), because these types of verbs are particularly difficult for children with language impairments
The Enhanced Block Party: Investigation Based Teaching Practices to Foster Engineering Play Behaviors in Young Children	Jim Elicker HDFS, and Zack Gold	Teachers	Increased preschool teachers' knowledge about and use of constructive play materials, including blocks, observation skills, and recognition of young children's engineering play behaviors, and increase preschool teachers' awareness of the value of blocks and other constructive play materials for young children's early learning.
Developing on-site food gardens at early childhood education centers	Sarah Schmitt HDFS and Frank Snyder Dept. Health and Kinesiology	Teachers	Develop and intervention designed to improve young children's fruit and vegetable prefaces and access to healthy foods through developing an on-site food garden at an early childhood education center
Technology at Mealtimes: Exploring the Relationship Between Parental Feeding Practices, Technology Use and Child Eating Behavior	Moriah Gramm & Dr. Rachel Vollmer and Dr. Julie Schumacher & Dr. Tammy Harpel Department of Family and Consumer Sciences	Parents	How Parents interact with their children at mealtimes and technology use.

opportunities for early childhood teachers to provide ongoing expertise (Powell, Diamond, & Cockburn, 2013). Programs such as laboratory schools, where continual support, dialogue, investigation, and exploration occur, foster opportunities for ongoing professional development and education, which are a beneficial byproduct for teachers, children, and their families. In a field where observation, engagement, and intentional interactions are highly valued and necessary, the atmosphere for research supports such exposure to ideas and concepts.

Professional Preparation at MCDLS

MCDLS at Purdue University acts as an environment for innovation for ideas and understanding within the context of best practices. Hence, in addition to collaborating with various departments and faculty at the university, the MCDLS also engages in professional preparation of various university students. University students at graduate and undergraduate levels engage with the laboratory school staff to learn best practices in the field of early childhood education.

The strongest collaboration is with the Human Development and Family Studies department where MCDLS is housed. Students from all four majors in the department have opportunities to complete field work through practicum (part-time participation in the classroom settings) as well as capstone student teaching (full-time participation in the classroom settings). Additionally, university students may conduct part- or full-time field work with the director learning the administrative roles of a laboratory school.

In the classroom based field experiences, university students will observe and practice professional skills in best practice techniques such as positive guidance, planning for and implementing developmentally appropriate lessons and activities, assessment of young children, and engagement with families. Since MCDLS embraces an environment for innovation regarding best practice demonstration, university faculty have confidence in the staff to mentor university students to achieve a high level of knowledge of these best practices. University students then take these skills into their own professional lives in fields such as early childhood education, early intervention, human services, and research in child development and education, and family and consumer science education.

Collaboration for professional preparation with other departments and programs throughout the university also occurs at MCDLS. For example, university students from speech, language, and hearing sciences perform hearing screenings on the children in the program as well as engage in observation and research opportunities. University students in engineering create interactive activities including games, toys, and manipulatives that are then field tested in the laboratory school. These engineering students must spend time observing the play of the children prior to the creation so that they learn about child development and best practice in encouraging play and appropriate toy usage. The engineering students and the classroom teachers also collaborate on ideas and definitions of developmentally appropriate toys and development. Once the toys are built, the university students observe the MCDLS children playing with their designs to determine durability and success in the outcome related to the defined goals of the design. The students from the school of nursing implement the Denver Developmental Screening Test with the children to gain experience implementing the assessment tool. Pharmacy students join the laboratory school and talk with children about safety medications and the importance of handwashing as part of their course work in engaging the children and families. Lastly, students from food and nutrition science create recipes, collect data, and analyze food preferences of the children. All collaboration enhances not only the university students' professional preparation, in some cases builds input into research, but also the programming at MCDLS.

Service at MCDLS

The third arm (research, education, and service) is demonstrated through the exceptional programming for the children as well as the quality collaboration with the university. Service (among the various definitions from Merriam-Webster) is defined as "contributing to the welfare of others." In addition to being an available high quality early childhood education setting for children not necessarily associated with the university, the MCDLS serves as the example of what truly effective developmentally appropriate practice as well as collaboration across disciplines should look like. Administrators and teachers from state and local programs visit, learn about, and receive professional development training from the staff at MCDLS through on-site visits as well as state presentations. Additionally, university students who have field and research experiences at MCDLS are then able to share their knowledge and skills with other programs as they complete field and research in other areas of the region and state. MCDLS is revered throughout the state as an exceptional early childhood education program that not only provides extraordinary programming for young children but also for university students in their training programs.

CONCLUSION

The bottom line is that the laboratory style school on a university campus has the platform to engage in contemporary and innovative approaches to research, professional preparation, and educational practices contributing to advancement of the university, early childhood education field, and community at large. Early childhood laboratory schools are contexts in which adults and children engage in shared inquiry and professional growth. These experiences promote the notion of university laboratory schools as the ideal environment from which innovations in research, professional preparation, and demonstration of effective practices emerge in particular for the field of early childhood education but may also impact research, education, and service.

The research chronicled in this manuscript is open ended and ongoing because the studies have been developed from a value or a priority in the culture and community of the program to continually examine best practices. As well, the professional preparation of both the program staff and university students is enriched by this priority of examining best practices meaning that professionals are always aware of new and innovative approaches to their professional practices.

University and program teachers, faculty, and staff are available and excited to work together at the laboratory school to participate in a partnership and/or leadership in research and demonstration of best practices. A calling to implement such innovative approaches at all levels necessitates the need for a mission and vision that many universities and colleges must protect by supporting the financial well-being of a program. Early childhood laboratory schools are not intended to financially profit from the studies implemented in their environments; however, similar to university libraries or research labs across campuses, they are intended to provide a resource for the ongoing pursuit of knowledge, discovery, and implementation. Innovations in research, education, and service at laboratory schools engages individuals in a community that is committed to the task, joy, and responsibility of exploration.

REFERENCES

Bank Street School for Children. (n.d.). History & philosophy. Retrieved from https://www.bankstreet.edu/school-children/about-sfc/our-history/

Barbour, N. E. (2003). The early history of child development laboratory programs. In B. McBride (Ed.), *Bridging the gap between theory, research and practice: The role of child development laboratory programs in early childhood education* (pp. 9–29). Bingley, England, Emerald Group.

Barbour, N. E., & McBride, B. A. (2016). *The future of child development lab schools: Applied developmental science in action.* New York, NY: Psychology Press.

Beatty, B. (1995). *Preschool education in America: The culture of young children from the colonial era to the present.* New Haven, CT: Yale University Press.

Berk, L. (1986). Relationships of educational attainment, child-oriented attitudes, job satisfaction, and career commitment to caregiver behavior towards children. *Child Care Quarterly, 14,* 103–129.

Bir, C., Widmar, N., & Schlesinger-Devlin, E. (2018). *Personal gardens: Who is growing their own in the U.S.?* West Lafayette, IN: Purdue Extension, Purdue University. Retrieved from https://mdc.itap.purdue.edu/item.asp?itemID=23017

Boegehold, B. D., Cuffaro, H. K., Hooks, W. H., & Klopf, G. J. (Eds.). (1977). *Education before five: A handbook on preschool education.* New York, NY: Bank Street College of Education.

Boor, B. & Wu, T. (2018). Real-time monitoring of microbes and mold in buildings. Indoor Air Quality Association (IAQA) 21st annual meeting, Chicago, IL January 2018.

Caines, J. (1988). *I need a lunch box.* New York, NY: Harper Collins.

Elicker, J., Anderson, T., Choi, J., Schlesinger-Devlin, E., & Gold, Z. (2013). *Children's social competence, physical activity, and early engineering thinking in the Imagination Playground™, traditional playground, and dramatic play area.* Final Report KaBOOM! Retrieved from https://s3.amazonaws.com/media-kaboom/docs/documents/pdf/ip/purdue_imaginationplayground_full_2013.pdf

Elicker, J., & Barbour, N. (2015). *University laboratory preschools.* Oxford, England: Routledge.

File, N. (2012). Identifying and addressing challenges to research in university laboratory schools. *Early Education and Development, 23*(2), 143–152.

Fleming, C., & Karas, B. (2002). *Muncha! Muncha! Muncha!* New York, NY: Simon & Schuster Children's.

Galdone, P. (1973). *The little red hen.* New York, NY: Clarion Books.

Gold Z. S., Elicker, J., & Beaulieu, B. A. (2017). *The enhanced block party: Fostering engineering play behaviors in young children* [Web-based training materials]. Produced by Purdue University Department of Agriculture Communications. Disseminated by Purdue University Cooperative Extension Service, West Lafayette, IN.

Gold, Z. S., Elicker, J., Choi, J. Y., Anderson, T., & Brophy, S. P. (2015). Preschoolers' engineering play behaviors: Differences in gender and play context. *Children, Youth and Environments, 25*(3), 1–21. doi:10.7721/chilyoutenvi.25.3.0001

Harms, T., & Tracy, R. (2006). Linking research to best practice: University laboratory schools in early childhood education. *Young Children, 61*(4), 89–93.

Iowa State University. (n.d.). *History.* Retrieved from http://www.cdls.hs.iastate.edu/history

Johnson, W. (2006). *The laboratory school: Yesterday, today, and tomorrow* (Doctoral dissertation). Retrieved from ProQuest Database. (Accession No. 3232513)

McBride, B. A., Groves, M., Barbour, N., Horm, D., Stremmel, A., Lash, . . . Toussaint, S. (2012). Child development laboratory schools as generators of knowledge in early childhood education: New models and approaches. *Early Education & Development, 23*(2), 153–164. doi:10.1080/10409289.2012.651068

Miller, D. (2007). The seeds of learning: Young children develop important skills through their gardening activities at a Midwestern early childhood program. *Applied Environmental Education & Communication, 6*(1), 49–66.

Monroe, L. (2009). *Evaluation of a laboratory preschool: Utilizing a theory approach logic model* (Doctoral dissertation). Retrieved from ProQuest Database. (Accession No. 3355799)

National Farm to School Network. (n.d.). *Getting started with farm to early care and education.* Retrieved from http://www.farmtoschool.org/Resources/Getting%20Started%20with%20Farm%20to%20ECE.pdf

Nimmo, J., & Hallett, B. (2008). Childhood in the garden: A place to encounter natural and social diversity. *Young Children, 63*(1), 32–38.

Phillips, D. (Ed.). (1986). *Quality in child care: What does research tell us?* Washington, DC: National Association for the Education of Young Children.

Powell, D., Diamond, K., & Cockburn, M. (2013). Promising approaches to professional development for early childhood educators. In O. N. Saracho & B. Spodek (Eds.), *Handbook of Research on Education of Young Children* (385–392). New York, NY: Taylor & Francis.

PUExtenstion. (2013, November 6). *Block Party: The importance of play* [Video File]. Retrieved from https://www.youtube.com/watch?v=olV5Cla-j_g&feature=youtu.be

Purdue University. (n.d.). *Mission Statement.* Retrieved from http://www.purdue.edu/hhs/hdfs/MCDLS/about_us/mission.html

Richardson, S. E., & Bofferding, L. (2015). Through their eyes: Early childhood teachers as learners and teachers of mathematics. In T. G. Bartell, K. N. Bieda, R. T. Putnam, K. Bradfield, & H. Dominguez (Eds.), *Proceedings of the 37th annual meeting of the North American Chapter of the International Group for the Psychology of Mathematics Education* (pp. 804–811). East Lansing, MI: Michigan State University.

Scales, B., Perry, J., & Tracy, R. (2012). Creating a classroom of inquiry at the University of California at Berkeley: The Harold E. Jones child study center. *Early Education & Development, 23*(2), 165–180.

Schmitt, S. (n.d.). A randomized controlled trial of a preschool intervention to enhance self-regulation and dietary behaviors among young children (Unpublished manuscript). Purdue University, West Lafayette, IN.

Tanner, L. (1997). *Dewey's laboratory school lessons for today.* New York, NY: Teachers College Press.

University of California–Berkeley. (n.d.). *History.* Retrieved from https://ece.berkeley.edu/content/about-ecep

University of Minnesota. (n.d.). *Shirley G. Moore Lab School: About us.* Retrieved from http://lab-school.umn.edu/about-us/

Wood, D., & Wood, A. (1984). *The little mouse, the red ripe strawberry, and the big hungry bear.* New York, NY: Scholastic.

Zeichner, K. (2009). Rethinking the connections between campus courses and field experiences. *College- and University-Based Teacher Education, 61*(1/2), 89–99. doi:https://doi.org/10.1177/0022487109347671

CHAPTER 6

FROM THE SCIENTIFIC CHILD TO THE RECONCEPTUALIZED CHILD IN CANADIAN UNIVERSITY AND COLLEGE EARLY CHILDHOOD LABORATORY SCHOOLS

Rachel Langford

ABSTRACT

Laboratory schools for young children in colleges and universities have a long and rich history in Canada. Over this history, an understanding of the child has shifted. The purpose of this chapter is to examine, through a critical analysis of literature, the shift from a scientific view of the child associated with the child study and progressive education movements to a reconceptualized view of the child. The premise of the chapter is that different understandings of the child are entangled in the history of Canadian laboratory schools. Examining this shifting perspective is important because, as Moss (2014) argues, the paradigm or mindset early childhood researchers and educators adopt to

Contemporary Perspectives on Research on Child Development Laboratory Schools in Early Childhood Education,
pages 101–116

understand the child in a laboratory school tells us about their research and pedagogical priorities and practices.

Laboratory schools for young children in colleges and universities have a long and rich history in Canada (Brophy, 2000; Clark, Gleason, & Petrina, 2012). Over this history, an understanding of the child has shifted. The purpose of this chapter is to examine, through a critical analysis of literature, the shift from a scientific view of the child associated with the child study and progressive education movements to a reconceptualized view of the child. To reconceptualize refers to the desire to "critique, rethink, and reimagine early childhood and childhood studies in ways that encourage deeper analysis, new ways to reason and to act" (Bloch, Swadener, & Cannella, 2014, p. 2). The premise of the chapter is that different understandings of the child are entangled in the history of Canadian laboratory schools. Examining this shifting perspective is important because, as Moss (2014) argues, the paradigm or mindset early childhood researchers and educators adopt to understand the child in a laboratory school tells us about their research and pedagogical priorities and practices. The chapter was inspired by Prochner's and Doyon's (1997) claim that an investigation into what has remained the same and what has changed in the history of Canadian university and college early childhood laboratory schools is worthwhile.

TERMS AND TYPES

For the purposes of this chapter, the term *early childhood laboratory school* is used as an all-encompassing reference to a laboratory school for young children located at a Canadian university or college. Brophy (2000) explains that the history (and terminology) of Canadian university and college early childhood laboratory schools reflect different disciplinary traditions. One type of laboratory school typically referred to as a *child study center* (CSC) emerged from psychology and medical traditions focused on the scientific study of child development and child rearing (Brophy, 2000; Prochner, 2014; Wright, 2000). These laboratory schools typically offered half-day or full-day nursery school programs for preschoolers. Clark et al. (2012) report that beyond the child study center (CSC) at the University of British Columbia (UBC), there were over twenty other CSCs established in Canadian universities during the 1960s and 1970s that were "a strange hybrid of school and clinic, educational classroom and psychological lab, a place intended to cultivate both cutting edge research and children's imaginations" (Clark et al., 2012, p. 29). The number of CSCs in Canada has fallen significantly since the 1970s.[1]

A second type of Canadian laboratory school offering full-day childcare programs for infants, toddlers, and preschoolers evolved out of home economics and education traditions focused on the training of early childhood educators (Brophy, Callahan, Campbell, & Reid, 2013). Beginning in the late 1960s, many Canadian colleges established early childhood education post-secondary programs connected to a laboratory school. Brophy (2000) notes that, in contrast to CSCs, research was not initially conducted in these laboratory schools. Throughout the 2000s, a number of college laboratory schools, particularly in the province of Ontario, were closed because of high operational costs. Currently, five Canadian universities and 17 colleges have a laboratory school that provides a full-day program (Langford, 2017).

THE SCIENTIFIC CHILD

The history of Canadian CSCs has been characterized by Clark et al. (2012) as "understudied" (p. 30). Nevertheless, available literature does sufficiently capture how young children and their development have traditionally been viewed through a scientific lens in CSCs (Clark et al., 2012; Prochner & Doyon, 1997; Prochner & Hwang, 2008; Strong-Boag, 1982; Varga, 1997; Wright, 2000). The underlying belief of scientific child study was that "*scientific* investigation of development would provide essential knowledge about children, enabling the solving of 'problems of development'—that is knowing what are the typical behaviors displayed at particular ages, what promoted or inhibited them" (Varga, 1997, pp. 39–40; emphasis in the original). In CSCs, the concept of the scientific child was born and developed through the child study and progressive education movements influencing—perhaps dominating—research and pedagogical practices across the Canadian early childhood landscape (Dahlberg, Moss, & Pence, 2010).

Child Study Movement

The Institute of Child Study, established in 1925 and directed by William E. Blatz who was housed in the Department of Psychology at the University of Toronto until his retirement in 1960, is the best known Canadian CSC. Strong-Boag (1982) writes that the Institute was part of a North American scientific community that debated ideas about the preschool child that were considered radical for their time.

The scientific theories of Blatz and his collaborators on child development, child rearing, and educational curriculum were highly influential in Canada well into the 1970s, disseminated through speaking engagements and publications both within academia and in the popular press (e.g., Blatz,

1944; Blatz, 1966; Blatz & Bott, 1929; Fletcher, 1974). Varga (1997) describes the scientific approach used in the institute's nursery school:

> It was designed as a laboratory for systematic observations of children's behavior and development including their eating, sleeping and toileting behaviors, for carrying out experimental methods of child care, and for providing a model of care for parents and other caregivers. (p. 46)

Blatz maintained that "proper, informed child-rearing" in early childhood would produce normal and productive adults; the nursery school as a laboratory could be a "pragmatic tool" for realizing these social aims (Strong-Boag, 1982, p. 172).

In the 1930s, the birth of the Dionne quintuplets provided an opportunity to extend these aims. For 2 years Blatz and Institute graduate students observed the Dionne children, who were housed in a controlled environment away from their parents (Prochner & Hwang, 2008; Wright, 2000). Mary Wright (2000), an Institute graduate student, writes that through the ideas of maturation theory, behaviorism, mental hygiene, and scientific observations, Blatz developed his innovative theory of security (Prochner & Hwang, 2008; Wright, 2000). All children are theorized as developmentally progressing from a dependent security to an independent security in which the child can make decisions and accept consequences for his/her actions. The theory translated into a precisely organized and timed nursery school curriculum (Varga, 1997). During the school day, teachers provided an environment in which the limits of children's freedom were expanded as the children gained greater security, knowledge, and skills. In this environment, Blatz was adamantly opposed to punishment, extrinsic rewards, and competition among children (Wright, 2000), although in his work with the Dionne quintuplets the practice of isolation when the children misbehaved was used (Prochner & Hwang, 2008, p. 520).

Progressive Education Movement

In the 1960s, inspired by theories of Piaget, Bruner, McVicker, Hunt, and Bloom, educators' views about the nature of the child shifted from the earlier focus on socio-emotional development resulting from biological maturation (i.e., Blatz's security theory) to a focus on intellectual development emerging out of interactions with the environment (Prochner & Robertson, 2012; Varga, 1997, p. 116). Varga (1997) writes that at the University of Western Ontario laboratory preschool, for example, the implementation and assessment of a cognitive-developmental education program based on Head Start assumptions was researched. These theoretical and curricula changes can be characterized as innovations within a scientific or developmental (a more contemporary term) construct of the child progressing through ages and stages (Varga, 1997). Developmentally appropriate practice (DAP), which rose in prominence during the 1990s in the United States and Canada, was aligned with this scientific paradigm and normative developmental model of childhood.

Clark et al.'s (2012) account of the establishment and closing of the CSC at UBC in the 1960s illustrates this continuation of "the science of the child" in laboratory schools (p. 29). The CSC project was based on Blatz's views that "a child must find his way to maturity, at his own rate, with his individualized capacity and limitation . . . a teacher must not stunt or distort personality development or overdevelop it prematurely" (Clark et al., 2012, p. 40). At the same time, Clark et al. noted nascent concerns about scientific research *on* children at CSCs. Struggles ensued amongst various stakeholders over the purpose of the CSC—was it a site for scientific research or an innovative educational program based on progressive education goals for children at risk in their development, or both? And how was this balance to be achieved? Clark et al. (2012) suggest that certain directions taken by the CSC emphasized the value of education over research. For example, the administrator responsible for CSC is quoted as saying "parents would not want their children used as guinea pigs with too little attention given to normal education process" (p. 53). Here, the concept of the scientific child was beginning to be questioned even though it was through the perspective of the parent.

The future of the Institute for Child Study at the University of Toronto became precarious after the retirement of William Blatz in 1960. However, through several institutional mergers, by 1996 the Institute's thriving focus was on teacher training, research, and curricula innovations (Wright, 2000). Recent research projects (Carver, McConnaha, Messina, Morley, & Wang, 2017) at the Institute include an investigation of the Japanese Lesson Study as a process of teacher development (Moss, Hawes, Naqvi, & Caswell, 2015; Moss, Messina, Morley, & Tepylo, 2012) and a developmental examination of a rigorous block-play program (Tepylo, Moss, & Stephenson, 2015). Curricula innovations include a pedagogical framework based on a knowledge-building approach that focuses on environmental inquiry for early years and elementary teachers (Bereiter & Scardamalia, 2014; The Laboratory School at The Dr. Eric Jackman Institute of Child Study, 2011). In describing Institute curricula projects, Carver et al. (2017) write that "children are challenged to use their natural curiosity to critically investigate the social and natural world, to gain the skills to communicate with others, to think independently, and to become engaged citizens" (p. 290). While innovations are evident in descriptions of these projects, they are consistent with a scientific paradigm in which developmental knowledge of the child is applied to teaching the child (Carver et al., 2017). As the next section explains, literature that adopts a reconceptualizing perspective of the child critiques this approach.

THE RECONCEPTUALIZED CHILD

An Emerging and Growing Literature

Inspiration for reconceptualizing the child in Canadian laboratory schools comes from Reggio-Emilia pedagogy, Aotearoa/New Zealand and the reconceptualizing early childhood education (RECE) movement. While a full explanation of the theoretical complexities of the RECE movement is beyond the scope of this chapter, it can be said that the movement draws extensively on post-foundational ideas that Ryan and Grieshaber (2005) say question:

> ...the modernist belief in the power of science to objectively determine the universal laws of human development. Instead science is viewed as a social construction, imbued with the values of its creators and therefore enacting a particular set of power relations in its application (Lubeck, 1998, p. 35; as cited in Pacini-Ketchabaw, Nxumalo, Kocher, Elliot, & Sanchez, 2015, p. 207).

Literature that interrogates the power of science and conceptualizes a different kind of child—a 21st century child—in Canadian laboratory schools can be characterized as emerging and growing. In the late 1990s, research on multi-age groupings in the laboratory school at Ryerson University signaled an early departure from the scientific approach to studying the child and DAP (Bernhard, Pollard, Eggers-Pierola, & Morin, 2000). In this research, the scientific notion articulated by maturationists and developmentalists that children should be separated into educational groupings that match their developmental age and stage was questioned. Underpinning multi-age groupings was a principle of fundamental heterogeneity in human development with culture and other social factors producing different developmental pathways (Bernhard, 1995). In addition, a Canada-wide study, *Paths to Equity*, first piloted at the Ryerson laboratory school, investigated early childhood educators' preparation for working with minority children and families (Bernhard, Lefebvre, Chud, & Lange, 1995). As Pacini-Ketchabaw and Pence (2006) note, reconceptualizing the child and family as culturally, linguistically, and racially diverse is a particularly Canadian focus, reflecting the country's values of multiculturalism and pluralism.

Reconceptualist publications began to increase. Presentations exploring reconceptualist ideas at national conferences on Canadian university and college early learning laboratory schools held in 2009, 2012, and 2014 were developed into publications (Langford & Di Santo, 2013). In British Columbia, the Investigating Quality (IQ) Project led by researchers from the University of Victoria[2] and funded by the provincial government cultivated researcher/practitioner groups who focused on examining and rethinking practices with young children (Pence & Pacini-Ketchabaw, 2012). Out of this critical and intellectual climate emerged publications focused on reconceptualizing research and pedagogical practices in early childhood laboratory schools in British Columbia (e.g., Atkinson, 2016; Elliott & Yazbeck, 2013; Grove & Lirette, 2013; Hodgins, Atkinson, & Wanamaker, 2017; Kind, 2010; Land & Danis, 2016; Pacini-Ketchabaw et al., 2015). The journal *Canadian Children* (now the *Journal of Childhood Studies*), provides an important venue for these publications.

The innovation of provincial early learning curriculum frameworks in British Columbia, Alberta, and New Brunswick (Langford, 2012) also played a key role in shifting images of the child and generating publications about innovative curricula in laboratory schools and some community programs.[3] In these provinces, this early childhood policy work funded by provincial governments was put into practice by laboratory schools. For example, in 2008, the development of a post-foundational early learning curriculum framework by faculty at the University of New Brunswick resulted in publications that documented the processes of questioning DAP and considering alternative practices in the university's laboratory school as well as community programs (Whitty, 2009; Rose & Whitty, 2013). More recently, published research has explored a shift in research methodologies in the laboratory school that take into account children's rights and capabilities to meaningfully participate in research (Binder 2012; Binder & Kotsopoulos, 2011; Binder, Sorin, Nolan, & Chu, 2015; Hodgins, 2012; Hodgins, Kummen, Pacini-Ketchabaw, & Thompson, 2013; Koller & San Juan, 2014; MacNevin & Berman, 2017; Underwood, Chan, Koller, & Valeo, 2015).

Reconceptualizing Research

Briefly, scientific research uses an experimental, interventionist and/or developmental assessment design that assumes[4] objectivity to study children. In contrast, reconceptualizing research uses qualitative research methods, such as interviews with children or methods in which research and practice are intertwined, for example in action research or pedagogical documentation. An underlying assumption of reconceptualizing research is that the researcher "is not neutral and situated in apolitical contexts;" rather, values and context are considered important in research (Pacini-Ketchabaw et al., 2015, p. 211).

To illustrate, Hodgins et al. (2013) describe their work in British Columbia laboratory schools as entangling and reconceptualizing research/prac-
tice and objective/subjective binaries. Informed by post-foundational perspectives, they conduct research through pedagogical narrations described
in their province's early learning curriculum framework (Government of
British Columbia, 2008). As a research tool, pedagogical narrations require
"dialoguing, listening, and reflecting with others," including children, to
deepen understandings of practices (Hodgins, 2012; Pacini-Ketchabaw et
al., 2015, p. 205). The word *narrations* is plural to emphasize the dialogic
nature of researching and documenting pedagogical practices and the "ongoing and multiple nature of the process" (Hodgins et al., 2013, p. 43).

In reconceptualizing research, the child is accorded participation rights
and is viewed as an active social agent in research processes. Reconceptualizing research further employs theoretical perspectives (i.e., sociology of
childhood, capacity theory [Sen, 1999], and critical race theory) in which
competent children are understood to be part of society and draw on "discourses available to them in the historical, social, and political context in
which they live" (MacNevin & Berman, 2017, p. 829). The following examples illustrate the reconceptualization of the child in research practices
in laboratory schools.

- Drawing on the work of Paley's (1991) storytelling curriculum,
  Binder's qualitative research project involved working with a group
  of children over eight weeks and documenting with the children
  their stories told, acted, and visually represented. Binder found a
  multimodal approach to literacy that enabled the children to create
  texts about themselves and link them to others and the world.
- Drawing on critical race theory and post-structural theories, MacN-
  evin and Berman (2017) used child observations (i.e., patterns of
  play, social relationships) to locate a map of the dynamics of race
  across a group of children. Findings indicate that the children have
  a clear understanding of racial categories and exhibit preferences
  for White play materials, thereby reproducing the power dynamics
  of the larger society in their play.
- Other university researchers have explored young children's perspectives on inclusion and identified methods that are effective for
  increasing children's involvement in this research (Koller & San
  Juan, 2014; Underwood et al., 2015; Underwood, Valeo, & Wood,
  2012). Framed by the sociology of childhood, Koller and San Juan
  (2014) found that young children of different ages can "identify
  and discuss multifaceted issues associated with the inclusion of children with disabilities when play-based methods are administered"
  (p. 18). Research conducted by Underwood et al. (2015) involved

multiple activities and forms of communication to promote young children with disabilities' participation. Findings indicate that children with disabilities could "provide information about their experiences and capabilities and communicate their views on activities that reflect their own wellbeing" (p. 15).

Reconceptualizing Practice

In reconceptualizing practice in Canadian early childhood laboratory schools, five key understandings of the child contrasted with a scientific/developmental viewpoint are evident in literature: (a) the child is a capable individual rather than limited developmentally; (b) knowledge of the child is subjective, partial, and provisional rather than objective and comprehensive; (c) the child is an active participant in curriculum-making rather than a consumer of the teacher's curriculum; (d) knowledge is co-constructed between a child and educator rather than simply a result of developmental progression; and (e) the child is fundamentally relational and interdependent rather than independent as a result of his or her developmental progress. Examples of literature below capture these five understandings of the reconceptualized child translated into practice.

Many educators writing about their pedagogical experiences in Canadian early childhood laboratory schools reflect on the complexities and challenges of thinking differently about the child (e.g., see Williams et al., 2013). Leaning on ideas from reconceptualist scholars such as MacNaughton, Hughes, and Smith (2008) and Olsson (2009), Grove and Lirette (2013), educators from MacEwan University, document how projects that respond to the children's dislikes, concerns, and requests enhance "a more profound awareness of children's theories and how these theories complicate and make complex our image of the child...the child as an active citizen who is skilled, accomplished and socially responsible" (Grove & Lirette, 2013, p. 27). Kind (2010) describes her reconceptualizing journey as an *atelierista* (art studio teacher) in Capilano University's Children's Center as one of finding "rhythms of creative difficulty" in order "to more deeply understand children's artistic languages—that is, how to read, interpret, respond to, enrich, problematize and *encounter* the visual processes and artistic engagements of children" (p. 115; emphasis in the original).

The following more detailed example illuminates the complex thinking—at the interpersonal, political, and environmental levels—involved in reconceptualizing the child: at the University of Victoria, Atkinson (2016) explores how a toddler painted her nose while experimenting with paint in a forest, thereby "transgressing unspoken boundaries about how paint must be used by children" (p. 60). Atkinson struggles with what to do: DAP recommends the child be redirected to more appropriate materials. But drawing on Rinaldi's (2006) pedagogy of listening, Atkinson finds that "educators [need to be] open to children's thinking, their wonderings, their theories" (p. 63). Moreover, Atkinson ponders how an understanding of the transgressing child is entangled in everything else in the forest environment, from its land as the traditional territories of the Coast and Straits Salish and Lekwungen peoples and the colonization of the land by settlers to the forest air and dampness of the forest floor.

Other literature draws on a socio-material theoretical perspective (Lenz-Taguchi, 2010) to explore how children's encounters with other people and more-than-human materials, such as forests and toys, form and reform children's identities (Atkinson, 2016; Kind, 2010; Pacini-Ketchabaw et al., 2015). In one example, Hodgins et al. (2017) report on moments of practice from the IQ Project (Pence & Pacini-Ketchabaw, 2012) in which children's encounters with dolls provoke thinking about children's "misuse" (hitting, pounding, etc.) of them and educator responses (Hodgins et al., 2017; see also Bezaire & Cameron, 2009 on toys as text, critically reading children's playthings). As Hodgins et al. state, educators "responses to the unexpected doll encounters are infused with our images of children, educators, and ECEC itself" (p. 23). Within the IQ Project's pedagogical development model, thinking about pedagogy is not to locate the right or best practice but to consider how children's encounters with others and materials are connected to larger social, cultural, and political issues.

Similarly, Rose and Whitty (2013) explore how the simple clock's "tyranny of time" affects children's engagement in and with the learning environment (p. 38). In their work with educators, these researchers (2013) asked what it would mean if children's encounters with others and materials "took time" and if educators' "attention shifted from the clock to the children"—challenging the structured, routine-bound days of early childhood programs first established at the Institute of Child Study at the University of Toronto in the 1920s and persisting until today (p. 39).

A recent survey[5] (Langford 2017) on full-day Canadian university and college early childhood laboratory schools found that survey informants consider their laboratory schools to be dynamic places of innovation and a testing ground for new curricula ideas.[6] This finding is consistent with evidence from this chapter's literature review that reconceptualizing ideas are prevalent in university laboratory schools[7] that evolved out of an education tradition. In some provinces, researchers and educators in these laboratory schools have been able to demonstrate in practice curricula innovations (e.g., early learning curriculum frameworks) initiated by provincial governments. Survey informants indicate that the status and value of their laboratory schools, particularly in university settings, is always precarious, requiring a delicate balance between the education of young children and innovation in pedagogy and research.

CONCLUSION

On the surface, this chapter reviews literature that documents the history of university and college early childhood laboratory schools in Canada. But under the surface, the review reveals a change in how the young child in the laboratory school is conceptualized—a change from a scientific child to a reconceptualized child. At the same time, understanding this change as simply a scientific child/reconceptualized child binary ignores innovations in thinking about the scientific child (Prochner, 2014; Clark et al., 2012).

Literature describes innovations *within* the scientific paradigm: from Batz's theory of security in the 1920s (Wright, 2000) to the view that children's experiences influence their development in the 1960s (Varga, 1997) to an inquiry-based curriculum in the 2000s (The Laboratory School at The Dr. Eric Jackman Institute of Child Study, 2011). The current move in literature to reconceptualize the child using post-foundational theoretical perspectives in some Canadian university and college early childhood laboratory schools can be considered a paradigmatic shift in the concept of the child.

It remains to be seen, however, if future literature will document this shift as having significantly influenced pedagogical practices and research in the wider Canadian ECEC field in the light of the pervasiveness of the "science of the child" as a taken-for-granted singular truth about the child (Clark et al., 2012). As the literature review indicates, laboratory schools can be more influential when educational policy supports dissemination of new ideas about the child and pedagogy. At the same time, a dialogue about differing conceptualizations of the child—the scientific child and the reconceptualized child—needs to be asserted and intentional across Canadian university and college early childhood laboratory schools and in the ECEC communities. By analyzing literature that documents the history of these conceptualizations of the child, the chapter seeks to contribute to this dialogue.

NOTES

1. The two types of laboratory schools described in this chapter are distinguished from campus childcare services that do not engage in research and curricula innovation.
2. Childcare centers at the University of Victoria are not formally linked to an academic program. However, the early childhood education faculty in the School of Youth and Child Studies works closely with educators in the centers, and many educators have authored and/or coauthored publications.

3. Canada is a federated state; education and childcare are the responsibility of provinces and territories. Each early learning curriculum framework is unique to a province or territory.

4. This is not to suggest that Canadian child study centers do not use qualitative methods (see, for example, Pyle & Danniels, 2015). To engage in reconceptualist research means holding a set of assumptions that are grounded in post-foundational theories.

5. The survey selection criteria excluded university laboratory schools at the University of Alberta, University of Concordia, and the University of Toronto/Ontario Institute in Studies in Education, which offer half-day programs.

6. Not all college laboratory schools engage in reconceptualist practices.

7. The literature review indicates that researchers or educators at universities (rather than at colleges) are more likely to write about their research or practices.

REFERENCES

Atkinson, K. (2016). A touch of paint: Transgressing unspoken boundaries. *Journal of Childhood Studies, 41*(2), 60–65.

Bereiter, C., & Scardamalia, M. (2014). Knowledge building and knowledge creation: One concept, two hills to climb. In S. C. Tan, H. J. So, & J. Yeo (Eds.), *Knowledge creation in education* (pp. 35–52). Singapore: Springer.

Bernhard, J. (1995). The changing field of child development: Cultural diversity and the professional training of early childhood educators. *Canadian Journal of Education, 20*(4), 415–436.

Bernhard, J., Lefebvre, M.-L., Chud, G., & Lange, R. (1995). *Paths to equity: Cultural, linguistic and racial diversity in Canadian early childhood education.* Toronto, Canada: York Lanes.

Bernhard, J. K., Pollard. J., Eggers-Pierola, C., & Morin, A. (2000). *Infants and toddlers in Canadian multi-age childcare centres: Age, ability and linguistic inclusion.* Ottawa, Canada: Research Connections Canada.

Bezaire, K., & Cameron, L. (2009). Toys as text: Reading children's playthings. In L. Iannacci & P. Whitty (Eds.), *Early childhood curricula: Reconceptualist perspectives* (pp. 271–298). Calgary, Canada: Detselig Enterprises.

Binder, M. (2012). The storied lives children play: Multimodal approaches using storytelling. *Canadian Children, 39*(2), 11–20.

Binder, M., & Kotsopoulos, S. (2011). Multimodal literacy narratives: Weaving the threads of young children's identity through the arts. *Journal of Research in Childhood Education, 25*(4), 367–384.

Binder, M., Sorin R., Nolan, J., & Chu, S. (2015). Multimodal meaning-making for young children: Partnerships through blogging. In S. Garvis & N. Lemon (Eds.), *Understanding digital technologies and young children: An international perspective* (pp. 92–111). New York, NY: Routledge.

Blatz, W. E. (1944). *Understanding the young child.* Toronto, Canada: Clarke, Irwin.

Blatz, W. E. (1966). *Human security: Some reflections.* Toronto, Canada: University of Toronto Press.

Blatz, W. E., & Bott, H. (1929). *Parents and the preschool child.* New York, NY: William Morrow.

Bloch, M., Swadener, B., & Cannella, G. (Eds.). (2014). *Reconceptualizing early childhood care and education: A reader: Critical questions, new imaginaries and social activism.* New York, NY: Peter Lang.

Brophy, K. (2000). A history of laboratory schools. In L. Prochner & N. Howe (Eds.), *Childhood care and education in Canada* (pp. 96–115). Vancouver, Canada: University of British Columbia Press.

Brophy, K., Callahan, J., Campbell, R., & Reid, L. (2013). An approach to student training: Opportunities for emergent learning. In R. Langford & A. Di Santo (Eds.), *Leading the way: Recognizing the role of early learning lab schools in Canadian universities and colleges* (pp. 18–21). Toronto, Canada: Ryerson University.

Carver, S., McConnaha, W., Messina, R., Morley, E., & Wang, Y. (2017). Laboratory schools: Bridging theory, research, and practice to improve education. In J. Horvath, J. Lodge, & J. Hattie (Eds.), *From the laboratory to the classroom: Translating science of learning for teachers* (pp. 279–296). Abingdon, Oxon: Routledge.

Clark, P., Gleason, M., & Petrina, S. (2012). Preschools for science: The Child Study Center at the University of British Columbia. *History of Education Quarterly, 52*(1), 29–61.

Dahlberg, G., Moss, P., & Pence, A. (2010). *Beyond quality in early childhood education care: Languages of evaluation.* London, England: Routledge.

Elliot D., & Yazbeck, S-L. (2013). Navigating change through wonder and dialogue. In R. Langford & A. DiSanto (Eds.), *Leading the way: Recognizing the role of early learning lab schools in Canadian universities and colleges* (pp. 34–41). Toronto, Canada: Ryerson University.

Fletcher, M. I. (1974). *The adult and the nursery school child* (2nd ed). Toronto, Canada: University of Toronto Press.

Government of British Columbia. (2008). *British Columbia early learning framework.* Victoria, Canada: Ministry of Education, Ministry of Health, Ministry of Children and Family Development & Early Learning Advisory Group.

Grove, A., & Lirette, T. (2013). Children and citizenship. In R. Langford & A. DiSanto (Eds.), *Leading the way: Recognizing the role of early learning lab schools in Canadian universities and colleges* (pp. 22–28). Toronto, Canada: Ryerson University. Hodgins, B. D. (2012). Pedagogical narrations' potentiality as a methodology for child studies research. *Canadian Children, 37*(1), 4–11.

Hodgins D., Atkinson, K., & Wanamaker, L. (2017). (Re)Imagining and (re)ngaging in relational encounters: Communities of practice for (re) vitalizing pedagogies. *Association of Early Childhood Educators Ontario, 1*(1), 23–34.

Hodgins, D., Kummen, K., Pacini-Ketchabaw, V., & Thompson, D. (2013). Entangling and reconceptualizing research/practice binaries in laboratory schools in British Columbia. In R. Langford & A. DiSanto. (Eds.), *Leading the way: Recognizing the role of early learning lab schools in Canadian universities and colleges* (pp. 42–48). Toronto, ON: Ryerson University.

Kind, S. (2010). Art encounters: Movements in the visual arts and early childhood education. In V. Pacini-Ketchabaw (Ed.), *Flows, rhythms and intensities of early childhood education curriculum* (pp. 113–132). New York, NY: Peter Lang.

Koller, D., & San Juan, V. (2014). Play based interview methods for exploring young children's perspectives on inclusion. *International Journal of Qualitative Research in Education, 28*(5), 610–631. doi:10.1080/09518398.2014.916434

Land N., & Danis, I. (2016). Movement/ing provocations in early childhood education. *Journal of Childhood Studies, 41*(3), 26–37.

Langford, R. (2012). Innovations in provincial early learning curriculum frameworks. In N. Howe & L. Prochner (Eds), *Recent perspectives on early childhood education and care in Canada* (pp. 206–228). Toronto, Canada: University of Toronto Press.

Langford, R. (Spring 2017). Canadian university and college early learning laboratory schools: What are they all about? *AECEO eceLINK*, Toronto, Canada: Association of Early Childhood Educators Ontario. 18–23.

Langford R., & DiSanto, A. (Eds.). (2013). *Leading the way: Recognizing the role of early learning lab schools in Canadian universities and colleges.* Toronto, Canada: University of Toronto Press.

Lenz-Taguchi, H. (2010). *Going beyond the theory/practice divide in early childhood education: Introducing an intra-active pedagogy.* London, England: Routledge.

Lubeck, S. (1998). Is developmentally appropriate practice for everyone? *Childhood Education, 74*(5), 283–92.

MacNevin, M., & Berman, R. (2017). The Black baby doll doesn't fit the disconnect between early childhood diversity policy, early childhood educator practice, and children's play. *Early Child Development and Care, 187*(5/6), 827–839. doi: 10.1080/03004430.2016.1223065

MacNaughton, G., Hughes, P., & Smith, K. (Eds.). (2008). *Young children as active citizens: Principles and practices and pedagogies.* London, England: Cambridge Scholars.

Moss, P. (2014). *Transformative change and real utopias in early childhood education: A story of democracy, experimentation and potentiality.* Abingdon, England: Routledge.

Moss, J., Hawes, Z., Naqvi, S., & Caswell, B. (2015). Adapting Japanese lesson study to enhance the teaching and learning of geometry and spatial reasoning in early years classrooms: A case study. *ZDM Mathematics Education, 47*, 377–390.

Moss, J., Messina, R., Morley, E., & Tepylo, D. (2012). Sustaining professional collaborations over 6 years: Using Japanese lesson study to improve the teaching and learning of mathematics. In J. Bay-Williams (Ed.), *Professional collaborations in mathematics teaching and learning: Seeking success for all: The National Council of Teachers of Mathematics Teaching and Learning 70th Yearbook* (pp. 297–309). Reston, VA: National Council of Teachers of Mathematics.

Olsson, L. M. (2009). *Movement and exploration in young children's learning: Deleuze and Guattari in early childhood education.* New York, NY: Routledge.

Pacini-Ketchabaw, V., & Pence, A. (2006). Contextualizing the reconceptualist movement in Canadian early childhood education. In V. Pacini-Ketchabaw & A. Pence (Eds.), *Canadian early childhood education: Broadening and deepening discussions of quality* (pp. 5–20). Ottawa, Canada: Canadian Child Care Federation.

Pacini-Ketchabaw, V., Nxumalo, F., Kocher, L., Elliot, E., & Sanchez, A. (2015). *Journeys: Reconceptualizing early childhood practices through pedagogical narration.* Toronto, Canada: University of Toronto Press.

Paley, V. G. (1991). *The boy who would be a helicopter: The uses of storytelling in the classroom*. Cambridge, MA: Harvard University Press.

Pence, A., & Pacini-Ketchabaw, V. (2012). The investigating quality project: Innovative approaches to early childhood education. In N. Howe & L. Prochner (Eds.), *Recent perspectives on early childhood education and care in Canada* (pp. 229–244). Toronto, Canada: University of Toronto Press.

Prochner, L. (2014). Shaping minds as soon as possible: Two centuries of preschool in Canada. *Canadian Issues*, Spring, 44–48. Retrieved from http://connection.ebscohost.com/c/articles/110899540/shaping-minds-as-soon-as-possible-two-centuries-preschool-canada

Prochner L., & Doyon, P. (1997). Researchers and their subjects in the history of child study: William Blatz and the Dionne quintuplets. *Canadian Psychology, 38*(2), 103–110.

Prochner, L., & Hwang, Y. (2008). "Cry and you cry alone": Timeout in early childhood settings. *Childhood, 18*(4), 517–534.

Prochner L., & Robertson, L. (2012). Early childhood education and care in Canada in the 1950s and 1960s. In N. Howe & L. Prochner (Eds.), *Recent perspectives on early childhood education and care in Canada* (pp. 15–49). Toronto, Canada: University of Toronto Press.

Pyle, A., & Danniels, E. (2015). Using a picture book to gain assent in research with young children. *Early Child Development & Care, 186*(9), 1438–1452. doi:10.1080/03004430.2015.1100175

Rinaldi, C. (2006). *In dialogue with Reggio Emilia: Listening, researching and learning*. London, England: Routledge.

Rose, S., & Whitty, P. (2013). Valuing subjective complexities disrupting the tyranny of time. In L. Prochner & V. Pacini-Ketchabaw (Eds.), *Re-situating Canadian early childhood education* (pp. 35–52). New York, NY: Peter Lang.

Ryan, S., & Grieshaber, S. (2005). Shifting from developmental to postmodern practices in early childhood education teacher education. *Journal of Teacher Education, 65*(1), 34–45.

Sen, A. (1999). *Development as freedom*. Oxford, England: Oxford University Press.

Strong-Boag, V. (1982). Intruders in the nursery: Childcare professionals reshape the years one to five, 1920–1940. In J. Parr (Ed.), *Childhood and family in Canadian history* (pp. 160–178). Toronto, Canada: McClelland & Stewart.

Tepylo, D. H., Moss, J., & Stephenson, C. (2015). A developmental look at a rigorous block play program. *Young Children, 70*, 18–25.

The Laboratory School at the Dr. Eric Jackman Institute of Child Study. (2011). *Natural curiosity: A resource for teachers*. Toronto, Canada: Miracle Press.

Underwood, K., Valeo, A., & Wood, R. (2012). Understanding inclusive early childhood education: A capability approach. *Contemporary Issues in Early Childhood, 13*(4), 290–299.

Underwood, K., Chan, C., Koller, D., & Valeo, A. (2015). Understanding young children's capabilities: Approaches to interviews with young children experiencing disability. *Child Care in Practice, 2*(3), 220–237. doi:10.1080/13575279.2015.1037249

Varga, D. (1997). *Constructing the child: A history of Canadian day care*. Toronto, Canada: James Lorimer.

Whitty, P. (2009). Towards designing a postfoundational curriculum document. In L. Iannacci & P. Whitty (Eds.), *Early Childhood Curricula: Reconceptualist Perspectives* (pp. 35–86). Calgary, Canada: Detselig.

Williams, J., Farzaneh, T., Simon, M., Salau, L., Francisco, L., & Perera-Jones, N. (2013). Our learning story: Journey of transformation. In R. Langford & A. DiSanto (Eds.), *Leading the way: Recognizing the role of early learning lab schools in Canadian universities and colleges* (pp. 5–9). Toronto, Canada: Ryerson University.

Wright, M. J. (2000). Toronto's Institute of Child Study and the Teachings of W. E. Blatz. In L. Prochner & N. Howe (Eds.), *Childhood care and education in Canada* (pp. 107–114). Vancouver, Canada: University of British Columbia Press.

CHAPTER 7

KEEPING RELEVANT IN CHANGING TIMES

The Evolution of a University Laboratory School

Monica Miller Marsh, Martha Lash, Pam Hutchins, and Rochelle Hostler

---

ABSTRACT

The Kent State University Child Development Center (CDC), an internationally known laboratory school, has evolved over time as it strives to stay relevant in a university setting that is constantly shifting and changing in response to social, economic, and political forces. More closely aligning the laboratory school with the Early Childhood Education program by becoming an authorized International Baccalaureate Primary Years Program (IB PYP) world school has strengthened the children's program, moved the work of the CDC into the international realm, and aligned the CDC with the university's strategic plan. Simultaneously, the CDC continues to make an impact at the local level upholding John Dewey's original intentions for laboratory schools. Here we document and analyze the effects of the changes with the introduction of the IB PYP to both the Center and the Kent State Early Childhood Education program.

Contemporary Perspectives on Research on Child Development Laboratory Schools in Early Childhood Education,
pages 117–133
117

Historically, one can study the definition of a laboratory school from many perspectives. Some views are consistent with that of a traditional scientific laboratory, while others focus more on the role of the school as a place of teacher education and demonstration. Dewey's vision of a laboratory school aligns with the scientific laboratory, "staffed with college trained teachers and devoted to research, experiment, and educational innovation" (Knoll, 2014, p. 455). In his laboratory school at the University of Chicago, Dewey "tested his hypothesis on knowledge and learning, established a community and devised a curriculum capable of reconciling individual freedom and collective well being" (Durst, 2010, p. 46). Dewey's belief that the most important work of the university education department is "the scientific— the contribution it makes to the progress of educational thinking" (Dewey, 1915, p. 87) makes clear his thought that the laboratory school and university should be strongly connected.

Throughout the first half of the 20th century, a number of university programs around the country began to follow Dewey's lead and called themselves laboratory schools. Many of those schools have since closed (Barbour & McBride, 2017), and of those that remain many do not operate true to the Deweyan philosophy (Jackson, 1990). In the latter half of the 20th century, as college of education laboratory schools were in decline, reform efforts such as clinical schools, professional development schools, and campus child care centers began to emerge, where the focus shifted to teacher education and service to families (Bersani & Hutchins, 2003). As we enter the 21st century, the world of higher education is rapidly changing. Kostelnik (2017), in her recent chapter entitled "What Child Development Laboratories Need to Do to Thrive: An Administrator's Perspective," contends that laboratory schools have the potential to be valuable vehicles for 21st century scholarship, if they are able to respond effectively and provide value to institutions of higher education (p. 96). In her words:

> To do their work well, CDLs [child development laboratories] must be in tune with the ecosystem in which they function. Of course that involves a complex mesosystem of their home colleges and departments; affiliate administrators, students and faculty; as well as the children and families served. However, higher education is the overarching ecosystem in which CDLs are embedded and to which they must respond effectively if they are to provide value to the institutions and professions they serve. In turn, higher education functions within a larger societal macrosystem that cannot be ignored. (Kostelnik, 2017, p. 96)

In other words, the days of laboratory schools being independent, stand-alone programs are over. In order to remain viable, laboratory schools need to be supported by and supportive of other programs and departments across campus.

Kostelnik (2017) highlights five major trends in higher education that have significant implications for laboratory schools. These trends include: (a) the shift from higher education being perceived as a public good to a vehicle for private gain, (b) the creation of flexible learning environments in order to meet the demands of a new generation of student learners, (c) the creation of "branding" and niche programs in order to stand out from other programs offering similar degrees, (d) the shift from privileging individual researchers to valuing intentionally designed and strategically supported teaching and research collaborations, and (e) responding to the lack of common training across the early childhood workforce.

In this chapter we share how the Kent State University CDC's vision of a laboratory school has evolved over time and how we are currently addressing two of the trends specified by Kostelnik in order to stay relevant: adopting a niche program and building global and local collaborations. In the following paragraphs we briefly describe the history of the CDC and discuss how we came to adopt the International Baccalaureate Primary Years Program (IB PYP) curriculum framework, a niche program that has become integrated into university programs beyond the CDC and the early childhood education (ECE) program and aligns with the current mission and priorities of Kent State. We then illustrate how the IB PYP framework has strengthened the children's program at the CDC, bolstered research opportunities, and provided us with the opportunity to share our exemplary teaching practices with IB PYP educators around the world. A brief look at the CDC's involvement in community service demonstrates the school's continued efforts to stay true to Dewey's notion of a laboratory school being a space in which children and adults work together to find solutions to real world problems that benefit their own communities.

BRIEF HISTORY OF THE KENT CHILD DEVELOPMENT CENTER

The Kent State University (KSU) CDC is a five-star Step Up to Quality award-winning school, which is the highest rating possible on the quality rating and improvement system administered in the state of Ohio. The laboratory school originated in 1972 as a program serving preschool age children and grew over the years as a kindergarten and toddler program were added in the 1980s and 1990s, respectively, as the demand for high quality early childhood programs persisted. The CDC, taking inspiration from the Reggio Emilia approach to education, has a school community that values individual identity and reflection. Collaboration among the faculty supports this community of learners and sustains the reflective and analytic work of the group, generating new knowledge and growth in learning. This collaborative work contributes to a system of interactions and relationships that are continuously constructed as teachers, children, and families work together (Fraser & Gestwicki, 2002).

The environment, both physical spaces and the social/emotional climate, is viewed as incredibly important in the learning process as they equally support the children's learning and development. Located on the edge of the expansive KSU campus, the CDC is within walking distance to a hiking path, wetlands, meadow, and many lovely garden areas. Special emphasis is given to the children's relationships with the natural world. Children have daily access to an outdoor learning laboratory designed with their interests in mind (Sisson & Lash, 2017). This space fosters open-ended experiences among native plants and grasses while supporting children's love of the natural world.

The school's curriculum is an inquiry-based, emergent curriculum driven by the interests of children, families, and teachers. Each classroom has one full-time licensed mentor teacher, a part-time graduate student, and up to five ECE field students and interns. The program is further supported by two part-time afternoon teachers and a myriad of undergraduate assistants who work between 10 and 15 hours each week. Teachers offer children high-quality and complex materials that support the children's efforts to represent and communicate ideas in multiple ways. Children are encouraged to participate with others through listening, negotiation, and turn taking while learning to accept the perspective of others. Inspired by studying the Reggio Emilia approach beginning in the 1990s and the implementation of the IB PYP in 2014, the faculty at the school have constructed an educational program that extends the understanding of developmentally appropriate practices and supports individuality, participation, inquiry, and critical thinking. This approach is guided by core values that are grounded in social constructivism that include learning based on the children's interests, experimentation, and cooperation (Devries & Zan, 2012).

The program currently serves 150 children from 18 months of age through kindergarten from a variety of cultural, socioeconomic, and linguistic backgrounds. English and 18 other languages are spoken in the homes of the families, representing the United States and 20 other countries. Approximately 30% of the families currently attending identify themselves as culturally diverse. Families are considered integral in the daily life of the school. They are viewed as partners in the education of their child where family attitudes, beliefs, and values are held in high regard. The respect given to this concept ultimately supports the goal of understanding the impact of the child's experience at home as it relates to the school. This ensures that the school is providing the best learning experiences for children.

Since its inception, the CDC has been affiliated with the ECE department, in what is now the School of Teaching, Learning, and Curriculum Studies in the College of Education, Health, and Human Services at KSU.

The CDC laboratory school has a three-prong mission of service, research, and teacher education (Lash & Miller-Marsh, 2017). An integral part of the CDC's mission includes the professional preparation of teachers and related professions and research to inform teacher practice in tandem with the ECE program at KSU. In the following section we more fully describe the ECE program and explain the relationship between the CDC and the ECE program.

CONTEXTUALIZING AND SHIFTING KENT'S EARLY CHILDHOOD TEACHER EDUCATION PROGRAM

KSU's ECE program is situated in a teaching and research public university with 30,000 university students at the main campus and an additional 14,000 students across seven regional campuses; the geographical setting is suburban, near two urban areas and surrounded by small towns and rural communities in the midwest United States. The 2015 Carnegie Classification of Institutions of Higher Education (http://carnegieclassifications.iu.edu/) categorizes KSU as a doctoral university: Higher research activity. Over the past decade KSU has diligently aligned policies for faculty responsibilities and merit review to move to the highest category of doctoral university: Highest research activity (i.e., faculty tenure and promotion moved from the Boyer model to research, teaching and service, merit and special awards favor research). Thus, in all program and field efforts, the mission and strategic goals of the university must be considered; we saw the same shift at the KSU CDC laboratory school (Lash & Miller-Marsh, 2017). The ECE program is nationally recognized, most recently in 2015 by the National Association for the Education of Young Children (NAEYC) and the Council for the Accreditation of Educator Preparation (CAEP). Faculty beliefs and research derive from and are enacted in an inquiry-based constructivist approach to teaching and learning that merges theory and practice to help preservice teachers become effective critical educators and teacher leaders.

Striving for Social Justice and International Education in Teacher Education

The ECE conceptual framework emphasis historically has focused on social justice. Through faculty self-study and reassessment of preservice teachers' needs and development, the conceptual framework and program was expanded in 2011 to include a strong emphasis on international mindedness (James & Davis, 2010), as can be recognized in the KSU ECE program's conceptual model (see http://www.kent.edu/ehhs/tlcs/eced/

philosophy-early-childhood-education), which positions novice teachers as critical educator-teacher leaders who are committed professionals, curriculum experts, democratically accountable leaders, culturally relevant pedagogical experts, reflective thinkers, and co-decision makers. The KSU ECE conceptual framework encompasses the specialized domains for national and state accreditations as indicated by the NAEYC and CAEP and the teacher performance domains of the Ohio Department of Education, respectively. Early childhood preservice teachers earn the IB Certificate for Teaching and Learning, as specified in the IB mission statement:

> The International Baccalaureate aims to develop inquiring, knowledgeable and caring young people who help to create a better and more peaceful world through intercultural understanding and respect. To this end the organization works with schools, governments and international organizations to develop challenging programmes of international education and rigorous assessment. These programmes encourage students across the world to become active, compassionate and lifelong learners who understand that other people, with their differences can also be right. (IB, n.d.)

This philosophy has allowed the faculty to move beyond state standards into more globally recognized objectives and concepts in teaching and learning and the young child. A more thorough explanation of this in-depth conceptual work is described in the following paragraphs.

The IB concept of international mindedness—an openness to and curiosity about the world and people of other cultures and a striving toward a deep level of understanding of the complexity and diversity of human interaction—demonstrates itself through the IB Learner Profile attributes: inquirers, knowledgeable, thinkers, communicators, principled, open-minded, caring, risk-takers (courageous), balanced (spiritual), and reflective. These concepts and attributes mirror and enhance faculty approaches to teaching and learning for our preservice teachers and for the children in early childhood programs. Preservice teachers, supported to realize that even very young children have feelings about fairness and justice (Hyland, 2010; Wardle, 2013), can move to a more global realization that taking effective action demonstrates responsibility and respect for self, others, and the environment (International Baccalaureate, 2009). KSU coursework includes a foundation in children, families, communities, curriculum, content, and methods; furthermore, field and student teaching experiences for the ECE students occur both in preschool and primary grades for five different placements and approximately 1,400 hours.

The coursework and classroom fieldwork are intertwined over five semesters to support the transition from theory to practice; that is, all classes each semester entail field assignments to seal the university classroom learning. These assignments include weekly reflections and processing of field experiences. Given the university's geographical location, a wide variety of area schools allow for diverse pedagogical, sociocultural, and socioeconomic experiences that are discussed in the university classroom (Anderson, 2016; Lash & Kroeger, 2018; Vartuili, Snider, & Holley, 2016). Additionally, through the PYP affiliation, the preservice students can begin to use the IB language, concepts, principles, and questioning in various field placements, particularly our own CDC. Soon after the affiliation, the CDC master teachers were receiving specific questions regarding the IB PYP curriculum framework that were beyond their daily knowledge base in a Reggio Emilia-inspired approach program, because while these programs are complementary they do not share the same pedagogical language (Cancemi, 2011). In the meantime, the CDC faculty continue to strive to update and expand their knowledge base to include the PYP framework.

Striving for Social Justice and International Education in Teacher Practices

These KSU preservice teachers' questions in their CDC lab school field placements serve as provocations for the CDC teachers to find more specific information about the IB PYP. We quickly learned that although our ECE faculty take great pains to keep the teacher education program current and global, and we make sure to communicate and collaborate with the CDC lab school faculty, these efforts were not robust enough to adequately serve the CDC teachers in their daily practices and mentoring of preservice teachers earning the IB PYP certificate. The CDC faculty requested a 2-day, faculty led training entitled "Internationalizing the Curriculum: Engaging with Ideas and Concepts of the International Baccalaureate Primary Years Programme and Adaptations for Environments Serving Children 0–6 year." Additionally, while members of the CDC leadership team had attended IB PYP trainings, we realized it was time to send all of the CDC mentor teachers to IB workshop trainings. Concurrently, we reexamined and modified how the IB PYP Certificate for Teaching and Learning was being embedded throughout the preservice teacher education program.

During the shared *Internationalizing the Curriculum* workshop, gains were made in learning, collaboration, and the reaffirmation that the teacher education program and the CDC share a social constructivist, inquiry-based learning approach as realized by the IB PYP and the Reggio Emilia-inspired approach. Specific objectives for the training were for teachers to: obtain a basic introduction to the IB PYP with an emphasis on the early years (3–6 years old); to understand the PYP curriculum, mission statement, international mindedness, learner profile, six transdisciplinary themes, five essential elements, key concepts, attitudes, inquiry cycle, and transdisciplinary skills; to gain a basic knowledge on the IB PYP written, taught, and assessed curriculum framework; to discuss and learn new inquiry-based teaching strategies; and to have a better understanding of the diverse perspectives of the international families attending child care programs. Evaluations of our shared work showed that teachers were able to articulate and had a basic understanding of the main components of the IB PYP curriculum framework, explored a self/programmatic understanding of international mindedness, were more familiar with the basic PYP materials and when/where/why they are used, learned additional teaching strategies for inquiry-based learning, and were open to a global curriculum approach. In retrospect, we look at this training as the first formal step in the CDC's feasibility study into becoming an IB World School.

The journey had begun, the advantages were beginning to make themselves apparent, and the lab school began to struggle with those important issues of relevancy articulated by Kostelnik in the opening paragraphs of this chapter. After a 2-year feasibility study, the CDC formalized their efforts and moved into IB candidacy, and in May of 2018, the CDC became an authorized IB PYP World School.

Aligning With Kent State University's Mission and Vision

While the CDC already offered an exemplary program based on the Reggio Emilia approach for over two decades, the program was firmly entrenched within the laboratory school rather than being integrated throughout the ECE program or other related program areas. This meant there was little investment in the lab school by those who worked beyond its walls. The IB PYP program provided the CDC with an opportunity to build collaborations with ECE faculty and to firmly align itself with the newly crafted mission and vision of KSU.

The IB PYP is an example of what Kostelnik (2017) describes as a niche program. As she explains, "True niches are hallmark programs recognizable to specific programs because they stand out from the rest (p. 100). While the core early childhood curriculum remains similar to program offerings at other institutions, the IB PYP provides Kent State with opportunities for growth in enrollment, international exchanges, increased hiring opportunities for graduates, and global research possibilities. All of these aspects of the ECE program make the partnership with the IB attractive to undergraduate students and their families, graduate students, ECE and other related faculty, as well as other departments on campus. In fact, the Middle Childhood Education program followed the lead of the ECE program and now offers the IB Middle Years Program (MYP) certification. The

IB is also partnering with our career-related program, and other programs are in conversation with the IB. These IB offerings are in place at various branch campuses as well as at the Kent campus. Most importantly, the adoption of the IB PYP clearly aligns the CDC with President Beverly Warren's *Strategic Roadmap for a Distinctive Kent State* (Kent State University, 2015).

The Strategic Roadmap is being used to guide the operating plan for the entire eight-campus university system. The president and provost, with oversight from the board of trustees, are tasked with implementation of the plan. The goal of the roadmap is to identify strategies that can be employed "to further propel a pathway to a nationally distinctive blend of teaching, research, and creative excellence" (2015, p. 1). A new vision, mission statement, and core values were adopted along with five major priorities. The vision and mission statement excerpted from the Strategic Roadmap are:

> Vision: "To be a community of change agents whose collective commitment to learning sparks epic thinking, meaningful voice and invaluable outcomes to better our society." (2015, p. 1)
>
> Mission: "We transform lives and community through the power of discovery, learning and creative expression in an inclusive environment." (2015, p. 1)

The CDC's adherence to an inquiry-oriented, play-based curriculum inspired by the Reggio Emilia approach and guided by the IB PYP framework clearly supports the vision and mission of the university. In addition, two of the five priorities detailed in the Strategic Roadmap—Students First and Regional Impact—are already a part of the culture of the CDC, as will be explicated throughout the rest of the chapter. The remaining three priorities, *global competitiveness, organizational stewardship,* and *a distinctive Kent State,* are priorities that we see as being directly addressed through our affiliation with the IB.

In the following section we describe how the IB PYP framework has helped us to create a shared language between the CDC and ECE program, strengthened the CDC's assessment practices and the type of support made available to English language learners (ELL), while also providing opportunities for research and to shape professional development for early years practitioners around the world.

BECOMING AN INTERNATIONAL LABORATORY SCHOOL

As field placement students and student teachers entered the classrooms at the CDC, they began to introduce new phrases and terminology into the discourse of our school, such as references to transdisciplinary themes or learner profile attributes. Over time, we developed a shared language within the school, strengthening the relationships among the teachers at the CDC as well as our collaborations with faculty in the ECE program. In addition to this new vocabulary, the IB PYP framework challenged us to critically examine some areas of our laboratory school curriculum, which was one of the reasons we chose to adopt the IB PYP framework. We knew, for example, that our assessment policy could be strengthened, so we embraced the IB PYP requirement of writing a formal assessment policy.

The IB PYP requires a written assessment policy identifying school-wide assessment practices that must be implemented by teachers and shared with all school constituents (International Baccalaureate, 2009). This requirement addresses one of the major criticisms of the Reggio Emilia approach: "In the absence of a written curriculum there is a lack of accountability to the wider society" (Soler & Miller, 2003, p. 65). To this point, accountability at our school, like in other Reggio-inspired schools, was achieved through detailed documentation of children's inquiries through mediums such as photography, video, and audiotaping. This documentation is made visible to others in written daily reflections, installations throughout the school, family meetings and/or curriculum chats, and individual student portfolios. Portfolios were compiled by teachers, sometimes in consultation with children, yet there was an unevenness across classrooms in terms of the degree to which teachers included their own interpretations regarding children's learning or offered feedback upon an agreed upon set of habits of mind (Costa & Kallick, 2008). In addition, there were no designated spaces for children or families to provide feedback for the teacher to consider as curriculum emerged.

As a response to these shortcomings, and in order to meet the requirements articulated in the PYP, we recently adopted the learning story framework as a narrative assessment that meaningfully assesses children *in situ* (Carr, 2001). Learning stories, developed by Margaret Carr to align with the sociocultural focus of New Zealand's Te Whāriki Early Childhood Curriculum, meaningfully incorporate four characteristics of assessment: it occurs in context, it includes discussion with children, it requires teacher interpretation relative to a set of dispositions, and it drives learning and teaching (Carr, 2001). At the CDC, we use the learner profile attributes to interpret children's learning within the learning story, and this type of feedback has improved both the frequency and the quality of feedback to children from teachers. Creating the IB PYP assessment policy unified our assessment practices and strengthened our commitment to enact rigorous, authentic narrative assessment.

The creation of a school language policy has also strengthened our school curriculum and more importantly strengthened our relationship with parents. A parent survey was created with the support of one of our international doctoral students and distributed to all parents. The results of the survey led to the implementation of some new classroom practices. For example, classroom teachers now offer office hours throughout the week so that parents who may need more time to express themselves or a more detailed explanation about an issue will have a private space in which to speak. In addition, families who are new to the school are being paired with families who speak the same primary language so that they can act as resources for one another, and the returning families can help orient new families to the school.

We also came to realize through our discussions pertaining to language with international families that terms such as "parent involvement" and "parent volunteer" are unfamiliar to most of the international population. These and other revelations gleaned through survey responses led to a more robust research study being conducted by Miller Marsh and Raimbekova (2018) on how international parents perceive their roles and responsibilities in the education of their young children. Understanding international parent perceptions will help the CDC and other school personnel serving this population to build stronger links between home and school.

There are additional research studies currently taking place at the CDC, which have specifically stemmed from our association with the IB PYP. One such study is focused on how children, parents, and teachers respond to the IB Learner Profiles. Another study seeks to document and understand how CDC teachers and leaders mentor the KSU ECE preservice teachers and communicate curriculum to the parents and larger community as they transition into utilizing the IB PYP framework. These types of research studies have the potential to impact international early childhood programs and policies as well as early childhood teacher education.

While the above studies have been highlighted because of their relationship to the IB PYP, it is important to note that over the last 5 years the CDC has been moving from collaborative self-study toward an applied developmental science model (Barbour & McBride, 2017; Cutler et al., 2012; Lash & Miller-Marsh, 2017; McBride et al., 2012). This means that there are many other studies being conducted at the CDC by both external and internal researchers, including visiting scholars from abroad. Making these inquiries public (Baldwin, 2018; Borgerding, 2015; Miller-Marsh & Zhulamanova, 2016; Myers, Hostler, & Hughes; 2017; Raven, 2016; Sisson & Lash, 2017; West, Guillot Miller, & Moate, 2017) is another one of the ways that the CDC is striving to keep relevant in a research institution.

While the IB PYP has helped to fortify the pedagogical, curricular, and research aims of our school, we are also helping to strengthen the IB PYP with commissioned work focused on the professional development of early years practitioners. This work includes a guide that outlines the scope of technical and ethical guidelines that teachers and administrators should be considering when capturing visual data in educational contexts. We are also creating three toolkits to be used in IB PYP workshops: the first provides a rationale for, and examples of, children's play; the second serves to illustrate children's participation and agency through a morning meeting routine; and the third articulates, and gives examples of, the vitality of narrative assessment in early childhood education. This commissioned work will be used by early years educators in contexts around the world to illustrate quality teacher practice and exceptional curricular processes within the PYP framework.

Characterizing an International School

Is it simply the adoption of an international curricular framework such as the IB PYP that defines a school as an international school? Currently, there is no common definition of an international school. According to Hayden and Thompson (2017), "the term has not been well-defined in the past, and the lack of definition appears to be growing rather than diminishing as the 21st century progresses" (p. 4). International schools include a wide variety of systems, curricula, organizations, and approaches. Hayden and Thompson (2017) list eight criteria that should be met in order to consider a school an international school:

1. transferability of students' education across international schools,
2. a moving population (higher than in national public schools),
3. multinational and multilingual student body,
4. an international curriculum (i.e., International Baccalaureate),
5. international accreditation (e.g., Council or International Schools, International Baccalaureate Organization, Western Association of Schools and Colleges, etc.),
6. a transient and multinational teacher population,
7. non-selective student enrollment, and
8. usually English or bilingual as the language of instruction.

In terms of an international school, the CDC meets all of the above criteria aside from a transient and multinational teacher population. While some of our associate teachers are international students who come to Kent State to work on their graduate degrees and are hired at the CDC to teach, our current lead teachers are all citizens of the United States. In addition, while we do serve multinational and multilingual families who would be considered a moving population, at this point in time our internationally mobile population is constituted of about a quarter of our school community.

Acting Locally and Impacting Globally

Becoming an international world school does not mean that the KSU CDC has turned away from studying local problems and issues. Dewey's notion of a laboratory school being a space in which children and adults work together to think critically and creatively to identify and find solutions to real-world problems in their own communities is as relevant today as it was at the turn of the 20th century. Just as Dewey understood that a democracy is the result of actively involving people in the decision-making process of governing, Malaguzzi's Reggio Emilia approach is built on the premise that children develop through their interactions with others, including those with parents, teachers, peers, and the environment (Edwards, 2002). As Carla Rinaldi states, the "child generates changes in systems in which he or she is involved" and becomes a "producer of culture, values, and rights" (as cited in Edwards, 2002, p. 5). This notion that children are an integral part of society who have the right to actively participate in their communities and in their world is also mirrored in the IB PYP. Consider the following excerpt from *Making the PYP Happen*:

> In the PYP it is believed that not only is it possible for students to identify appropriate action, but also that teachers have a responsibility to enable them to choose their action carefully, to facilitate this action, and to encourage them to reflect on the action they undertake. This is viewed as an important part of students' active participation in their own learning." (International Baccalaureate, 2009, p. 26)

Dewey, Malaguzzi, and the philosophy of the IB PYP all position young children as capable individuals who are aware of the needs of others in their schools and communities and are concerned with world events (Hall & Rudkin, 2011). This focus on social justice work is integral to the ECE program. At the CDC, children routinely engage in community service experiences with a social action focus.

We define community service as "helping others in ways that benefit those beyond our school" (Miller Marsh, Cardy, & West, 2018). These experiences have included participating in diaper and book drives, preparing and serving food at a soup kitchen, and launching an anti-littering campaign, complete with posters and a radio advertisement. Our research findings illustrate that with the support of adults, children are capable of addressing issues in the school and community that are important to them, discussing those issue with adults outside of the school community, reflecting on their actions, and realizing that their voices can be heard beyond the walls of the school (Miller Marsh, Cardy, & West, 2018).

The anti-littering campaign exemplifies the commitment the school has made to the pursuit of global environmental sustainability. Children are taught to be stewards of the Earth through caring for the school gardens, participating in the school-wide composting program, and working with the university Office of Sustainability to reduce, recycle, repurpose, and reuse materials. Caring for the school gardens means that children make decisions about what will be planted, where things will be planted, and how harvested fruits and vegetables will be used. Our outdoor educator, in collaboration with the Portage County Master Gardeners—volunteers who have undergone intensive training in the art and science of gardening—work alongside the children in these gardening efforts.

The children work to reduce their use of water and electricity and recycle whenever possible. Teachers repurpose and reuse items for various purposes including artwork, building materials, investigations in math, science, literacy, and physical education. For example, cereal boxes become covers for writing journals, old tires are used for large motor activities, and pallets and large burlap coffee bags become forts in the classroom. As the children learn about sustainability, they teach the prospective teachers as well as their families about the practices taking place at school. Oftentimes these practices become a part of children and adults' home lives.

The school's efforts at the local level have been recognized and honored over the last 2 years. In May of 2017 the laboratory school was awarded the Portage County Environmental Conservation Award in the Stewardship category from the Portage Park District for "stewarding future environmentalists." In April of 2016 the school was awarded the Kent State University Office of Experiential Education and Civic Engagement Engaged Department Award for "providing assistance to others and building community." While these awards were given to our school based on local efforts, they exemplify the IB spirit of international mindedness. Administrators, teachers, students, and families at the CDC understand that we are all interconnected, and we assume a sense of responsibility for a global community that is facing many challenges.

CONCLUSION

The original intentions of laboratory schools according to Dewey were "creating communities dedicated to change, experimentation and social reform" (Durst, 2010, p. 9). The IB PYP framework embraces this spirit of innovation and collective action, as is evidenced by the statement of aims for all IB programs, "to develop internationally minded people who, recognizing their common humanity and shared guardianship of the planet, help to create a better and more peaceful world" (International Baccalaureate, 2009, p. 1) These sentiments, which have historically been embedded in the philosophies of both the ECE program and the CDC made the IB PYP an obvious choice for specialization in both programs. The adoption of the IB PYP has strengthened the collaborations between the ECE program and CDC faculty and more closely aligned both programs with the University's mission and vision.

The IB PYP has revitalized and provided increased visibility for all three prongs of the CDC's mission: service, professional development, and research. The IB PYP framework has provided the faculty with a tool to strengthen an already strong children's program in the areas of assessment and language, which built stronger relationships with parents. Our community-based partnerships continue to flourish through the service experiences enacted by children and their teachers. The faculty of the CDC has been provided with the opportunity to showcase exemplary teaching practices through a series of videos used around the world by the IB PYP for professional development. Research opportunities and collaborations in the areas of early childhood and teacher education as well as in a variety of other areas abound. As a laboratory school, the CDC is poised to become a research hub with the ability to support and advance the work of researchers across domestic university campuses and abroad. During rapidly changing times, when a plethora of significant and challenging questions need to be addressed, we find ourselves in an advantageous position.

REFERENCES

Anderson, E. (2016). Confronting existing challenges and meeting new demands in early childhood education using program-university collaborative models. *Journal of Early Childhood Teacher Education, 37*(1), 3–24.

Baldwin, K. (2018). The power of using international picture books with young children. *Young Children, 73*(2) 74–80.

Barbour, N., & McBride, B (Eds.). (2017). *The future of child development lab schools: Applied developmental science in action.* New York, NY: Routledge.

Bersani, C., & Hutchins, P. (2003). Reconceptualizing the child development laboratory school. In B. A. McBride & N. E. Barbour (Eds.), *Bridging the gap between theory, research, & practice: The role of child development laboratory programs in early childhood education* (pp. 113–139). Bingley, England: Emerald.

Borgerding, L. A. (2015). Dig into fossils! A Series of Activities Helps Young Students Learn about Fossils. *Science and Children, 52*(9), 30–37.

Cancemi, J. (2011). A dialogue between the Reggio Emilia experience and the IB Primary Years Programme. *International Schools Journal, 31*(1) 32–41.

Carr, M. (2001). *Assessment in early childhood settings: Learning stories.* London, England: Paul Chapman.

Costa, A. L., & Kallick, B. (Eds.). (2008). *Learning and leading with habits of mind: 16 essential characteristics for success.* Alexandria, VA: Association for Supervision and Curriculum Development.

Cutler, K., Bersani, C., Hutchins, P., Bowne, M., Lash, M., Kroeger, J., . . . Venhuizien, L. (2012). Laboratory schools as places of inquiry: A collaborative journey for two laboratory schools. *Early Education and Development, 23*(2), 242–258.

Devries, R., & Zan, B. (2012). *Moral classrooms, moral children: Creating a constructivist atmosphere in early education.* New York, NY: Teachers College Press.

Dewey, J. (1915). *The school and society.* Chicago, IL: University of Chicago Press.

Durst, A. (2010). John Dewey and the beginnings of the laboratory school. In *Women Educators in the Progressive Era: The women behind Dewey's laboratory school* (pp. 9–24). New York, NY: Palgrave Macmillan.

Edwards, C. P. (2002). Three approaches from Europe: Waldorf, Montessori, and Reggio Emilia. *Early Childhood Research and Practice, 4*(1), 1–14.

Fraser, S., & Gestwicki C. (2002). *Authentic childhood: Exploring Reggio Emilia in the classroom.* New York, NY: Delmar Thomson Learning.

Hall, E. L., & Rudkin, J. K. (2011). *Seen and heard: Children's rights in early childhood education.* New York, NY: Teachers College Press.

Hayden, M., & Thompson, J. (2017). International schools: Some issues for the future. *The Journal of the Advancement of International Education, 44*(123), 1–7.

Hyland, N. E. (2010). Research in review. Social justice in early childhood classrooms: What the research tells us. *Young Children, 65*(1), 82–90.

International Baccalaureate. (n.d.). *Mission.* Retrieved from http://www.ibo.org/about-the-ib/mission/

International Baccalaureate. (2009). *Primary years programme: Making the PYP happen: A curriculum framework for international primary education* (rev. ed.). Cardiff, Wales: International Baccalaureate.

Jackson, P. W. (1990). Introduction. In J. Dewey, *The school and society and the child and the curriculum* (pp. ix–xxxii). Chicago, IL: University of Chicago Press.

James, J., & Davis, G. (2010). Striving for international education: One program's journey. *Ohio Social Studies Review, 46*(1), 39.

Kent State University. (2015). *A strategic roadmap to a distinctive Kent State.* Retrieved from http://strategicroadmap.kent.edu/

Knoll, M. (2014). Laboratory school, university of Chicago. In D. C. Phillips (Ed.), *Encyclopedia of educational theory and philosophy* (Vol. 2, pp. 455–458). Thousand Oaks, CA: SAGE.

Kostelnik, M. (2017). What child development laboratories need to do to thrive: An administrator's perspective. In N. Barbour & B. McBride (Eds.), *The future of child development lab schools: Applied developmental science in action* (pp. 95–112). New York, NY: Routledge.

Lash, M., & Kroeger, J. (2018). Seeking justice through social action projects: Preparing teachers to be social actors in local and global problems. *Policy Futures in Education.* Retrieved from https://doi.org/10.1177/1478210317751272

Lash, M., & Miller-Marsh, M. (2017). Expanding research from collaborative self-study to an applied developmental science model. In N. Barbour & B. A. McBride (Eds.), *The future of child development laboratory schools: Applied developmental science in action* (pp. 23–37). New York, NY: Routledge.

McBride, B. A., Groves, M., Barbour, N., Horm, D., Stremmel, A., Lash, . . . Toussaint, S. (2012). Child development laboratory schools as generators of knowledge in early childhood education: Models and approaches. *Early Education and Development, 23*(2), 153–164.

Miller Marsh, Cardy, T. & West, E. (2018). "My voice is too small": Supporting young children's civic participation in the early childhood classroom. Unpublished manuscript, Department of Teaching, Learning, and Curriculum Studies, Kent State University, Kent, Ohio.

Miller Marsh, M., & Raimbekova, L., (2018, April). *International parent perceptions of their role and responsibility in the education of their young children.* Paper presented at the International Network of Scholars conference. New York, NY.

Miller-Marsh, M., & Zhulamanova, I. (2016). Follow the leader: Attending to the curriculum making potential of preschoolers. *Early Child Development & Care, 187*(5/6), 1004–1014.

Myers, C. Y., Hostler, R., & Hughes, J. (2017). "What does it mean to care?" Collaborative images of care within an early-years center. *Global Studies of Childhood, 7*(4), 369–372.

Raven, S. (2016). Understanding the body: A series of activities to teach preK children about human anatomy. *Science and Children, 53*(9), 52–57.

Sisson, J. H., & Lash, M. (2017). Outdoor learning experiences to connect children to nature: Perspectives from Australia and the United States. *Young Children, 27*(4), 8–15.

Soler, J., & Miller, L. (2003). The struggle for early childhood curricula: A comparison of the English foundation stage curriculum, Te Wha riki and Reggio Emilia. *International Journal of Early Years Education, 11*(1), 57–68.

Vartuili, S., Snider, K., & Holley, M. (2016). Making it real: A practice-based early childhood teacher education program. *Early Childhood Education Journal, 44*(5), 503–514.

Wardle, F. (2013). U.S. early childhood multicultural education. In O. N. Saracho & B. Spodek (Eds.), *Handbook of research on the education of young* children (3rd ed., pp. 275–298). New York, NY: Routledge.

West, E. M., Guillot Miller, L., & Moate, R. (2017). Single mothers' experiences of support at their young children's school: An interpretative phenomenological approach. *Early Childhood Education Journal, 45*(3), 379–391.

PART III

FUNCTIONS OF CHILD DEVELOPMENT
LABORATORY SCHOOLS

CHAPTER 8

THE ROLE OF THE CHILD DEVELOPMENT LABORATORY SCHOOL IN A 21st CENTURY LIBERAL EDUCATION

Sharon Carnahan

ABSTRACT

This review concerns the role of the child development laboratory school in a 21st century liberal education. A summary of the historical context of laboratory schools, and the parallel development of campus children's centers, is followed by a discussion of the modern mission of the child development laboratory school, and how this is developed in a campus context as part of a strategic plan. The American Association of Colleges and Universities High Impact Practices are linked to lab school implementations. Campus concerns about a child development lab's mission are next, followed by two plans for the liberal arts child development lab schools of the future: (a) increased interdisciplinary initiatives and (b) cooperatives for applied developmental science and social entrepreneurship.

Contemporary Perspectives on Research on Child Development Laboratory Schools in Early Childhood Education,
pages 137–156
137

Child development laboratory schools are campus-based places which provide early childhood care and education, while offering sites for teaching, research, community service, and professional development for students and educators. They are found at state and private universities, community colleges, and technical schools across the country (McBride et al., 2012). While laboratory schools can extend through secondary education, this review focuses on those serving children from birth through kindergarten.

A select number of child development laboratory schools are at liberal arts institutions. These schools engage in a steady struggle to justify their work as a part of the liberal arts ethos. Yet today, child development laboratory schools are more relevant on campuses than ever before. They embody the high impact practices recommended by the American Association of Colleges and Universities (AAC&U; Kuh, 2008), which support a constructivist approach to undergraduate education, invite interdisciplinary collaborations, and produce relevant research. This review concerns the theoretical and practical place of child development laboratory schools in higher education, beginning with an historical context, moving through the challenges of the past and present, and suggesting two models for the future: (a) increased interdisciplinary initiatives and (b) applied developmental sciences and social entrepreneurship.

HISTORICAL CONTEXT

In the United States, John Dewey is credited with beginning the first laboratory school, at the University of Chicago. It was in 1896, an exciting time in the progressive era in education, just a few years before the great Chicago exposition that lit the way for the new millennium. Dewey directed this experimental school until 1904—just 8 years to forge a new pathway for education that influences us still. A laboratory school was both a part of a university department *and* a place where parents sent children to be educated. This dual purpose has been woven into the fabric of the movement (see Barbour, 2003; for a review of early lab school history).

Dewey's experimental school was steeped in the emerging school of thought called pragmatism, of which Charles Peirce, William James, and Dewey were among the prominent figures. In philosophy, pragmatics is an approach that assesses the truth of meaning of theories or beliefs in terms of the success of their practical application. It is an approach that frames ideas about truth in terms of real life. If one side of an argument can be demonstrated to be practically true, then it is correct. If neither can be supported by experience, then the argument is unimportant. As Peirce wrote, "the opinion which is fated to be ultimately agreed to by all who investigate is what we mean by the truth, and the object represented in this opinion is the real. That is the way I would explain reality" (Houser & Kloesel, 1992, p. 139).

Pragmatism arose out of concerns about the purely theoretical and esoteric philosophical approaches of the previous century, and connected topics like the origin of knowledge (epistemology) to their practical applications. Environments and their demands change; so do people, and truth is what works for the people, in that particular environment. Truth is neither discovered (absolutism) nor invented (subjectivism) but constructed through an individual's interactions with the environment. Note that Dewey was born the year Darwin's *On the Origin of Species* was published. In fact, 50 years later, Dewey wrote *The Influence of Darwin on Philosophy*, and stated that education should sharpen the intellect, and give people tools with which to positively adapt to and influence an ever changing environment (Madigan, 2009).

Both James and Peirce used "pragmatism" as the name of a method for clarifying concepts and hypotheses and for identifying empty disputes. A "pragmatic education" has come to mean a system in which children or adults engage directly with problem solving in a particular environment or social context, identifying what is successful and practical, rather than learning abstract principles by memory or in isolation. This is not to be confused with a vocational education, based only on learning "practical" tasks such as farming, woodworking, or cooking for their own sake. Rather, in Dewey's lab school, these occupations were studied for the complete *integration* of grammar, rhetoric, logic, geometry, arithmetic, music, and science into everyday education, which was based on projects and practical activities. These are analogous to the trivium and quadrivium of a classical education.

The teachers at Dewey's lab school also embraced the scientific method of observation and experimentation, as their everyday magical way of helping children discover important aspects of reality—the truth about how things work. Today, we would call this a constructivist, holistic education, and it would line up with developmentally appropriate practice, which includes learning through active interaction with the physical environment and asking questions that are appropriate for the level of the child. As Friedrich Froebel (1826/1885) wrote in *The Education of Man*, "The prime purpose throughout is not to impart knowledge to the child but to lead the child to observe and to think (1885, p. 77).

More recently, faced with pressure to produce a trained workforce and demonstrate learning outcomes, and in response to the provisions of the No Child Left Behind Act of 2001 and its sequelae, public schools in the United States have increasingly adopted more adult-centered, didactic approaches to education. Yet child development lab schools and many early childhood educators have steadily resisted this approach. Supported by evidence from reviews of literature and national organizations, they have advocated an active, constructivist, hands-on approach to early education in laboratory schools and the wider community (Lake & Jones, 2008). This means that undergraduate students who study in these environments are also exposed to a pragmatic education, and lessons learned by viewing early education transfer back into the undergraduate classroom.

Dewey's lab school was an experiment in community life, where children were a part of a democratic whole. Modern conventions such as morning meetings, classroom votes, and choices about activities have their roots in Dewey's school, as does seeing teachers as part of a community of learners, a central tenet of laboratory schools today. Dewey's teachers also recorded the process of learning, not just its result. In an early precedent to the "documentation" of the learning process of children that we see now, Katherine Camp Mayhew and her sister Anna Camp Edwards left behind 12 volumes of logbooks and curricula. Then and now, observational data allow teachers to reflect on the educational process of each child, enabling activities based on the motivation and excitement of each one. Documentation also supports reflective practice, as teachers and children together think about what works and does not work in the classroom.

Dewey also saw that learning occurs in a social context. For him, that context had to be democratic, because every individual needed to be a part of the educational process, and every child needed a different education. According to Anne Durst, the democratic argument was that "the good of the individual lies in the happiness that comes with the full development of his [*sic*] capacity and powers, and the good of society lies in the promotion of this self-realization for every individual" (Durst, 2010, p. 4). Differentiation remains a central tenet of early education.

Although Dewey's original school lasted just 8 years, laboratory schools proliferated in the early 1900s as centers for teacher preparation. Schools increased in colleges and universities, especially prior to WWII, and university based laboratory schools filled an important role in research and teaching in places offering degrees in education or family and consumer sciences. Most laboratory schools began as campus schools for normal or teachers' colleges (Barbour, 2003). In the Jim Crow south, laboratory schools at historically Black colleges and universities (HBCU) served as centers of excellence in the provision of high quality education for African Americans from 1920–1960. While the published literature of the time took a deficit approach to describing the inferior schooling, these laboratory schools created excellent, academically rigorous educational opportunities for African American children, led by teachers trained in the pragmatic, progressive educational theories of the day (Pierson, 2014).

A parallel development was that of campus children's centers, created for the care of children of undergraduates, staff, and faculty. Most of these lab schools and children's centers were at large, land-grant universities.

However, a small group of liberal arts schools also developed these model/ demonstration sites.

Child Development Lab Schools: Professional Organizations

Today, two major international professional organizations represent child development lab schools: The National Coalition of Campus Children's Centers and The International Association of Laboratory Schools.

The National Coalition of Campus Children's Centers (NCCCC) is a non-profit organization supporting excellence in campus child care, with over 600 members. Created during the 1970s as a part of the feminist movement, seeking greater access to childcare for students, the organization established chapters in the 1990s, and was instrumental in the passing of CCAMPIS legislation (Child Care Access Means Parents in School). Child care is an important resource for parents trying to complete an education, when students on campus have children of their own.

According to the Institute for Women's Policy Research (IWPR), the share of 2- and 4-year public institutions with campus child care centers has declined, from about 54% in 2002 to 44% on 2015 (Berman, 2016). While many of these centers stand alone as sites for child care, most are affiliated with the departments of education or family and consumer sciences at their universities. Campus Children's Centers often have an affiliative relationship with universities, and are sites for research and writing curricula, but their primary purpose is to ease the path towards an education for students who have young children.

Most children's centers have histories similar to that of the Campus Children's Center at Indiana University Bloomington, as described on their website. The original idea grew out of the increased number of women with young children in the workplace, making it to consideration by a campus staff council in 1980. The program proposal was funded, and a full day childcare facility replaced the smaller Indiana University Nursery School in 1983. It has grown slowly over the years, and now occupies a renovated space with nearly 50 children. Infant and toddler care were expanded in 2006. The common elements among many campus children's centers are the origin in the 1980s, a focus on child care, gradual growth, and the replacement of part-time nurseries with more extended care (Smith, 2008).

The International Association of Laboratory Schools (IALS) is a smaller and more focused professional organization which includes schools offering early education, elementary school, and K–12 programs. They have defined the lab school, as distinct from the children's center, as a site where researchers conduct educational research, provide professional development, develop unique curricula, and experiment with education.

The literature about these schools as producers of research is slim. Aldrich (2014) reviewed laboratory schools, and noted that mention is seldom made of the site of research in journals publishing educational research done at these centers. Little is known about the influence of liberal arts lab schools per se on child development outcomes, as the schools are heterogeneous. University-based sites often produce research and publications about their experimental curricula or intervention projects, but these are not identified by school (For examples, see the Frank Porter Graham Child Development Institute; www.fpg.unc.edu). It is easier to find information about the centers themselves, published in specialty journals. The child development lab schools at liberal arts colleges are likely members of IALS, and may also join NCCCC.

The Role of a Child Development Laboratory School in a Liberal Education

Defining Our Role

Lab schools struggle with the often competing priorities of providing early care and education to the children of working parents, and conducting research, teaching, professional development, and curricular experimentation. Especially at the small liberal arts campus, the child development lab school must constantly seek to justify its presence. Leaders are asked, "Why are there children on campus? Why is our small college, with its competing priorities and market issues, in the child care business? We don't even offer a degree in early childhood education—how many of our undergraduates will benefit? If faculty and staff get priority in admission, isn't that a benefit that favors parents over single people?" Among the top small liberal arts schools in the United States, as identified by *U.S. News and World Report* (2019), examination of their websites shows that only about half have laboratory schools (Mount Holyoke, Smith, Williams, Hood, Claremont McKenna, Colby Sawyer, Colgate, Wellesley, Brandeis), while half (Middlebury, Swarthmore, Carleton, Pomona, Davidson, Washington, and Lee) do not. Defining and justifying their role is important for the future.

William Van Til (1969) reviewed the status of laboratory schools at the end of the 1960's, and concluded that their mission was blurry and their goals in conflict. For example, a school striving to be an exemplary site for student teachers may not be compatible with research and innovation, in which mistakes will be made and not all goes smoothly. He concluded, "The friends of the laboratory school will either learn from the past. . . . or drift towards extinction. . . ." (p. 5). Since then, some have learned and continue to thrive, while others have closed their doors or become campus child care centers only (Nielson, 1986; Sparks, 2015). How have some lab schools thrived? Wilcox-Herzog & McLaren (2012) provide a list of components of successful laboratory schools. These include: A clear mission, a defined curriculum, multiple streams of funding, relationships through networking, links with academic programs, and meet indicators of high quality in staff and facilities (Wilcox-Herzog & McLaren, 2012).

One continued area of concern is the cloudy mission, mashing together child care and research purposes. In a review of child development laboratory schools as generators of knowledge, McBride et al. (2012) also noted the difficulties in the blurring of roles as schools were pressured into becoming full day providers of child care to working parents. The diverse nature of lab schools, the shrinking base of financial support, and a mechanism for balancing service and research, are challenges confronting many liberal arts lab schools. An emphasis on service and full day care reduces the time teachers can spend in training, maintaining best practices, assisting researchers, or experimenting with curricula. Similarly, Branscomb & McBride (2004) described the difficulties faced by a laboratory school which expands to full day programming, to meet the need for revenue streams and child care for campus employees. It is a struggle to balance academic, outreach, and service demands when staff are fully engaged with children from 8:00 a.m. to 5:00 p.m. plus. The authors included the importance of the research mission, an interdisciplinary outreach on campus, and the primacy of maintaining an optimal caregiving and early education environment. The lack of affordable, high quality childcare in the United States is endemic, and so the issue will continue to be explored on campuses.

The first job of the laboratory school, therefore, becomes to clarify its mission. Carnahan and Doyle (2012), in a review of college mission alignment, noted the importance of having a clear mission and set of priorities for the laboratory school, and of contributing to the strategic plan of the college. Undergraduate education, provision of child education, research, and community outreach are all parts of the laboratory school mission, but their order should reflect the realities of the host institution. The school must take steps to make resource allocations mission driven. At Rollins College, our Hume House Child Development and Student Research Center expanded in 2017 from a half day program serving 20 children to a full day program serving 45. While undergraduate student involvement, interdisciplinary access, research projects, and community outreach expanded in the new facility, the program needed to hire more teaching staff than expected to assure that lead teachers had time to meet the demands of full day care and maintain highest standards of planning and providing an experimental, constructivist education. Resource allocations were adjusted to further the mission; this is an iterative process.

The second priority of the lab school is to secure multiple streams of stable funding to fulfill its chosen mission. From a high of more than 200 schools in the mid-1990s, the IALS has fewer than half those members today, though the actual number of operating lab schools is probably about twice that (Sparks, 2015). As liberal arts schools seek ways to stay competitive and relevant in the changing landscape of higher education, lab schools must adapt and diversify, or die, and some have closed as a result of budget cuts; exact numbers are not available. Most child development lab schools are funded by a combination of the college's general facilities and operations budget, faculty salaries and stipends, parent tuition, and grant funds, while some offer online classes, conferences, or other training to increase revenue (Carnahan & Doyle, 2012). When the child development lab school is interdisciplinary, networked, and mission-minded, the number of potential partners expands.

The lab school must also take responsibility for educating its constituency of parents, staff, faculty, and administrators, marketing its mission and purpose loud and clear. Lab schools should develop talking points that answer the frequently asked questions of those naïve to the mission. Social media, testimonials, newsletters, online parent groups, guest speakers, open house events, and dissemination of research results and publications can remind the community of the lab's importance to the college's mission and culture.

A final priority of the child development lab school is to identify areas of excellence, in teaching, research, or practice, where it can be innovative and transformational. In order to fulfill Dewey's vision, and the promise of improvement of children's lives, lab schools have to be able to give up what they are doing for something better. They must be flexible, nimble sites for creativity and testing of new ideas, which can be translated from research to practice.

Linking Child Development Laboratory Schools and Liberal Education

What is a Liberal Education? According to the AAC&U:

Liberal Education is an approach to learning that empowers individuals and prepares them to deal with complexity, diversity, and change. It provides students with broad knowledge of the wider world (e.g., science, culture, and society) as well as in-depth study in a specific area of interest. A liberal education helps students develop a sense of social responsibility, as well as strong and transferable intellectual and practical skills such as communication, analytical and problem-solving skills, and a demonstrated ability to apply knowledge and skills in real-world settings. (Kuh, 2008)

Today, Dewey's ideals have been rebirthed in the guise of the pragmatic liberal arts education. As a representative of an active, play-based approach, the child development laboratory school is a partner in this vision for undergraduates. First, the academic study of child development, as a dimension of the study of psychology and education, is a discipline central to liberal inquiry into the human condition. How we, as a society, care for our children is an issue of global importance across disciplines. Next, we know from research in every discipline that academic study is deepened by experiential learning. The AAC&U has identified teaching and learning practices that have been tested and repeatedly identified as improving academic learning. Table 8.1 is a crosswalk of these high impact practices as seen in child development lab schools, including collaborative assignments and projects, community-based learning, mentorship of individual students in research or practice, capstone courses, and internships (AAC&U, n.d.). While these can all be accomplished without lab schools, the service excellence, supervision, scaffolding, and population of the lab school makes it an ideal high impact practices partner.

In an early effort at an interdisciplinary model for a lab school, Van Voorhis and DeMarie-Dreblow (1995) described a major in early childhood education within a liberal arts education at a small liberal arts college in Muskingum, Ohio. They brought together the resources of sociology, psychology, and education, forming an interdisciplinary system. The psychology department led research specialization, while human services and systems level approaches came from the sociologists. They listed challenges in interdepartmental scheduling, faculty funding, and cooperation, but accomplished a successful program with three departments at a liberal arts institution. Their efforts were prescient, as today, interdisciplinary missions in lab schools tie directly in with a liberal education. In today's liberal arts laboratory schools, faculty and directors work hard to include multiple departments across campuses, spreading out the pragmatic use and campus support for working with children.

While undergraduates studying at lab schools may be primarily from psychology or education, nearly every discipline can make use of the laboratory setting. The majority of students will not have careers in working with children, but nearly 80% will become parents during their lifetimes, and knowledge of child development milestones is a protective factor against child maltreatment (Administration for Children & Families, Protective Factor 2). In addition, Bowers (2000) explored the effectiveness of hands-on work in a laboratory preschool for students enrolled in courses in developmental psychology, as well as early childhood education. She found a significant difference in changes in knowledge and attitudes about infants and toddlers for an interactive group, but not for a group who merely watched children through a one-way mirror.

TABLE 8.1 American Association of Colleges and Universities Selected High Impact Practices: Crosswalk With the Laboratory School

Recognized High Impact Practices (AAC & U)	Child Development Laboratory School Match
Place Based Education	• Educating students about the mission, vision and goals of the lab school and how this reflects the culture and values of the host institution • Student projects linked to local needs of children and families: health, education, ecology
Learning Communities	• Creating learning communities of directors, faculty, families, teachers and students who meet regularly to learn and plan • Short term communities around research interests: Diversity and inclusion, social emotional development, math skills, teaching children about LGBTQ issues
Writing Intensive Courses	• Course work in objective observation and case study methodology, data collection, research writing
Collaborative Assignments and Projects	• Collaborations between faculty, teachers and students on research and dissemination • Interdisciplinary projects around social entrepreneurship and societal change • Co-authored presentations & publications with faculty, students and staff • Small group assignments in child-focused courses
Undergraduate Research, Mentorship, and Internships	• Research as a part of faculty collaborative school year or summer research • Yearly student contributions to lab-initiated longitudinal studies • Internships in teaching, child assessment, curriculum & instruction, or discipline-specific projects
Service Learning and Community Based Learning	• Using the lab school as a fulcrum to leverage community based trainings based on knowledge development at the lab school • Training undergraduates in adult-child interaction skills prior to their community engagement/service learning with children
Capstone Courses	• Senior undergraduate seminars designed to study or solve a major issue

CONCERNS ABOUT CHILD DEVELOPMENT LAB SCHOOLS

Lab schools have received some criticism as elitist, nonrepresentative of the real world, and exclusive in their practices. Indeed, the lab school of the University of Chicago (Dewey's home) charges an annual tuition for 5-year-olds that is half the median income in that community, although financial aid is available (The University of Chicago, n.d.). Lab schools must weigh the priorities of being exemplars of best practices, and supportive sites for undergraduate learning and research, versus conducting models of research and education which can be replicated in the real world.

Several approaches address this stress. One approach is to strive for excellence in environment, education, and research, and to fund this in part through high tuition for families. In this model, generalization of knowledge to other settings is not a primary concern. A second is to separate the functions of child development laboratory and child care center, as Carnegie Mellon University has done with the Cyert Center (for full daycare) and The Children's School (for part-day and laboratory-based courses and research), and have separate funding and admissions criteria. A third is to increase the reach of the program by partnering with community based preschools or by choosing children from a wider pool than is represented by college faculty and staff. For example, the Early Childhood Development Centers at Texas A&M Corpus Christi conduct a public school sponsored lottery each year, and assign 60% of their openings to children who qualify for free/reduced school lunch in the community (Cassidy & Sanders, 2002). A lab school exists for particular pedagogical, financial, and political reasons, and campus culture is an important factor in strategic planning for the mission and reach of each one.

Thus, the child development lab school, with its roots in constructivism and its historic place on college campuses at the intersection of teaching, research, and child care, faces a challenging future. Following are two plans for the future of these special places.

Plan 1: Everyone's Laboratory School: Increase Interdisciplinary Initiatives

One vision of the future for laboratory schools in the liberal arts environment is to be a site for observation, research, or service to as many departments on campus as possible—to be everybody's lab school, offering high impact practices or training for community engagement work to as many disciplines as possible. Here are a few examples, grouped by topic or discipline.

Diversity and Inclusion Initiatives

When the laboratory school places an emphasis on representing a cross section of the college community, students gain through getting to know people (children and families) from a variety of linguistic, ethnic, and socioeconomic backgrounds. College campuses are typically more diverse than their immediate surrounding population. Through lab school experience, students interact with children and families from other cultures in the United States and internationally, with many languages spoken amongst the children. In addition, by virtue of its university supported adult child ratio, child development lab schools typically pay higher salaries and have more qualified staff and more classroom assistance than most schools. They are prime places for inclusion of children with disabilities, both those who are identified prior to admission and those who are identified within the first 6 months of the year.

In a review of the justification for inclusion of children with disabilities in laboratory schools, East and Clopton (2009) point out that all teachers and psychologists in U.S. schools are expected to accommodate the needs of students with disabilities, and must become knowledgeable about their education and development. The National Association for the Education of Young Children (NAEYC) defines inclusion as a combination of elements which benefit children and families: access to environments, participation in all activities, and supports such as professional development, communication, and collaboration with parents (Division of Early Childhood Education, 2009).

The Hume House Child Development and Student Research Center at Rollins College (Hume CDC) has included children with disabilities since 1993, gradually developing an evidence based plan of inclusion. In the early 1990s, the center included 10% children with disabilities, developing an individual plan for each one with the assistance of therapists. In order to be admitted, a child must have an Individual Family Services Plan in place, relationships with therapists, and be willing to authorize therapies in the natural environment, the preschool classrooms, for the benefit of undergraduate student observation and exposure to the therapeutic milieu. A grant from a private donor provided consultation from an applied behavior analyst, and beginning in the decade after 2000, we became a Positive Behavior Support (PBS) training site (Frey, Park, Brown-Ferrigno, & Korfhage, 2010). Today, we have a fully articulated inclusion admission policy. We include children with disabilities in each classroom, have a half-time inclusion specialist, and full integration with undergraduate students (Carnahan & Strickland, 2018). The goal of exposing undergraduates to complexity, diversity, and change is met at the laboratory school.

In addition, it is the policy of institutions of higher education not to discriminate on the basis of sex, disability, race, age, religion, color, national or ethnic origin, ancestry, sexual orientation, gender identity, gender expression, genetic information, physical characteristics, or any other category protected by law. These policies lead to a diverse staff, faculty and student body, plus strong support for anti-bias practices and curricula at child development laboratory schools.

Psychology and Education

Research and practice skills are acquired at a lab school by students in courses such as child development, child assessment, statistics and methods, sensation and perception, cognitive psychology, introductory psychology, gender roles, caring for others (sociology and psychology interdisciplinary), curriculum and instruction, and internships. Most child development laboratory centers are designed as a *school-within-a school*. As teachers lead children through a typical preschool day, some students are in the classroom, practicing hands-on skills, conducting observations, or running experiments. Behind the one-way mirror stands another cohort of students, videotaping or collecting data, watching the teaching along with their professors, or discussing aspects of children's development. Thus, a cascading, teaching waterfall is in progress, with professors and teachers modeling, shaping, and scaffolding undergraduate student behaviors, as teachers and students in turn support the learning of the young children. The children are teaching the adults, too.

Developmental Psychologist Lev Vygotsky described the job of the teacher or older peer who comes between the object or lesson and the child as mediation; the practice is called mediated learning. He described a taxonomy of mediation which is illustrative of many of the parts of the lab school teaching process. A "mediated learning experience" (MLE) happens when a student is guided in thought or action by someone more competent. Several curricula exist for developing these teaching skills, and a wealth of research indicates the benefits of a mediated learning approach (Kozulin et al., 2003). Lab schools enable the learning to cascade from teachers and faculty, to students, to children, and back again, in a controlled environment where best practices are expected.

Philosophy

Strong and transferable intellectual and practical skills such as communication, analytical thinking, and problem-solving are acquired by students through interactions with master teachers in innovative programs like *Philosophy for Children*. This program has introduced preschool children to philosophical content and deep thinking through picture books, play, and dialogue. Following the guidelines of work by Thomas Wartenberg (2014), student researchers at Rollins College, Tufts University, and many other schools teach undergraduates to use picture books and play to address ideas like moderation, caring, generosity, and courage by presenting philosophical puzzles illustrated in childrens' picture books. Researchers Erik Kenyon and Diane Doyle have developed three simple rules for their preschool ethics curriculum: *We Listen, We Think, and We Respond.* These rules work together to nurture dialogue and respectful disagreement among 3–5-year-old children. They note that teachers and students who engage in philosophical conversations have to let go of a pattern of child asks/teacher replies in favor of an open ended conversation in which the answers must be discovered together. Their multi-year project began with pilot testing and curriculum development at the Hume CDC lab school, with 30 undergraduates over several years (Kenyon & Terorde-Doyle, 2017). Philosophy for children has been an incubator for early education, with undergraduates teaching these skills to preschoolers, engaging over 120 students across five community-based schools (Kenyon, 2019).

Environmental Studies

Bogert (2016) has described the Jackman Institute of Child Study Laboratory School, which was founded in 1925 based on inspiration from John Dewey's views. In collaboration with the University of Toronto, the school began building a teacher resource and development program called *Natural Curiosity: Building Children's Understanding of the World Through Environmental Inquiry* (Bogert, 2016). Through the work, the students and teachers have connected the laboratory school to environmental scientists, and their next version will also include the views of indigenous peoples.

Techakosit (2011) describes an experimental laboratory school curriculum centered on the purpose-built Kasetsart School Botanical Garden in Thailand, which serves as an outdoor lab for conservation, sample collection, research, drawing and painting, and data analysis. Positive child results from their research include improved adaptation to working in groups, a systematic way of working, self-discipline, and knowledge of nature (Somsak, 2011).

Modern Languages

Based on mission and context, many child development lab schools use multilingual instruction, and study the process of language learning. For example, the Early Childhood Learning Center at the Abu Dhabi Campus of Zayed University provides bilingual classes in Arabic and English from the earliest enrollment, while developing dual language materials for undergraduate education (Dillon & Pinedo-Burns, 2017). In a simpler manner of community visits, undergraduates from French, Spanish, Arabic, and German classes read stories or present plays to children at the Rollins College lab school. By tailoring their interactions to the audience, the students gain child development knowledge and presentation skills.

Creative Arts

At the Lab School of Washington, which is partnered with American University, students are taught by doing rather than telling, via arts-infused, project-based learning. Graduate students in Special Education: Learning Disabilities do coursework at night, and then have a hands-on, yearlong internship in a lab classroom working with a master teacher. Faculty members in education and special education work together to bring cutting edge practices to the lab school, and the college partnership has been active for 40 years (see https://www.labschool.org/page)

At Rollins College, students in theater arts use *commedia dell'arte*, a form of theater from the 15th century characterized by a story read aloud and improvisation by colorful, costumed characters, to adapt classic stories for presentation to children. Students use journal entries to reflect on the success of their adaptations to the ages of the children in the audience. The Hume CDC lab school also follows a Reggio Emilia art-inspired preschool curriculum (Edwards, Gandini, & Forman, 2010). The Department of English sponsors a reading program, where undergraduates pair with preschool children to write and illustrate a fictional tale, creating a coauthored book at the end of the term. English department undergraduates thus learn adult–child interaction and scaffolding skills, gain an understanding of the developmental level of each child, connect with families, and produce a praise worthy display of books, plus contributing to research on children's storytelling abilities. Finally, students in art history take children on campus museum tours, acting as docents to develop lessons at the level of their preschool aged friends.

STEM Disciplines

Carnegie Mellon University's Children's Center is the laboratory school for the Psychology Department, and the main focus is research on cognitive development. Faculty, research associates, graduate students, and undergraduates have first priority in studies there. The emphasis on STEM related resources has resulted in a consistent program of research, including Laski and Siegler (2014), about kindergartener's learning of numbers, and Hicks and Carver's (2015) presenting ways to teach math to young children. A 50-year retrospective of the program reviews these and other projects (Carver, 2018).

STEM discipline students may also use the child development lab for mere exposure to young children and the epistemology of relevant subjects. For example, our students in a course in Developmental Psychobiology make a onetime lab visit to observe gender differences in very young children's play, and roll this into a unit on the biological and environmental origins of these hypothesized differences.

Summary

As the child development lab school becomes everybody's lab in the liberal arts environment, the lab provides increased access to high impact practices in a controlled setting for undergraduate students, facilitates faculty research, and gives opportunities for interdisciplinary courses and communities of learners. As the constituency of the liberal arts lab school widens to include many departments, its chances to survive and thrive may improve (Carnahan & Doyle, 2012).

Plan 2: Cooperatives for Applied Developmental Science

Small liberal arts child development lab schools engage faculty and students who produce significant research, but they often lack the resources to make contributions to policy or practice while acting alone. The liberal arts lab school's goal is not to mimic the R1 university, but to be an excellent part of the liberal arts, while still contributing to the body of new knowledge about children. Like Dewey, we are meliorists, believing that the world can be improved through our efforts.

In their influential book concerning the future of child development lab schools, Barbour & McBride (2016) propose an alignment with applied developmental science (ADS), which is scholarship that seeks to advance the integration of developmental research with policies and programs that promote the positive development of children and families. In this volume, McBride et al. (2012) point out that applied developmental science could be "a powerful ally" to laboratory schools. They suggest the development of a consortium of lab schools that would collaborate to engage meaningful issues in need of research and pilot testing of practices (Lerner, Fisher, & Weinberg, 2000; McBride et al., 2012). Similarly, Schwartz and Gerlach (2011) proposed a coalition of universities, lab schools, and public schools, gathered to study the confluence of mind, brain (neuroscience), and education, called a *Research Schools Network*. This network would develop a clear vision for improvement of education; build relationships between universities, labs, and community schools; set a standard for scholarship, and develop meaningful assessment tools for use in education (Schwartz & Gerlach, 2011).

Organizations such as NCCCC, the International Association of Laboratory Schools, the Association for Childhood Education International (ACEI), and the National Association for the Education of Young Children (NAEYC) each present a vision, publish scholarship, and develop meaningful curricula and tools for research and practice. However, none have galvanized the coalescence of liberal arts laboratory schools around a unifying principle or thrust for research. This remains as a goal for the organizations.

The paradigm of ADS is similar to a new mission taken on by business and economics majors at liberal arts institutions: the programs in social entrepreneurship. On college campuses, we see the rise of the social innovation movement—the use of techniques by companies and other entrepreneurs to develop, fund, and implement solutions to social, cultural, or environmental issues. In recent years, advocates for social change have turned to business schools and programs to provide them with the skills and competence they need to develop an idea, manage resources, conduct research, and bridge the gap between research and practice (Howorth, Smith, & Parkinson, 2012). Important "hub" issues sit squarely in the lab school's circle of expertise: developing a trained child care workforce, access to workplace children's care, illness reduction, and optimal early education (Grindal & McCoy, 2016). Combining entrepreneurial energy and the opportunities for experimentation and expertise of the child development lab school will create an incubator for new ideas for children and families.

Grindal and McCoy (2016) found ways in which social entrepreneurs are already offering new approaches to challenges in child development. In 2015, the Hult Prize Accelerator sponsored six teams to address worldwide problems of children. Their ideas included educational laundromats, using mobile devices to encourage daily reading with children, and working with college students, lab schools, and community organization to pioneer innovative approaches. Student entrepreneurs won with a radical approach to getting child development teaching skills to women in the developing world (Thorpe, 2015).

In 2017, the Social Capital Markets (SOCAP) flagship conference focused on a burgeoning new field for social innovation and entrepreneurship: early childhood education and care. Their goal is to engage communities, businesses, universities, and colleges in entrepreneurial solutions to early childhood problems, such as parent's literacy and involvement, access to high quality education, and social-emotional support for children (SOCAP, 2017). What better site for developing and pilot testing such initiatives than the child development laboratory school?

CONCLUSION

A summary of the historical context of laboratory schools, and the parallel development of campus children's centers, leads us to focus on clarifying the mission of child development lab schools on liberal arts campuses. AAC&U High Impact Practices are linked to lab school implementations, making the lab school a valuable partner in undergraduate education, as well as a workplace benefit for families. Plans for *increased interdisciplinary initiatives* and *cooperatives for applied developmental science and social entrepreneurship* can carry us onward. Wonder at the miracle of child development, and curiosity about its mechanisms, propel us forward. Future research should address means and models of collaboration between liberal arts laboratory schools.

REFERENCES

Aldrich, J. (2014). *Lab school trends: A survey of programs.* Unpublished manuscript.

Association of American Colleges and Universities. (2019, April 4). *High impact practices.* Retrieved from https://www.aacu.org/resources/high-impact-practices

Barbour, N. E. (2003). The early history of child development laboratory schools. In Brent A. McBride & N. E. Barbour (Eds.), *Bridging the gap between theory, research and practice: The role of child development laboratory programs in early childhood education* (pp. 9–29). Bingley, England: Emerald.

Barbour, N. E., & McBride, B. (Eds.). (2016). *The future of child development lab schools: Applied developmental science in action.* New York, NY: Routledge.

Berman, J. (2016, September 1). *Campus child care declining in most states despite growing numbers of college students with children* [Press release]. Retrieved from https://iwpr.org/campus-child-care-declining-in-most-states-despite-growing-numbers-of-college-students-with-children/

Branscomb, K., & McBride, B. (2004). Academics versus service: Balancing competing missions in laboratory schools offering full day programming. *Journal of Early Childhood Teacher Education, 25*(2), 113–121.

Bogert, C. (2016). The Eric Jackman institute of child study laboratory school. *International Association of Laboratory Schools Journal, 6*(1), 24–26.

Bowers, S. (2000). Are campus children's centers obsolete? *College Student Journal, 34*(1), 6–8. Retrieved from https://www.questia.com/library/journal/1G1-62839410

Carver, S. M. (2018). Campus Learning Laboratory. Carnegie Mellon University Children's School. *Exchange, 40*(3), 26–30.

Cassidy, J., & Sanders, J. (2000). A university lab school for the 21st century: The early childhood development center. In J. Cassidy and S. Garrett (Eds.), *Early childhood literacy: Programs & strategies to develop cultural, linguistic, scientific and healthcare literacy for very young children & their families.* CEDER Yearbook (pp. 1–19). Corpus Christi, TX: Center for Educational Development, Evaluation and Research.

Carnahan, S., & Doyle, D. (2012). College mission alignment: Lessons for laboratory schools. *National Association of Laboratory Schools Journal, 4*(1), Article 2. Retrieved from https://digitalcommons.ric.edu/nals/vol4/iss1/2

Carnahan, S., & Strickland, C. (2018). Everyday inclusion: A handbook for working with children and families. Unpublished manuscript, Rollins College, Winter Park, FL.

Dillon, A., & Pinedo-Burns, H. (2017). Intercultural conversations: Fulfilling the mission of laboratory schools in the United Arab Emirates and United States. *International Association of Laboratory Schools Journal, 7*(1), 14–23.

Division for Early Childhood Education and the National Association for the Education of Young Children. (2009, April). *Early childhood inclusion: A summary* [Position statement]. Retrieved from https://www.naeyc.org/files/naeyc/file/positions/DEC_NAEYC_ECSummary_A.pdf

Durst, A. (2010). *Women educators in the progressive era: The women behind Dewey's laboratory school.* New York, NY: Palgrave McMillan

East, K., & Clopton, K. (2009). Why laboratory schools must enroll students with diverse abilities. *National Association of Laboratory Schools Journal, 31*(2), 27–30.

Edwards, C., Gandini, L., & Forman, G. (Eds.). (2010). *The hundred languages of children: The Reggio Emilia experience in transformation* (3rd ed.). Santa Barbara, CA: Praeger.

Fallace, T. (2012). Review of the book *Women educators in the Progressive Era: The women behind Dewey's laboratory school* by Anne Durst. *History of Education Quarterly, 52*(3), 430–432. doi:10.1111/j.1748-5959.2012.00406.x

Frey, A. J., Park, K. L., Browne-Ferrigno, T., & Korfhage, T. L. (2010). The social validity of program-wide positive behavior support. *Journal of Positive Behavior Intervention, 12*(4), 222–235.

Froebel, F. (1885). *The education of man* (W. N. Hailman, Trans.) New York, NY: Dover. (Original work published 1826)

Grindal, T., & McCoy, D. (2016). Social entrepreneurs offer new thinking on old challenges in early childhood. *Huffington Post.* Retrieved from https://www.huffingtonpost.com/todd-grindal/social-entrepreneurs-offe_b_8156062.html

Hicks, S., & Carver, S. (2015). *Teaching math to young children* [PowerPoint slides]. Retrieved from www.psy.cmu.edu/cs/educators/HicksCarverEarlyMathNAEYC2015PDI.pdf

Houser, N., & Kloesel, C. J. W. (Eds.). (1992). *The essential Peirce, selected philosophical writings, vol. 1 (1867–1893) by C. S. Peirce.* Indianapolis: Indiana University Press.

Howarth, C., Smith, S., & Parkinson, C. (2012). Social learning and entrepreneurship education. *Academy of Management Learning & Education, 11*(3), 371–389.

Kenyon, E. (2019). Teaching undergraduates teaching PreK philosophy. In T. Wartenberg (Ed.), *Big students, Little kids, and picture Books: Bringing philosophy into classrooms.* Lanham, MD: Rowman & Littlefield.

Kenyon, E., & Terorde-Doyle, D. (2017). The three Rs of thinking: nurturing discussion in preschool. *The Roots of Learning, 12*(10). Retrieved from http://www.ascd.org/ascd-express/vol12/1210-kenyon.aspx

Kozulin, A., Gindis, B., Ageyev, V., & Miller, S. (Eds.). (2003). *Vygotsky's educational theory in cultural context.* Cambridge, England: Cambridge University Press.

Kuh, G. D. (2008). High impact educational practices: What they are, who has access to them, and why they matter. Washington, DC: American Association of Colleges and Universities. Retrieved from http://provost.tufts.edu/celt/files/High-Impact-Ed-Practices1.pdf

Lake, V., & Jones, I. (2008). Service-learning in early childhood teacher education: Using service to put meaning back into learning. *Teaching and Teacher Education: An International Journal of Research and Studies, 24*(8), 2146–2156.

Laski, E. V., & Siegler, R. S. (2014). Learning from number board games: You learn what you encode. *Developmental Psychology, 50*(3), 853–864.

Lerner, R., Fisher, C., & Weinberg, R. (2000). Toward a science for and of the people: Promoting civil society through the application of developmental science. *Child Development, 71*(1), 11–20.

Madigan, T. J. (2009). Dewey and Darwin. *Philosophy Now.* Retrieved from philosophy now.org/issues/71/Dewey_and_Darwin

McBride, B., Groves, M., Barbour, N., Horm, D., Stremmel, A., Lash, ... Toussaint, S. (2012). Child development laboratory schools as generators of knowledge in early childhood education: New models and approaches. *Early Education and Development, 23*(2), 153–164. doi:10.1080/10409289.2012.651068

Nielson, R. A. (1986). Laboratory schools: Blueprint for success. *National Association of Laboratory Schools Journal, 10*(3), 49–64.

Pierson, S. G. (2014). Laboratory of learning: HBCU laboratory schools and Alabama State College lab high in the era of Jim Crow. New York, NY: Peter Lang.

Schwartz, M., & Gerlach, J. (2011). Guiding principles for research network: Successes and challenges. *Mind, Brain, and Education, 5*(4), 172–179.

See the 2019 Best Liberal Arts Colleges (2019, April 4). *usnews.com.* Retrieved from https://www.usnews.com/best-colleges/rankings/national-liberal-arts-colleges

Social Capital Markets. (2017). SOCAP17 guest curator spotlight: Gary community investments' early childhood session. Retrieved from http://socialcapitalmarkets.net/2017/07/socap17-guest-curator-spotlight-gary-community-investments-early-childhood-session/

Smith, C. (2008). *History of the campus children's center.* Retrieved from https://childcare.indiana.edu/Centers/Campus%20Childrens%20Center.html (History)

Sparks, S. (2015). Amid changing landscapes, lab schools search for new roles. *Education Week, 34*(22), 12–13. Retrieved from https://www.edweek.org/ew/articles/2015/02/25/lab-schools-search-for-new-roles.html

Techakosit, S. (2011). The botanical garden at Kasetsart University Laboratory School Center for Educational Research and Development. *Journal of Developments in Sustainable Agriculture, 6,* 131–135.

The University of Chicago. (n.d.). Childcare resources. Retrieved from https://childcare.uchicago.edu/

Thorpe, D. (2015). Student entrepreneurs win Hult Prize with radical early childhood education model. *Forbes.* Retrieved from https://www.forbes.com/sites/devinthorpe/2015/10/13/student-entrepreneurs-win-hult-prize-with-radical-early-childhood-education-model/#66cd1d854d04

Van Voorhis, J., & DeMarie-Dreblow, D. (1995, November). An interdisciplinary early childhood major at a four-year liberal arts college: A quest for quality and communication among departments. Paper presented at the Annual Conference of the National Association of Early Childhood Teacher Educators. Washington, DC. Retrieved from the ERIC database. (ED392785)

Van Til, W. (1969). The laboratory school: Its rise and fall? Chicago, IL: Laboratory School Administrators Association, Indiana State University. Retrieved from ERIC database. (ED034703)

Wartenberg, T. (2014). *Big ideas for little kids.* Plymouth, England: Rowman & Littlefield.

Wilcox-Herzog, A., & McLaren, M. (2012). Lessons learned: Building a better laboratory school. *National Association of Laboratory Schools Journal, 4*(1), 1–8.

CHAPTER 9

THE ROLE OF LABORATORY PRESCHOOLS IN THE PROMOTION OF HIGH-QUALITY SOCIAL-EMOTIONAL GUIDANCE PRACTICES

Rebecca Anne Swartz

ABSTRACT

Laboratory preschools play an important role in training teachers and disseminating appropriate practices for guiding children's social-emotional development. These guidance practices encompass the ways that teachers are expected to respond to children's expression of ideas and display of emotions and support children's relationships with peers and adults (Gartrell, 2004). Laboratory preschools also generate knowledge about professional development for the early childhood education workforce. Social-emotional development and its associated guidance practices are a core focus in early childhood education theory, research, and practice. This chapter presents a review of the literature addressing adult-level, social-emotional factors that may influence social-emotional guidance practices. The affective organization of par-

Contemporary Perspectives on Research on Child Development Laboratory Schools in Early Childhood Education,
pages 157–171
Copyright © 2019 by Information Age Publishing
157

enting (Dix, 1991) and social convoy theory (Kahn & Antonucci, 1980) are presented as theoretical frameworks to elucidate the variations in adult social-emotional resources among teachers that may influence their social-emotional guidance practices during daily routines and activities. These frameworks provide direction for the development of future research and practices related to social-emotional guidance. Also discussed is the role of laboratory preschools in training teachers in effective social-emotional guidance practices, developing and disseminating teacher training pedagogy related to these practices, and demonstrating these practices to their communities.

Social-emotional development is foundational and supports the skills children acquire in other developmental areas. Young children first use their social-emotional capacities to settle into safe and trusting relationships with their teachers and peers. From that secure base they explore and learn in all other developmental areas (Hyson, 2004). Early childhood education programs of all types have the potential to foster children's social-emotional competence and provide a foundation for later learning and school success (Denham, 2006; Durlak & Weissberg, 2011). Programs aimed at fostering effective social-emotional guidance practices have expanded (Gunter, Caldarella, Korth, & Young, 2012; McLeod et al., 2017; Morris, Millenky, Raver, & Jones, 2013; Nix, Bierman, Domitrovich, & Gill, 2013). Longitudinal studies of social-emotional learning interventions have demonstrated positive health outcomes, higher levels of academic success, and a reduction of risk-taking behaviors in adolescence and adulthood (Bierman et al., 2010; Hawkins, Kosterman, Catalano, Hill, & Abbott, 2005). Social-emotional competence is also associated with success in early schooling (Denham, 2006). Given the strong association between social-emotional skills and positive outcomes, it is imperative that teachers of young children build a strong foundation of social-emotional guidance strategies and practices during training to carry into their classrooms. This chapter discusses the role of laboratory preschools in teaching best practices for improving social-emotional guidance methods to enhance knowledge during training and support practicing teachers. First, this chapter reviews the literature regarding teacher factors that may influence guidance practices. Second, this chapter presents theoretical frameworks that explore how adult psychosocial resources may influence social-emotional guidance practices. Finally, this chapter discusses the ways laboratory preschools may contribute to teacher training and professional support for positive social-emotional guidance practices.

The dissemination of best practices in early childhood education has historically been a core function of laboratory preschools although teachers are less frequently the focus of investigations in these settings (Barbour, 2003). A core area in teacher training has been appropriate practices for guiding children's social-emotional development. These guidance practices encompass the ways that teachers are expected to respond to children's expression of ideas and display of emotions and support children's relationships with peers and adults (see Gartrell, 2004; for a more thorough discussion). Laboratory preschools serve as living spaces for in-depth examinations of the factors that influence teacher practices and for the development of teacher education pedagogies that promote high-quality practices. Housed within research and training institutions, these schools bridge the gap between theory and practice in teacher education and occupy a unique position as programs for young children and their families. The contributions to early childhood education scholarship from laboratory preschools include building knowledge in the area of social-emotional guidance practices (henceforth referred to as "guidance practices"). The educators and researchers in university laboratory schools have direct access to interdisciplinary researchers who can bring other perspectives to bear in understanding social-emotional development and cultural and historical factors that may influence guidance practices. This includes scholars in psychology, sociology, and family science, all fields that contribute to our growing understanding of the factors that influence child development (Bersani & Hutchins, 2003; McBride et al., 2012; Stremmel, Hill, & Fu, 2003). Although guidance practices are only one area in which laboratory preschools contribute knowledge, this chapter focuses on ways these schools may contribute to advancing understanding of social-emotional development and associated guidance practices to support young children.

Many teachers and child-care providers in training (henceforth referred to as teachers) are first exposed to considering these practices as part of intentional teaching in early childhood classrooms while they observe and practice teaching in laboratory school settings. As a result, laboratory preschools are a setting in which researchers and teacher educators can build understanding of the factors that influence how guidance practices are carried out since such factors may influence the fidelity to which teachers are able to implement the positive guidance techniques they learn in training.

ADULT FACTORS AND THEIR INFLUENCE ON GUIDANCE PRACTICES

Positive relationships among all members of a school community combined with a nurturing environment are foundational for positive guidance practices. Recent research has linked quality of these guidance practices to the individual characteristics of adults providing care (Buettner, Jeon, Hur, & Garcia, 2016; de Schipper, Risken-Walraven, Guerts, & de Weerth, 2009; Gerber, Whitebook, & Weinstein, 2007; Hamre & Pianta, 2004; Li Grining et al., 2010; Swartz & McElwain, 2012). A recent report by the Institute of

Medicine and the National Research Council on the childcare workforce underscores the importance of understanding adult social-emotional factors influencing guidance practices (Institute of Medicine & National Research Council [IOM & NRC], 2015). The report identified teacher wellness and stress management as critical factors in promoting the stability and quality of practices in the child-care workforce. This suggests that improving guidance practices may depend on the types of support and training provided to teachers that increase their own social-emotional resources as a pathway to enhancing their practices with children.

The Improvisational Nature of Guidance Practices

Although best practices for building the social-emotional competence of children may be codified in textbooks, the implementation of these practices hinges on adult-level factors—adult "social-emotional resources"—that serve as a wellspring of positive energy teachers may draw upon in their spontaneous interactions with children. The nature of early childhood education work necessitates that these guidance practices are improvisational since teachers respond both cognitively and emotionally to children's emotional displays in real time. This is a key difference from best practices in other curricular areas such as math, science, or literacy for which a teacher can engage in detailed preplanning to carry out a lesson. Embracing the improvisational nature of adult responses in these moments allows the early education community an opportunity to examine the manner in which adult-level factors affect the ability of teachers to maintain supportive guidance practices throughout the daily routine. This focus also pertains to individual adult-level factors affecting guidance, a critical area of research and training, so that the correct supports are provided to teachers and they maintain environments that nurture young children (Zinsser, Christensen, & Torres, 2016).

Although the literature on teachers' influence on children's social-emotional competence is not extensive, investigations have demonstrated that parents have different effects on the socioemotional competence of their children that depend on their own emotion socialization practices (Eisenberg et al., 1998; Fabes et al., 2001; McElwain, Halberstadt, & Volling, 2007). Variances in emotion socialization practices are associated with differences in parental social-emotional resources such as emotion regulation styles, beliefs about children's emotional development, and the ability to engage in empathic perspectives (Clark, Kochanska, & Ready, 2000; Gottman, Katz, & Hooven, 1996; McElroy & Rodriguez; 2008; Wong, McElwain, & Halbserstadt, 2009).

There is emerging evidence in the literature that the social-emotional resources of non-parental caregivers demonstrate similar associations with practices and beliefs about emotion socialization practices found among parental caregivers (Ahn & Stifter, 2006; Hyson & Lee, 1996; Rothbaum, Nagaoka, & Ponte, 2006; Swartz & McElwain, 2012). Like parents, teachers engage in interactions with children across a variety of activities including physical care routines, play, meals, rest, and transitions. Throughout the day, teachers are responding to the emotional expressions of multiple children and their interactions in happy and challenging moments. A typical morning for a teacher may include supporting a tearful child having difficulty separating from a parent, helping frustrated children learn to negotiate over a coveted toy, helping a group of toddlers learn to modulate their excitement as they gently pat the classroom's guinea pig, and many other scenarios that quickly unfold minute by minute. Each of these moments is a valuable opportunity for providing positive guidance to children, but these moments also call upon teachers to modulate their emotional response along with their cognitive response since the child's emotional display also activates the adult's emotional state. In these moments, adult regulation and cognitive factors are at play that influence how teachers respond to each situation. Understanding the effect of emotional resources that might contribute to variance in daily practice is a first step to more targeted skill building in teacher training. This might include strategies to regulate adult emotion and examine emotion-related beliefs in addition to just having teachers explore the guidance practices. Effects of this type of self-reflective training may be greater than simply teaching the practices we hope to see used in the classroom. The existing literature indicates intentional teaching of social-emotional skills can improve child outcomes (Ashdown & Bernard, 2012; Gunter et al., 2012). Supporting teachers in this self-reflection may help them use improvisational moments as intentional instruction to children of strategies to manage emotions or resolve conflicts, similar to how they teach skills in other curricular areas.

ADULT FACTORS AND GUIDANCE PRACTICES: THEORETICAL MODELS

Because the caregiving context of early education shares many similarities with parenting and family life, two theoretical models from parenting and family studies literature can be brought to bear in understanding guidance practices in early childhood classrooms. First, we will look at the affective organization of a parenting model (Dix, 1991) to help us understand how teachers' emotional and cognitive factors may influence guidance practices. Then we will turn to the social convoy model (Kahn & Antonucci, 1980) to help us understand how professional social support networks can affect guidance practices.

Emotional Influences on Guidance Practices:
The Affective Organization of Parenting

Adults caring for young children engage in interactions across a variety of activities including physical care routines, play, meals, rest, and transitions. Throughout these interactions, adults continuously respond to the children in their care and experience their own emotions. In this regard, Dix (1991) conceptualized the affective organization of parenting as a complex, multidirectional process in which parents and children exercise mutual influence upon each other's experience and expression of emotion. The model explains how adult emotion resources combine to predict responses to children in emotional moments. The processes that Dix proposed are activation, engagement, and regulation. Activation of the parent's emotions occurs when encountering the child's expression and when the parent experiences thoughts and emotions and begins to appraise the situation. Engagement occurs as the parent begins cognitive processing of his or her own emotions and the situation. Moderating these two processes is the parent's own emotion regulation. The effectiveness of a parent's regulation of the emotional arousal stemming from the child's expression of emotion may not only influence the parent's response to the child but may also constrain the degree to which the parent's cognitive resources affect his or her response. In the same way, teachers' own emotion regulation style may be an important component of the emotional resources that teachers draw upon when responding to children. More positive regulation strategies enable teachers to effectively manage the emotional arousal stemming from children's emotional displays and respond in a manner that supports children's social-emotional development.

Emotion regulation processes are intertwined with cognitive processes. Dix (1991) theorized that parental emotion regulation moderates the effect of emotion-related cognition when responding to children's emotions. For example, parents who are distressed by their children's emotional displays may find themselves so overwhelmed by their own personal emotional arousal that they ignore their beliefs about validating a child's negative emotions. In a quiet moment when the child is not distressed, they may be able to articulate these beliefs or the parenting practice they would like to carry out in such situations. This underscores the joint contributions of emotion-related regulation and cognitive factors.

Although most of the literature on teacher beliefs and young children has focused on broad curricular practices, the few studies focusing on guidance practices report appreciable variance in beliefs about what is appropriate (Hyson & Lee, 1996; Swartz & McElwain, 2012). The parenting literature may be a rich source of information on how caregivers' beliefs influence their practices due to similarities in caregiving activities. The literature indicates that parents with more accepting beliefs and greater comfort with children's emotional displays provide and describe more supportive responses (e.g., labeling emotions, problem solving, validating child emotions); those uncomfortable with emotions provide and describe more non-supportive responses (e.g., ignoring, discouraging, punishing; Gottman et al., 1996; Wong et al., 2009). General orientation toward taking an empathic perspective also appears to be associated with more supportive responses to children's emotional displays and less harsh disciplinary practices (Clark et al., 2000; McElroy & Rodriguez, 2008). This further supports the idea that emotion-related beliefs are an important component in understanding why adults use particular guidance techniques.

Social Influences on Guidance Practices: The Social Convoy Model

Because guidance practices are implemented in a social space, a theoretical framework that explains the social context of teachers may also provide insight into how guidance practices are carried out. Social convoy theory (Kahn & Antonucci, 1980) is a life-course theory that seeks to explain the structure of the network of family, friends, and other people who support individuals in their daily lives. Social convoy theory brings together the tenets of attachment theory with the concept of social roles. Like attachment theory, social convoy theory views close relationships as a source of social-emotional support enabling individuals to meet everyday challenges. It examines the bonds that exist between an individual and the many social relationships embedded in his or her network. Social convoy theory also addresses multiple roles: family roles, work roles, and community roles that individuals fulfill as they mature, thereby increasing the complexity required to balance role-related demands.

Kahn and Antonucci (1980) assert that the structure of an individual's convoy is knitted together through the "transaction"—giving and taking—of three supportive elements: affect, affirmation, and aid. These transactions are the observable outputs of social support within the relationships that constitute the social convoy. Examining these transactions may provide insight into the strength and health of a teacher's social convoy. Affect transactions refer to the emotional expressions of shared respect, esteem, or caring. The amount of social support a person needs to be successful in meeting role-related expectations varies as a function of an individual's characteristics and the demands of the current situation. This may mean that at different times, the support of a particular group of convoy members is more critical than another group. For example, teachers may struggle more in meeting the role demands of providing care at the beginning of their careers due to a lack of specific knowledge or skills related to child development. The assistance of mentor teachers or faculty would be more critical as potential sources of aid at that time to help scaffold the individual teacher's knowledge. Once a knowledge base is established, these transactions may become less critical to daily functioning and transactions could become intermittent. Support may still be critical during times of stress when teachers must cope with children's challenging behaviors, adapt guidance practices to the needs of diverse learners and families, and manage times of personal stress.

By bringing the framework proposed by Dix (1991) and Kahn and Antonucci (1980) together, we are able to gain a better picture of how adult social-emotional resources combine to influence related guidance practices. Since guidance practices are motivated both by emotional and social factors on the part of teachers, we are better able to target the key factors to move teachers from less optimal guidance practices to those that build children's social-emotional competence. Some teachers will need greater support in building their understanding and belief system about children's social-emotional development and effective socialization strategies. Some teachers will need greater support in building their emotion regulation strategies, their ability to take someone else's perspective when experiencing another's emotional display, or their ability to manage their own psychological stresses. All teachers can benefit from building social support networks that value their role in building children's social-emotional competence through effective guidance practices and having opportunities for them to reflect upon the challenges of carrying out such practices. Creating these opportunities for adult learners should be considered essential when planning programming to promote effective guidance practices. Such opportunities should also be the focus of research and program development in laboratory preschools where many teachers receive their formal training as early educators and develop foundational dispositions for their professional practice.

LABORATORY PRESCHOOLS AND THE PROMOTION
OF HIGH-QUALITY GUIDANCE PRACTICES

Laboratory preschools play four key roles in promoting high-quality guidance practices. First, they are centers of teacher training and provide opportunities for teachers at all points in their career to view high-quality guidance in action. Second, they can be centers of professional networks in their own communities, providing opportunities for continued learning and reflection on guidance practices. Third, they can be places to examine mentoring processes for guidance practices. Finally, they can be hubs of research, documentation, and innovation in curriculum and practices that can be used in teacher training, policy development, and outreach (McBride et al., 2012).

Centers of Teacher Training

Laboratory preschools provide opportunities for preservice teachers to gain a foundational understanding of guidance practices. Laboratory preschools are spaces for preservice teachers at a variety of learning levels including high school child development classes, community college child development centers, and laboratory preschools in research or teaching-focused institutions. What ties these settings together as laboratory preschools is their core purpose of serving as standard-bearers for the field of early childhood education and for modeling key guidance practices. Teachers in training complete both observational and hands-on practice in laboratory preschools. Through these experiences, they are introduced to the best practices and standards of early childhood education. This includes watching the laboratory school faculty and staff interacting with children and families as they negotiate everyday routines and emotional moments.

Teacher training involves opportunities for preservice teachers to reflect upon their observation of and interactions with children, families, and colleagues through supportive conversations, reflective writing, and other activities with their course instructors, peers, and mentors. It is especially critical for guidance practices that these conversations occur since they are an opportunity for preservice teachers to engage in conversations about how intentional teaching practices occur in the classroom through the arrangement of the environment, responses to children's emotional expressions, and observation of the classroom climate. During these reflective interactions, the best practices in guidance are communicated to preservice teachers, and they become part of the foundational dispositions toward teaching young children that they will bring into their future classrooms and interactions (Scales, Perry, & Tracy, 2012). These conversations are also a critical time to introduce important concepts about emotion regulation, self-awareness, culture, and contextual factors that may influence a teacher's responses to children's emotional expressions in the classroom and in the future. It is critical that preservice teachers develop reflective dispositions that enable them to respond to the wide variety of experiences and expressions that young children and families bring into the classroom. This could include introducing explicit theoretical models such as the Dix (1991) model discussed earlier in this chapter. It could also include encouraging preservice teachers to reflect upon how their personal emotion socialization influences their expectations and responses when they encounter the emotional expressions of young children and families who may come from very different backgrounds than their own.

Additionally, during these conversations, mentor teachers and instructors can stress the importance of building social support networks that allow for collaborative inquiry and reflection that occurs among teams of teachers and interdisciplinary professionals when they are working through challenges with young children who may require targeted interventions or specialized practices. Thus, the laboratory school community becomes a living model of the collaboration that students will encounter as they begin their careers in early childhood education settings. With its mission of teacher training, the laboratory school is a safe space for preservice teachers to test various guidance strategies with the support of mentors. Relationships in the laboratory school form the beginnings of the supportive network they will need as they move forward in their teaching careers and face the dilemmas of daily practices of serving young children and families. Also, these interactions provide fertile ground for teacher educators and early education leaders to improve their mentorship skills (Monroe & Horm, 2012).

Centers of Professional Networks

Laboratory preschools can function as hubs of innovation and professional connection within their communities. They are places in which teachers can begin to build their professional network, or social convoy (Kahn & Antonucci, 1980), that will sustain them as they encounter challenges in their careers. Professionals can turn to laboratory preschools to model best practices and for resources to overcome challenges. Laboratory preschools, with the depth of human resources they contain in terms of faculty, teachers, and knowledge, are sources of new curricula and research. They also exemplify high-quality practices made visible through their commitment to communicating these practices to a dynamic and real community (Cutler et al., 2012). Within the laboratory school, teachers develop beliefs about their role as educators and effective practices in guidance within a professional support network that reifies and sustains the practice of that ideal. These opportunities to interact with colleagues are times for support and sharing within a network of professionals, creating ripple effects of quality guidance practices within networks of teachers. Some laboratory preschools in the United States also are funded through collaborative agreements with state prekindergarten, child-care subsidy, and Head Start programs. Thus, these laboratory programs also become places that model effective practices for helping teachers meet program standards in publicly funded programs.

Sources of Research, Documentation, and Innovation

Laboratory preschools are positioned to lead in the development and promotion of high-quality guidance practices with their depth of knowledge and human resources. First, laboratory preschools provide a critical setting for research aimed at understanding these teacher-level factors and for the development of teacher training and mentoring practices that will enable early childhood educators to have the critical skills to carry out effective guidance practices. Laboratory preschools are settings in which teacher educators can explore the development of supports for teachers and promote the flexible guidance practices necessitated by the improvisational nature of their work.

Laboratory preschools also can be a rich source of documentation that can be integrated into teacher training, policy, and community decision-making for early childhood education. They are important sites for piloting new curricula and research measures. For social-emotional practices, this means that laboratory preschools can provide a setting for creating training materials for curricula or measures, calibration of research scales, or the refinement of curricular or program standards. To support innovation training to improve guidance practices, laboratory preschools could investigate the process of teaching newer practices, such as mindfulness meditation, training program leaders in reflective supervision, or develop and evaluate curricula aimed at helping teachers of young children improve guidance practices. Laboratory preschools may communicate these ideas through a variety of different formats, such as videos, books, web resources, or documentation panels that make the strategies for developmentally appropriate social-emotional skills explicit, understandable, and replicable.

The laboratory preschool community has always been connected to the training of new professionals in the field of early childhood education. This includes disseminating basic information about child development and effective child guidance to learners beginning their studies in the field. The materials created by laboratory preschools are also useful in communicating the importance of positive guidance practices to community members and policy makers who may not have a background in child development or early education, yet by the nature of the roles in community leadership and government, they may have influence in decision-making in early childhood education.

Guidance practices are foundational practices for early education. Laboratory preschools are standard-bearers for the early childhood education community to develop and demonstrate inclusive guidance practices that can support children as they develop a strong foundation of social-emotional skills. Promoting the social-emotional wellness of teachers and caregivers, as discussed earlier in this chapter, is a key factor in promoting the stability and quality of practices carried out by the professionals in service of children. Through their research and outreach networks, laboratory preschools can share effective mentoring, training, and support practices that support high-quality guidance. The laboratory school community, therefore, plays a key role in workforce development and knowledge generation for efforts that enable high-quality guidance practices to be employed for young children and their families not only through their daily service to the children and families in their own schools but through their training, outreach, and scholarly contributions.

REFERENCES

Ahn, H. J., & Stifter, C. (2006). Child care teachers' response to children's emotional expression. *Early Education and Development, 17*(2), 253–270. doi:10.1207/ s15566935eed1702_3

Ashdown, D. M., & Bernard, M. E. (2012). Can explicit instruction in social and emotional learning skills benefit the social-emotional development, well-being, and academic achievement of young children? *Early Childhood Education Journal, 39*(6), 397–405. doi:10.1007/s10643-011-0481-x

Barbour, N. E. (2003). The early history of child development laboratory programs. In B. A. McBride & N. E. Barbour (Eds.), *Bridging the gap between theory, research, and practice: The role of child development laboratory programs in early childhood education* (pp. 9–29). Oxford, England: Elsevier

Bersani, C., & Hutchins, P. (2003). Reconceptualizing the child development laboratory school. In B. A. McBride & N. E. Barbour (Eds.), *Bridging the gap between theory, research, and practice: The role of child development laboratory programs in early childhood education* (pp. 113–139). Oxford, England: Elsevier.

Bierman, K. L., Coie, J. D., Dodge, K. A., Greenberg, M. T., Lochman, J. E., McMahon, R., & Pinderhughes, E. J. (2010). The effects of a multi-year universal social–emotional learning program: The role of student and school characteristics. *Journal of Consulting and Clinical Psychology, 78*(2), 156–168. doi:10.1037/ a0018607

Buettner, C. K., Jeon, L., Hur, E., & Garcia, R. E. (2016). Teachers' social-emotional capacity: Factors associated with teachers' responsiveness and professional commitment. *Early Education and Development, 27*(7), 1018–1039. doi:10.1080 /10409289.2016.1168227

Clark, L. A., Kochanska, G., & Ready, R. (2000). Mothers' personality and its interaction with child temperament as predictors of parenting behavior. *Journal of Personality and Social Psychology, 79,* 274–285. doi:10.1037/0022-3514.79.2.274

Cutler, K., Bersani, C., Hutchins, P., Bowne, M., Lash, M., Kroeger, J., & Black, F. (2012). Laboratory schools as places of inquiry: A collaborative journey for two laboratory schools. *Early Education and Development, 23*(2), 242–258.

Denham, S. (2006). The emotional basis of learning and development. In B. Spodek & O. N. Saracho (Eds.), *Handbook of research on the education of young children* (pp. 85–103). Mahwah, NJ: Erlbaum.

de Schipper, E. J., Riksen-Walraven, J. M., Geurts, S. A. E., & de Weerth, C. (2009). Cortisol levels of caregivers in child care centers as related to the quality of their caregiving. *Early Childhood Research Quarterly, 24*(1), 55–63. doi:10.1016/j.ecresq.2008.10.004

Dix, T. (1991). The affective organization of parenting: Adaptive and maladaptative processes. *Psychological Bulletin, 110*(1), 3–25. doi:10.1037/0033-2909.110.1.3

Durlak, J. A., & Weissberg, R. P. (2011). Promoting social and emotional development is an essential part of students' education. *Human Development, 54*(1), 1–3. doi:10.1159/000324337

Eisenberg, N., Cumberland, A., & Spinrad, T. L. (1998). Parental socialization of emotion. *Psychological Inquiry, 9*(4), 241–273. doi:10.1207/s15327965pli0904_1

Fabes, R. A., Leonard, S. A., Kupanoff, K., & Martin, C. L. (2001). Parental coping with children's negative emotions: Relations with children's emotional and social responding. *Child Development, 72*, 907–920. doi:10.1111/1467-8624.00323

Gartrell, D. (2004). *The power of guidance: Teaching social-emotional skills in early childhood classrooms.* Clifton Park, NY: Thomson/Delmar Learning.

Gerber, E. B., Whitebook, M., & Weinstein, R. S. (2007). At the heart of child care: Predictors of teacher sensitivity in center-based child care. *Early Childhood Research Quarterly, 22*(3), 327–346.

Gottman, J. M., Katz, L. F., & Hooven, C. (1996). Parental meta-emotion philosophy and the emotional life of families: Theoretical models and preliminary data. *Journal of Family Psychology, 10*(3) 243–268. doi:10.1037/0893-3200.10.3.243

Gunter, L., Caldarella, P., Korth, B. B., & Young, K. R. (2012). Promoting social and emotional learning in preschool students: A study of strong start pre-K. *Early Childhood Education Journal, 40*(3), 151–159. doi:10.1007/s10643-012-0507-z

Hamre, B. K., & Pianta, R. C. (2004). Self-reported depression in nonfamilial caregivers: Prevalence and associations with caregiver behavior in child-care settings. *Early Childhood Research Quarterly, 19*(2), 297–318.

Hawkins, J. D., Kosterman, R., Catalano, R. F., Hill, K. G., & Abbott, R. D. (2005). Promoting positive adult functioning through social development intervention in childhood: Long-term effects from the Seattle social development project. *Archives of Pediatric and Adolescent Medicine, 159*(1), 25–31.

Hyson, M. (2004). *The emotional development of young children: Building an emotion-centered curriculum.* New York, NY: Teachers College Press.

Hyson, M. C., & Lee, K. (1996). Assessing early childhood teachers' beliefs about emotions: Content, contexts, and implications for practice. *Early Education and Development, 7*(1), 59–78.

Institute of Medicine and National Research Council. (2015). Part IV: Developing the care and education workforce for children birth through age 8. In L. Allen & B. Kelly (Eds.), *Transforming the workforce for children birth through age 8: A unifying foundation.* Washington, DC: The National Academies Press. doi:10.17226/19401

Kahn, R. L., & Antonucci, T. C. (1980). Convoys across the life course: Attachment, roles, and social support. In P. B. Baltes and O. Brim (Eds.), *Life span development and behavior,* (Vol. 3; pp. 253–286). New York, NY: Academic Press.

Li Grining, C., Raver, C. C., Champion, K., Sardin, L., Metzger, M., & Jones, S. M. (2010). Understanding and improving classroom emotional climate and

behavior management in the "real world": The role of head start teachers' psychosocial stressors. *Early Education and Development, 21*(1), 65–94.
doi:10.1080/10409280902783509

McBride, B. A., Groves, M., Barbour, N., Horm, D., Stremmel, A., Lash, M., & Toussaint, S. (2012). Child development laboratory schools as generators of knowledge in early childhood education: New models and approaches. *Early Education and Development, 23*(2), 153–164. doi:10.1080/10409289.2012.651068

McLeod, B. D., Sutherland, K. S., Martinez, R. G., Conroy, M. A., Snyder, P. A., &
Southam-Gerow, M. A. (2017). Identifying common practice elements to improve social, emotional, and behavioral outcomes of young children in early
childhood classrooms. *Prevention Science, 18*(2), 204–213.

McElroy, E. M., & Rodriguez, C. M. (2008). Mothers of children with externalizing
behavior problems: Cognitive risk factors for abuse potential and discipline
style and practices. *Child Abuse & Neglect, 32*(8), 774–784. doi:10.1016/j.
chiabu.2008.01.002

McElwain, N. L., Halberstadt, A. G., & Volling, B. L. (2007). Mother- and father-
reported reactions to children's negative emotions: Relations to young children's emotional understanding and friendship quality. *Child Development,
78*(5), 1407–1425. doi:10.1111/j.1467-8624.2007.01074.x

Monroe, L., & Horm, D. M. (2012). Using a logic model to evaluate undergraduate
instruction in a laboratory preschool. *Early Education and Development, 23*(2),
227–241.

Morris, P., Millenky, M., Raver, C. C., & Jones, S. M. (2013). Does a preschool social
and emotional learning intervention pay off for classroom instruction and
children's behavior and academic skills? Evidence from the foundations of
learning project. *Early Education & Development, 24*(7), 1020–1042.

Nix, R. L., Bierman, K. L., Domitrovich, C. E., & Gill, S. (2013). Promoting children's social-emotional skills in preschool can enhance academic and behavioral functioning in kindergarten: Findings from Head Start REDI. *Early Education and Development, 24*(7), 1000–1019.

Rothbaum, F., Nagaoka, R., & Ponte, I. C. (2006). Caregiver sensitivity in cultural
context: Japanese and U.S. teachers' beliefs about anticipating and responding to children's needs. *Journal of Research in Childhood Education, 21*(1), 23.

Scales, B., Perry, J., & Tracy, R. (2012). Creating a classroom of inquiry at the University of California at Berkeley: The Harold E. Jones Child Study Center. *Early
Education and Development, 23*(2), 165–180.

Stremmel, A. J., Hill, L. T., & Fu, V. R. (2003). An inside perspective of paradigm
shifts in child development laboratory programs: Bridging theory and professional preparation. In B. A. McBride & N. E. Barbour (Eds.), *Bridging the
gap between theory, research, and practice: The role of child development laboratory
programs in early childhood education* (pp. 89 – 111). Oxford, England: Elsevier.

Swartz, R. A., & McElwain, N. L. (2012). Preservice teachers' emotion-related regulation and cognition: Associations with teachers' responses to children's
emotions in early childhood classrooms. *Early Education and Development, 23,*
206–223. doi:10.1080/10409289.2012.619392

Wong, M. S., McElwain, N. L., & Halberstadt, A. G. (2009). Parent, family,
and child characteristics: Associations with mother- and father-reported

emotion socialization practices. *Journal of Family Psychology, 23*(4), 452–463. doi:10.1037/a0015552

Zinsser, K. M., Christensen, C. G., & Torres, L. (2016). She's supporting them; who's supporting her? Preschool center-level social-emotional supports and teacher well-being. *Journal of School Psychology, 59,* 55–66.

CHAPTER 10

EARLY CHILDHOOD TEACHER-AS-RESEARCHER

An Imperative in the Age of "Schoolification": Harnessing Dewey's Concept of the Laboratory School to Disrupt the Emerging Global Quality Crisis in Early Childhood Education

Emer Ring, Lisha O'Sullivan, and Marie Ryan

ABSTRACT

High-quality early childhood education is associated with a compelling range of immediate and long-term benefits for children, families, and society. Play-based early childhood programs have been identified as the most conducive to achieving high-quality outcomes for children in the early years. However research continues to highlight the "schoolification" of young children's earliest experiences, whereby child-led curricula and playful pedagogy are replaced by a focus on pre-academic skills; direct instruction and standardized testing. Linked to the accountability agenda, this intensification of children's early years' experiences is leading to an emerging global quality crisis in early

Contemporary Perspectives on Research on Child Development Laboratory Schools in Early Childhood Education,
pages 173–194

childhood education that unless disrupted has the potential to negatively impact children's learning and development. In this chapter, it is suggested that situating the concept of the early childhood teacher-as-researcher within the framework of Dewey's laboratory school has the potential to support early childhood teachers in countering the threats to quality stemming from the schoolification movement.

High-quality early childhood education is associated with a compelling range of immediate and long-term benefits for children, families, and society (Girard, Pingault, Doyle, Falissard, & Tremblay, 2017; Heckman, 2013; Organisation for Economic Co-Operation & Development [OECD], 2017a). Definitions of quality however are inextricably associated with societal understandings of early childhood education and specific historical, political, social, and economic contexts (Ring et al., 2016; Urban, Robson, & Scacchi, 2017). While acknowledging the impact of these contextual influences, research has isolated the key dimensions of quality that have universal applicability. Melhuish et al. (2015) described these dimensions as positive and enriched teacher–child verbal interactions; teachers' knowledge and understanding of how young children learn; teachers' skills in supporting children in resolving conflicts and the degree to which parents are assisted in providing valuable learning interactions at home. Play-based early childhood programs have been identified as the most conducive to achieving high-quality outcomes and enabling all children to realize their full potential and achieve long-term developmental gains (O'Sullivan & Ring, 2016; Whitebread, Kuvalja, & O'Connor, 2015b). However, despite valid research demonstrating the negative impact of pressuring young children to employ nascent abilities in a developmentally inappropriate manner, a focus on pre-academic skills; direct instruction, and standardized testing continues to infiltrate early childhood programmes (Almon & Miller, 2011; Bassok, Latham, & Rorem, 2016; Carlsson-Paige, McLaughlin, & Almon, 2015; House, 2011; Moss et al., 2016; Wilhelmsen, 2016). The proposed introduction of a cross-national assessment by the OECD focused on measuring early learning cognitive, social, and emotional outcomes through testing children aged 4½ to 5½ further highlights the threat to the provision of high-quality early childhood education for young children (OECD, 2017b; Moss et al., 2016). In this chapter, it is suggested that aligning the role of the early childhood teacher-as-researcher with the concept of the laboratory school suggested by Dewey provides us with a much-needed remedy to avert, what the authors suggest, is an emerging global quality crisis in early childhood education. The chapter concludes by suggesting potential scaffolds for developing the teacher-as-researcher role, drawing in particular, on one online initiative which seeks to build a teacher-researcher community in the Irish context; the Research Expertise Exchange (REX; REX Consortium, 2016).

AN EMERGING GLOBAL QUALITY CRISIS
IN EARLY CHILDHOOD EDUCATION

Welcome pressure continues to be placed on governments internationally to invest in early childhood education (OECD, 2017a). However investment globally continues to be uneven, with the Scandinavian countries, Australia and New Zealand committing high levels of expenditure to early childhood education in comparison to other countries including the United States and Ireland (OECD, 2017a). Coinciding with government investment in early childhood education internationally and a concern to provide for structural and process quality is the emerging crisis of a "schoolification epidemic" (Ring & O'Sullivan, 2018, p. 1) propelled by the accountability agenda and exemplified by the school readiness movement. This crisis represents a serious threat to the concept of child-centred, high-quality early childhood education and equality of educational opportunity and access for all children. Accountability continues to be synonymous with high-stakes standardized testing rather than on creating supportive environments to improve practice and enhance children's learning and development (Graue & Johnson, 2011). Schoolification has emerged from this preoccupation with the promises of accountability and refers to a global trend whereby early childhood education is predominantly concerned with preparing children for school and maintains a focus on the development of children's academic skills to the detriment of child-centred curricula and playful pedagogy (Ring & O'Sullivan, 2018). It is critical however, when acknowledging the threat to quality early childhood education presented by the "schoolification epidemic" (Ring & O'Sullivan, 2018, p. 1) and school readiness discourse, that a targeted focus is maintained on equalizing opportunities for children from poorer backgrounds and children with disabilities. Research indicates that social origins continue to impact negatively on children's outcomes with many children experiencing less nurturant environments and limited opportunities, leading to reduced life chances (Melhuish, 2014; OECD, 2017a). Likewise, without intensive and directed quality early intervention, the developmental challenges experienced by children with disabilities become more pronounced, leading to lifetime consequences, increased poverty, and overwhelming exclusion (World Health Organisation [WHO] and United Nations Children's Fund [UNICEF], 2012). In a recent national evaluation of concepts of school readiness in Ireland and consonant with global patterns, school readiness was identified as a maturationist-environmental concept associated with a child's age and the acquisition of predetermined academic skills (Dockett & Perry, 2002; Ring et al., 2016). Sixteen prekindergartens; 16 kindergartens; 57 children, and 30 parents participated in the qualitative phase of the research with a response rate of 29.6% ($n = 148$) and 23.8% ($n = 114$)

Figure 10.1 Drawings of childrens' concept of early childhood education experiences.

to the quantitative survey distributed to a random sample of 500 prekindergartens and 500 kindergartens. Fifty-seven children, aged between three and four participated in 10 child conferences (Clark & Moss, 2011). The maturationist-environmental lens through which a significant majority of participants in the research study viewed the concept of school readiness was particularly evident in children's dialogue and drawings. Children articulated a perception of early childhood education as being concerned with homework, learning numbers and letters, and having limited availability for play. See Figure 10.1 for a sample of children's drawings.

Increasingly therefore early childhood education is being influenced by elementary education and school readiness measured by a child's age, cognitive skills, and social and behavioral dispositions (Ring et al., 2016; Ring & O'Sullivan, 2018). While this represents a worrying trend for all children, it is particularly problematic for children from poorer backgrounds and children with disabilities. Research and practice internationally indicate that specific historical, cultural, socio-economic, and political influences determine the early childhood education ecosystem a child experiences, with the three overlapping spheres of influence in Figure 10.2 clearly identifiable across all education systems.

At the macro-level, the rationale for early childhood education is shaped by specific policy priorities, which are implemented at the micro-level by early childhood teachers. The child, home, and community occupy the mesosphere and represent the interrelationships affecting and shaping the experience of early childhood education for all stakeholders. The effect of a specific education ecosystem on early childhood education is further demonstrated in the variation across countries in relation to compulsory school-starting age detailed in Table 10.1 and the associated introduction of more formal curricula with less focus on play-based approaches.

The emerging maturationist focus on early childhood education promotes a biological view of development, with failure to demonstrate

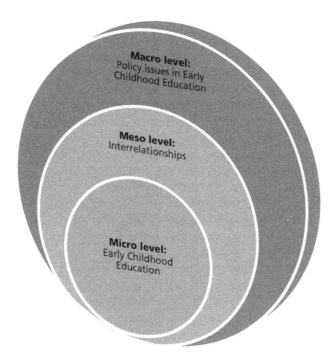

Figure 10.2   The early childhood ecosystem adapted from Bronfenbrenner (1979) and Ring et al. (2016)

TABLE 10.1 Compulsory School Starting Age Internationally Adapted from European Commission/ EACEA/ Eurydice (2017)	
School Starting Age	**Country**
4 Years	United Kingdom–Northern Ireland
5 Years	Bulgaria, Cyprus, United Kingdom–England, United Kingdom–Wales, United Kingdom–Scotland, Malta, United States
6 Years	Albania, Australia, Bosnia and Herzegovina, Belgium, Czech Republic, Denmark, Former Yugoslav Republic of Macedonia, France, Germany, Greece, Hungary, Iceland, Republic of Ireland, Italy, Liechtenstein, Luxembourg, Montenegro, Netherlands, Norway, Portugal, Romania, Serbia, Slovenia, Spain, Switzerland, Turkey
7 Years	Croatia, Estonia, Finland, Latvia, Lithuania, Poland, Sweden

Note: From European Commission/EACEA/Eurydice (2017). The structure of the European education systems 2017/18: Schematic diagrams: Eurydice facts and figures. Printed with permission from the author.

readiness for school attributed to the individual child, while ignoring the effect of the experiences provided for the child (Dockett & Perry, 2002). The environmental focus associates readiness with behaviors and skills such as a knowledge of colors, shapes, letters of the alphabet, counting, and behaving in a socially acceptable manner (Ring et al., 2016). Placing developmentally inappropriate demands on children may potentially affect children's future development through negatively affecting dispositions such as self-confidence, risk-taking, initiative, curiosity, cooperativeness, engagement, persistence, and enthusiasm, as children experience failure in tasks that they are not developmentally ready for (Ring & O'Sullivan, 2016). The seriousness of this practice was illustrated by Wilhelmsen (2016) who isolated up to 18 visual components that should be developed for a child to engage with print effectively, noting that these components do not begin to be fully developed until a child reaches 8 years. The growing standardization and narrowing of early childhood education promoted by the maturationsist-environmental focus will ultimately lead to an alignment of curricula with what is being measured and the emergence of a self-fulfilling system characterized by a teaching-to-the-test approach and with improvement being measured with reference to a range of narrow and predetermined criteria (Morris, 2016; Moss et al., 2016). Worryingly, this represents a return to the "traditional school" where the teacher is the custodian of a distinct body of knowledge to be transmitted in the form of a prescribed curriculum with children being tested for mastery. It ignores the appropriateness of an emergent curriculum, co-constructed by both children and adults, individualized and responsive to children's development and reflecting the increasing body of research on how children learn most effectively in the early years (Edwards, Gandini, & Forman, 2012; Jones, 2012; Zingoni, 2014; Wien, 2008). Critically allowing specific ecosystems combined with a maturationist-environmental concept of school readiness to be the propeller for early childhood education undermines the concept of child-centeredness as articulated by Dewey in terms of conceptualizing the child as the starting point, the centre, and the end of learning and teaching and ignores the incontrovertible research on the positive effect of implementing a playful pedagogy for children in the early years (Dewey, 1902; Ring & O'Sullivan, 2018).

A PLAYFUL PEDAGOGY: THE EVIDENCE?

While Dewey's views on play have received less attention than his other contributions, they provide an important blueprint for conceptualizing the role of play in education. In contrast to the laboratory school, which encouraged the use of play as a pedagogical tool, play is often sacrificed in favor of more prescriptive curricula and teacher-led instruction in to-day's kindergarten and elementary school classrooms (Graue, 2009; Ring & O'Sullivan, 2018). Graue (2009) observes that play when choreographed thoughtfully, represents a powerful learning context for children and cautions that play has been abandoned in favor of more formal instruction in literacy and numeracy. Dewey's ideas on play as freely chosen, intrinsically motivating, meaningful, and socially constructed, provide a strong rationale for a playful pedagogy in young children's education (Frost, Wortham, & Reifel, 2009). More recent research on the contribution of play to early learning affirms the Deweyan assertion that young children learn far more effectively through play than formal methods (López Boo, Caridad Araujo, & Tomé, 2016; Howard & McInnes, 2013; Whitebread & O'Sullivan, 2012).

Freedom is a key characteristic of play, and unlike many other classroom activities, children have the freedom to play and the freedom to quit (Gray, 2013). Dewey saw the actual experience of freedom in play as a prerequisite to understanding and appreciating its value in a democratic society (Frost et al., 2008). Closely linked to the idea of play as a freely chosen activity is the idea of play as an intrinsically motivating activity, with the activity itself being more motivating than any external goal (Frost et al., 2008; Howard & McInnes, 2013). Play as an intrinsically motivating activity leads to means being prioritized over ends, which is an important ingredient in effective early learning (Gray, 2013). The research on play and problem-solving, repeatedly finds that children in playful conditions perform better than children in more formal conditions (Sylva, Bruner, & Genova, 1976; Thomas, Howard, & Miles, 2006; Whitebread, Jameson, & Basilio, 2015a). Thomas et al. (2006), for example, undertook a comparison of 3- to 5-year-old children's problem-solving in formal and playful conditions through timing how long it took children to complete a jigsaw puzzle. A pretest involved timing all children completing a jigsaw before assigning them to a playful or formal 8-minute practice condition. Play cues identified by children in earlier research including the level of choice afforded, where the activity takes place (at a table or on the floor), and the presence or absence of adults were manipulated to design the play and formal conditions (Howard, 2010). In the play, condition children were asked if they wanted to try some more puzzles on the floor without adult presence and in the formal condition, children were asked to sit at a table and complete some more puzzles with adult presence. The children were retimed immediately after the practice condition and again 1 week later. While no significant difference was reported for both groups in pretest scores, children in the playful condition demonstrated a significant improvement in the time taken to complete the puzzle in both the immediate and delayed posttest (Thomas et al., 2006). Studies such as this, illustrate that children perform better when they tackle problems playfully. When they engage playfully, children try out a range of problem-solving strategies and novel combinations and the shifting of focus from ends to means appears to reduce concern with outcomes and fear of failure (Sylva et al., 1976; Thomas et al., 2006; Whitebread et al., 2015a). The message is clear, for novice learners, which young children clearly are, the pressure to perform and concern with outcomes adversely affects overall performance (Gray, 2013).

From a pedagogical perspective, freely chosen play provides important opportunities for children to become deeply absorbed in the process of their activity. Moreover, teachers who practice a playful pedagogical approach nurture freedom and intrinsic motivation in all classroom activities through offering authentic choices to children and emphasizing means over ends. Outcomes-driven curricula, which emphasize the product of learning, are clearly at odds with an approach that places equal, if not more, value on the process of learning. The contribution of play as an intrinsically motivating endeavor goes far beyond the early years. Dewey saw work (as distinguished from labor) as a natural outgrowth of play (Dennis, 1970). While Dennis (1970) distinguished work from play in so far as the activity becomes more intentional, optimally, when at work, the goals should still be intrinsic to the activity. From this perspective, a key contribution of play is the nurturance of the playful attitude (Howard & McInnes, 2013). This can also be conceived as a playful disposition. Children need support to strengthen desirable dispositions; thus, nurturing a playful disposition should be a priority in early childhood education (Katz, 2010). Many great innovators in disciplines as diverse as science, engineering, and the arts attribute much of their success to their enduring playful approach, further illustrating the contribution a playful pedagogy can make to life-long achievement (Bergen, 2009). It is critical, in this regard, that more attention be paid to how young children are learning, how they tackle problems and the conditions that support them persisting and adapting as they encounter challenges. As the research on young children's metacognition and self-regulation demonstrates, the extent to which children develop these abilities may be much more important for future learning success than the acquisition of formal academic skills and content (McClelland, Acock, Piccinin, Rhea, & Stallings, 2013; Whitebread et al., 2015a).

Long before modern neuroscience made the natural timetable of brain development more transparent, Dewey recognized that young children learn in a qualitatively different way than do older children and adults. Ironically, the tendency to impose a watered-down curriculum delivered by methods that are ill-suited to young children's learning needs remains common practice (Ring et al., 2016). Without a doubt, a rejection of prescriptive curricula and direct instruction is by no means an assertion that young children should not be supported to develop knowledge and understanding. Young children are curious and eager to learn new things

(Whitebread, 2015). As Dewey recognized, however, it is crucial that knowledge and understanding are fostered through developmentally appropriate pedagogy that builds on what is meaningful to children (Frost et al., 2008). Congruent with the thinking of Piaget (1962) and Vygotsky (Cole, John-Steiner, Scribner, & Sourberman, 1978), Dewey emphasized pretend play as a leading form of meaning-making during the preschool years (Frost et al., 2008). When children pretend they are actively making sense of feelings, thoughts, relationships, and experiences. As such, the content of play is always meaningful because it is distinctly embedded in children's own personal experiences. Play as a mechanism through which children come to understand their world, people, experiences, and relationships clearly contributes to a democratic society (Frost et al., 2008). The research in this area supports the view that young children perform better when tasks are meaningful and have a clear purpose (Mistry, Rogoff, & Herman, 2009; Whitebread, 2015). Istomona (as cited by Karpov, 2005), for example, undertook some research on children's ability to remember in irrelevant and meaningful contexts. This study compared how many words 3- to 7-year olds could remember in two situations. In the first situation, the adult read out a list of words that the children had to recall, and in the second, the adult was playing with the children and asked them to go to the "shop" and read a list of items to be bought (another adult took on the role of "shopkeeper" and asked the children what they wanted to buy). Children recalled more words in the play situation because the context was meaningful (shopping) and there was an obvious purpose to the activity (buying groceries rather than recalling for the sake of it (Karpov, 2005; Mistry et al., 2009). More recently, Whitebread et al. (2015a), found that opportunities to engage in free-play with story sacks (including dolls and props) in small groups after hearing a story led to children demonstrating greater confidence, more problem-solving, and creative behaviors in their own subsequent storytelling. This research, which suggested that an imaginative component makes learning more meaningful, corroborated Dewey's view of pretend play as a leading form of thought during the early years (Frost et al., 2008). From a pedagogical perspective, children should be provided with plenty opportunities to use their senses, physical skills, and imagination to learn how their world works (Blaustein, 2005). This informal knowledge base provides an important foundation for the acquisition of the more abstract and scientific knowledge introduced in formal schooling (Karpov, 2005).

Dewey further recognized that the inclusion of play in early years' curricula was critical to social engagement (Frost et al., 2008). Consistent with sociocultural perspectives (Cole, John-Steiner, Scribner, & Sourberman, 1978), Dewey saw the peer group itself as a microcosm of society where children practice important negotiation and perspective taking skills and have opportunities to both make and follow their own rules (Dennis, 1970; Frost et al., 2008). During the preschool years, play becomes increasingly social as children become more competent at communicating their personal play intentions and in understanding and accommodating the play intentions of peers. As play becomes more interdependent, children often invest as much time in collaborating about their play as they actually spend playing (O'Sullivan, 2016). This type of collaborative interaction is believed to be responsible for many of the gains associated with play (Broadhead, 2010). Manuelinko's (as cited by Karpov, 2005) early research in this area, for example, illustrated the role of peers in supporting self-control. In this experiment, 3- to 7-year olds were asked to stand still in a number of conditions (e.g., asked to stand motionless in an empty room, asked to stand motionless in an empty room but to pretend to be a "standing sentry," and asked to stand motionless in the role of a "sentry" in a room with playmates). All children, except the 6- to 7-year olds (who obviously had better-developed self-control) stood still for longer in the condition where they were in role, with peers present. While this research, once more, demonstrates the significance of meaningful conditions, it also illustrates the salience of social play with peers in the early years. More recent research on the social, cognitive, emotional, and motivational aspects of self-regulation has found that play activities involving pairs and small groups, which are characterized by high levels of collaboration and talk, are associated with high levels of self-regulation in preschool-aged children (Robson, 2016; O'Sullivan & Ring, 2016; Whitebread, Coltman, Jameson, & Lander, 2009). In many classroom activities, adults tend to assume the regulatory role, potentially reducing the children's opportunities to regulate their own interactions (Gray, 2013; Whitebread et al., 2009). Freely chosen play with peers, however, should be a core element of a curriculum which aims to nurture children's capacity to participate effectually in a community with a shared system of values and meanings (Frost et al., 2008). While freely chosen play with peers offers a unique context in which children develop important social skills, adult involvement in learning activities should not preclude children from practicing self-control, perspective taking, and collaboration. The idea of the co-constructed curriculum was, after all, at the heart of Dewey's philosophy (Frost et al., 2008).

Dewey believed there was no distinction between play and work for the young child (Dennis, 1970). The pedagogical practices we adopt, however, often encourage premature dichotomizing of play and learning (Howard, 2010). As Dewey proposed, play is the most meaningful learning context for the young child and uniquely fosters the dispositions and skills that are needed to engage in formal learning. His views are consistent with the contemporary view that high-quality early childhood education involves a delicate balance of free-play, guided-play (where play remains child-initiated but involves adults subtly guiding children's activity towards specific dimensions of learning), and playful structured activities (activities initiated by adults but are based on children's emerging interests and foster children's autonomy, control, and imagination; O'Sullivan & Ring, 2016; Weisberg, Kittredge, Hirsh-Pasek, Golinkoff, & Klahr, 2015). Freely-chosen play provides important opportunities for children to participate spontaneously in their social world and to engage in activities that are intrinsically motivating and meaningful to them. Dewey notably distinguished play from fooling, with the latter seen as more of an aimless and arbitrary endeavor (Dennis, 1970). This resonates with the view that just as play can be sustained and complex it can also be repetitive or stuck (Bodrova & Leong, 2015). Teachers have an obvious role in supporting children engaging in the type of play that is optimally challenging (O'Sullivan & Ring, 2016).

Dewey's non-binary position on play and work has important implications for learning activities that are more controlled by teachers. Learning in such contexts is clearly enhanced when children are afforded some freedom, when the task is meaningful and has a clear purpose, and when children have opportunities to learn collaboratively. A playful pedagogical approach, based on Dewey's principles, is in sharp contrast to an inflexible method that tightly controls learning, imposes external and inaccessible goals, relies on extrinsic rewards to encourage performance, and emphasizes individual performance (Dennis, 1970). Dewey's ideas are now more relevant than ever given that the learning agility considered fundamental to success in the 21st century is characterized by adaptability, creativity, innovation, and collaboration (Golinkoff & Hirsh-Pasek, 2016). In the earliest years of children's' learning, play is the context through which these emerging skills are most effectively nurtured. Those entrusted with responsibility for initial teacher education and continuing professional development will be well served by taking Dewey's lead and continuing to problematize, within their own practice, the pedagogical power of play (Frost et al., 2008). The concept of the laboratory school suggested by Dewey with its concern to locate educational practice within an empirical and theoretical framework provides a context within which to develop the teacher-as-researcher in early childhood education.

THE LABORATORY SCHOOL

Dewey's assertions on pedagogy and curriculum were grounded in action research. In the laboratory school established in 1884 by Dewey in the University of Chicago, the classroom was designed as a laboratory where teachers tested their ideas, methods, and values with the objective of improving both their own pedagogy and the child's learning (Pring, 2015). The aim of the laboratory school was to create a robust theoretical basis on which to build an educational practice and create a repository of critically grounded theory required of a true profession (Wirth, 1964). Linked to the university, its two main purposes were to allow teachers to exhibit, test, verify, and criticize educational theory and practice and thereby add to the corpus of emerging educational research (Mayhew & Edwards, 1936). It represented a radical departure from the principle that educational theory had been definitively established and required only further refinement for practice.

In his rejection of stimulus and response in favor of all members of a group having an equable opportunity to receive and take from each other, the role of the child and the teacher as co-constructors of knowledge emerged as central to the education practice advocated in the laboratory school (Dewey, 1916). Dewey was concerned with applying the principles implied in a democratic society to the enterprise of education, articulating a creative and responsive concept of democracy concerned with "the creation of a freer and more humane experience in which all share and to which all contribute" (Dewey, 1939, p. 4). Dewey conceptualized the school as an extension of the home and community, focused on the child's interests and including the child's voice (Pring, 2014).

The concept of the teacher-as-researcher is implicit in Dewey's belief that "the teacher is a learner, and the learner is without knowing it, a teacher" (Dewey, 1916, p. 160). Dewey promoted an empirical philosophy in advocating that all knowledge and understanding stem from experience in a democratic environment where children enjoyed the freedom to explore ideas and teachers had autonomy in exercising judgement (Dewey, 2002). The teacher is positioned between the child and the cultural inheritance embodied in the curriculum (Pring, 2014). The teacher's role is to link the child and the curriculum, not through transmitting the curriculum but rather through engaging in a process of inquiry, identifying the problem, formulating hypotheses, suggesting possible solutions and testing these experiences in practice with the learner. Dewey, it would appear, considered the teacher to be a scientist, continuously questioning, reviewing, reflecting on, and refining practice through an ongoing cycle of inquiry. Critically in the laboratory school and in collaboration with the university department to which it was linked, the teacher's role was to contribute to the development of an effective education system rather than simply to the practice within the four walls of his or her classroom.

THE EARLY CHILDHOOD TEACHER AS RESEARCHER

Despite Dewey's early insights and aspirations for the teaching profession as a self-evolving, knowledge-creating, democratic community of educational experts, somewhere along the way, the researching role of the teacher became more peripheral than essential, and the job of educational research was delegated to academic researchers. The loss of teachers' ownership of educational research has been lamented by researchers for years. Hargreaves (1996) identified the gap between educational researchers and teachers as the "fatal flaw" in educational research. Stenhouse (1975) cautioned against teachers being the "objects" of research and considered that teachers should be the researchers based on their privileged access to the data central to understanding the learning and teaching process. Unlike the collaborative relationship between Dewey's laboratory school and the university department where both parties collaboratively developed ideas and generated educational knowledge together, one-way, hierarchical relationships have developed between schools and universities; the school is seen as the place for teaching and the university is seen as the place for researching.

In recent years, both internationally and nationally, a number of initiatives have been taken to rebuild research partnerships between educational researchers and teachers (Darling-Hammond, 2005; Malone & Smith, 2010; McLaughlin & Black-Hawkins, 2007). In examining the effectiveness of these partnerships in the context of their own School University Partnership for Educational Research (SUPER) project, McLaughlin and Black-Hawkins (2007) noted that these partnerships generally involved teachers, not academics, deciding upon the types of research questions that they wished to address and how the findings should affect practice within their own schools. Meanwhile, researchers provided the settings with a range of research expertise, training, and resources to support settings in their inquiry activities. While this project was extremely beneficial for the settings involved with the researchers, dissemination of research findings beyond those intimately involved in the research process was identified as a significant challenge for university–school research partnerships. Led by a Higher-Education Consortium in Ireland, REX is a national, online infrastructure, developed in 2016, for supporting collaborative educational research sharing within the Irish context (REX Consortium, 2016). REX is a web-based platform, providing a means for student–teacher researchers; established researchers and practicing educational professionals to find one another and link research need with capability. REX enables teachers and student teachers to build their own research identities through their researcher membership profiles and facilitates collaboration with other academic and teacher researchers by providing a point of contact for those seeking research partners and helping to identify those already working in complementary areas. Through REX, educators have posed important real-world questions for research and have worked collaboratively with higher education researchers and teams of supervised students to conduct meaningful research, which has had an immediate impact on the lives and learning of children (McGann, Ryan, McMahon, & Hall, 2018). Utilizing technology, the REX model has the potential to transport Dewey's laboratory school into the 21st century through providing a blueprint for fostering research relationships, and scaffolding teacher research.

Additionally, significant attempts have been made in teacher education internationally to reestablish research as a core component of initial teacher education. Researchers suggest that the impact of engaging teachers and student teachers in the research process has been overwhelmingly positive (Cochran-Smith & Lytle, 2009; Coleman, 2007). Coleman (2007) attempted to explain the sense of confidence and empowerment experienced by teachers following engagement with research by suggesting that when teachers conduct their own research they often include their own perspectives in the process, which increases their sense of ownership within the profession of teaching because they feel that they are now active contributors to the field of education.

The confidence, empowerment, and sense of ownership inspired by teacher engagement with research can be juxtaposed with teachers' perceptions that they are under siege from surveillance and accountability agendas (Lingard, Martino, & Rezai-Rashti, 2013; Sahlberg, 2010). The use of assessment data as a tool to evaluate teachers has led to an untrusting relationship between teachers and data (Hargreaves & Braun, 2013). Rather than assessment data being mined enthusiastically by teachers to answer their questions, as envisaged by Dewey, assessment data has come to be resented by teachers (Roberts-Holmes, 2015; Shirley & Hargreaves, 2006). Assessment data is seen as a tool of external accountability rather than a tool for professional responsibility. A Deweyan perspective would advocate that early childhood teachers should be using assessment data as part of regular cycles of inquiry, examining, and improving their own practice, learning from the learners, for the learners, and for the wider teaching profession. In this way, data is not the toxic tool of accountability but rather is the antidote to external accountability agendas as it enables the teaching profession to be self-regulating and professionally responsible. Early childhood teachers are continuously collecting data on children's learning. Observations of children's learning progressions are documented daily. By incorporating this invaluable data into the inquiry cycle, early childhood teachers, particularly if they work collaboratively, can offer insights into the myriad of educational questions and problems that have eluded researchers and practitioners for years. Early childhood teachers need support to move beyond using assessment data as an instrument for evaluation and to using it as an instrument for research. From this Deweyan perspective, teaching should be research-informed, data-informed practice.

Dewey promoted the development of teaching as a profession and rejected the apprenticeship model in favor of teaching having a distinct and broad knowledge base, which is now recognized in the context of the emergence of teaching as a profession (Wirth, 1964). Following an extensive literature review, Sexton identified the eight components of teaching as a profession detailed in Figure 10.3.

In relation to early childhood teachers, two of the components related to high levels of remuneration and high status/prestige continue to present challenges in terms of poor working conditions and grossly inadequate remuneration for what is increasingly recognized as a highly complex role requiring distinct competencies (Moss, 2016; OECD, 2017a). Moss advised that addressing this issue is firstly a political and ethical choice related to how the work is understood and what values society subscribes to and prioritizes.

The concept of teacher-as-researcher can be linked to the profession having a recognized knowledge base, displaying a commitment to ongoing professional development, engaging in intellectually based/extended training, exhibiting a spirit of altruism, the role of personal responsibility, and adhering to a code of ethics and teacher-autonomy.

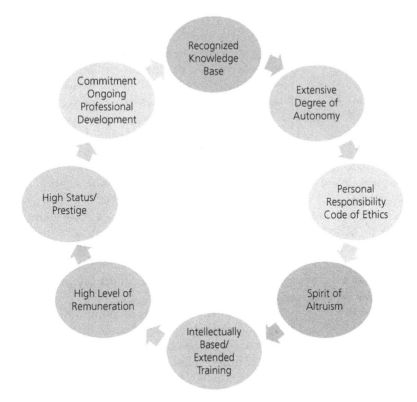

Figure 11.3 The eight components of teaching as a profession adopted from Sexton (2007).

In this era of globalization, competition, and accountability, external pressures are pushing teaching from a democratic profession to a technocratic one. Without research, teachers are without armor; armor to defend themselves from forces pushing agendas that are far removed from the needs of young children, such as the "schoolification" movement. As a knowledge-creating and evidence-collating profession, early childhood teachers are well positioned to be the custodians of a child-centred approach to education.

CONCLUSION

In the current climate of accountability, where the global education reform movement promotes a focus on core subjects, standardized testing, corporate management models, a reduction in teacher autonomy and the intensification of children's early years' experiences, the development of critically grounded early childhood education theory upon which to build practice and ensure quality provision is essential. The "schoolification" of the early years is symptomatic of the erosion of autonomy amongst teachers. In a top–down approach, early childhood teachers are continuously told what to do by political powers, national curriculum bodies, academic researchers, managers, and parents. Teachers should not be seen as mere implementers of the ideas of others (Breneseleović & Krnjaja, 2013) but should be encouraged to be creative, innovative experimenters as Dewey envisaged. As knowledge building professionals, early childhood teachers are better positioned to reclaim decision-making authority, to demonstrate and articulate the value of play-based pedagogical approaches and to justify co-constructed curricula to parents, managers, and supervisory bodies. Initial teacher education programmes have a central role to play if teacher research is to become embedded in the teaching role. University and practice links are essential for high-quality educational research that will have a real-world impact for early childhood education. Additionally, the authors suggest that promoting the role of the early childhood teacher-as-researcher has the potential to contribute to the professionalization of the early childhood teacher and move it to the top of the policy agenda. Harnessing Dewey's concept of the laboratory school and positioning the role of the early childhood teacher as researcher firmly in the early childhood quality agenda is imperative to ensure that teachers are in a position to interrogate and engage in data-informed, child-centred practice, with which to disrupt the prevailing zeitgeist, which is frequently driven by competing economic, political, and social imperatives rather than child-led pedagogy. Critically harnessing the concept of the laboratory school presents a much-much needed opportunity to highlight the importance of supporting early childhood teachers in engaging in valid interpretations, pedagogical decisions and actions that provide for effective instructional practices, and optimal outcomes for all children in the early years.

REFERENCES

Almon, J., & Miller, E. (2011). *The crisis in early education. A research-based case for more play and less pressure.* Annapolis, MD: Alliance for Childhood. Retrieved from http://habitot.org/museum/pdf/play_research/Crisis_EarlyEd.pdf

Bassok, D., Latham, S., & Rorem, A. (2016). Is kindergarten the new first grade. *AERA Open, 1*(4), 1–31. doi:10.1177/2332858415616358

Bergen, D. (2009). Play as the learning medium for future scientists, mathematicians, and engineers. *American Journal of Play, 1*(4), 413–428.

Blaustein, M. (2005.) See, hear, touch: The basics of learning readiness. *Beyond the Journal: Young Children on the Web.* Retrieved from https://pdfs.semanticscholar.org/39d0/553a5134e516044e021a2930247a761b7db5.pdf

Bodrova, E., & Leong, D. J. (2015). Vygotskian and post-Vygotskian views on children's play. *American Journal of Play, 7*(3), 371–388. Retrieved from https://files.eric.ed.gov/fulltext/EJ1070266.pdf

Breneselović, P., & Krnjaja, Ž. (2013). Transforming preschool teacher's role: From implementer toward researcher. *Journal of Faculty of Educational Sciences, 46*(1), 111–126.

Broadhead, P. (2010). Cooperative play and learning from nursery to year one. In P. Broadhead, J. Howard, & E. Wood (Eds.), *Play and learning in the early years: From research to practice* (pp. 43–60). London, England: SAGE.

Bronfenbrenner, U. (1979). *The ecology of human development.* Cambridge, MA: Harvard University Press.

Carlsson-Paige, N. McLaughlin, G. B., & Almon, J. W. (2015). *Reading instruction in kindergarten: Little to gain and much to lose.* Maryland, MD: Alliance for Childhood. Retrieved from https://deyproject.files.wordpress.com/2015/01/readinginkindergarten_online-1.pdf

Clark, A., & Moss, P. (2011). *Listening to young children: The mosaic approach* (2nd ed.). Oxford, England: Praeger.

Cochran-Smith, M., & Lytle, S. L. (2009). *Inquiry as stance: Practitioner research for the next generation.* New York, NY: Teachers College Press.

Cole, M., John-Steiner, S., Scribner, S, & Sourberman, E. (Eds.). (1978). *L. S. Vygotsky: Mind in society. The development of higher psychological processes.* Cambridge, MA: Harvard University Press.

Coleman, A. (2007). Leaders as researchers: Supporting practitioner enquiry through the NCSL research associate programme. *Educational Management Administration and Leadership, 35*(4), 479–497. doi:10.1177/1741143207002429

Darling-Hammond, L. (2005). Educating the new educator: Teacher education and the future of democracy. *The New Educator, 1*(1), 1–18. doi:10.1080/15476880490441379

Dennis, L. (1970). Play in Dewey's theory of education. *Young Children, 25*(4), 230–235. Retrieved from http://www.jstor.org/stable/42643331

Dewey, J. (1910). *The child and the curriculum: Including the school and society*, New York, NY: Cosimo. (Originally published 1902)

Dewey, J. (1916). *Democracy and education*. New York, NY: The Free Press.

Dewey, J. (1939). Creative democracy. The task before us. Retrieved from https://www.philosophie.uni-muenchen.de/studium/das_fach/warum_phil_ueberhaupt/dewey_creative_democracy.pdf

Dockett, S., & Perry, B. (2002). Who's ready for what? Young children starting school. *Contemporary Issues in Early Childhood, 3*, 67–89. doi:10.2304/ciec.2002.3.1.9

Edwards, C., Gandini, L., & Forman, G. (Eds.). (2012). *The hundred languages of children* (3rd ed.). Oxford, England: Praeger.

European Commission/EACEA/Eurydice (2017). *The structure of the European education systems 2017/18: Schematic diagrams: Eurydice facts and* figures. Retrieved from https://publications.europa.eu/en/publication-detail/-/publication/0e54460d-d585-11e7-a5b9-01aa75ed71a1/language-en/format-PDF/source-53918966

Frost, J. L., Wortham, S., & Reifel, S. (2008). *Play and child development* (3rd ed.). Upper Saddle River, NJ: Merrill Prentice Hall.

Girard, L. C., Pingault, J. P., Doyle, O., Falissard, B., & Tremblay, R. E. (2017). Expressive language and prosocial behaviour in early childhood: Longitudinal associations in the UK millennium cohort study. *European Journal of Developmental Psychology, 14*(4), 381–398. doi:10.1080/17405629.2016.1215300

Golinkoff, R. M., & Hirsh-Pasek, K. (2016). *Becoming brilliant: What science tells us about raising successful children*. Washington, DC: APA LifeTools.

Graue, E. (2009). Reimagining kindergarten. *School Administrator, 66*(10), 10–15. Retrieved from http://dm.education.wisc.edu/megraue/intellcont/Graue%20reimagining%20K%20School%20Administrator-1.pdf

Graue, E., & Johnson, E. (2011). Reclaiming assessment through accountability that is "just right." *Teachers College Record, 113*(8), 1827–1862.

Gray, P. (2013). *Free to learn: why unleashing the instinct to play will make our children happier, more self-reliant and better students for life*. New York, NY: Basic Books.

Hargreaves, D. H. (1996). *Teaching as a research-based profession: Possibilities and prospects*. London, England: Teacher Training Agency.

Hargreaves, A., & Braun, H., (2013). *Data-driven improvement and accountability*. Boulder, CO: National Education Policy Center. Retrieved from https://nepc.colorado.edu/publication/data-driven-improvement-accountability

Heckman, J. (2013, September 14). The great divide. Lifelines for poor children. *The New York Times*. Retrieved from http://opinionator.blogs.nytimes.com/2013/09/14

House, R. (Ed.). (2011). *Too much, too soon. Early learning and the erosion of childhood*. Hawthorn, NJ: Hawthorn Press.

Howard, J. (2010). Making the most of play in the early years: The importance of children's perceptions. In P. Broadhead, J. Howard, & E. Wood (Eds.), *Play and learning in the early years* (pp. 145–160). London, England: SAGE.

Howard, J., & McInnes, K. (2013). *The essence of play: A practice companion for professionals working with children and young people*. Abingdon, England: Routledge.

Jones, E. (2012). The emergence of emergent curriculum. *Young Children, 67*(2), 66–68. Retrieved from https://issuu.com/naeyc/docs/heritage_v67n2_0312_0

Karpov, Y. V. (2005). *The neo-Vygotskian approach to child development.* Cambridge, MA: Cambridge University Press.

Katz, L. G. (2010). A developmental approach to the curriculum in the early years. In S. Smidt (Ed.), *Key issues in early years education: A guide for students and practitioners* (2nd ed., pp. 11–17). Abingdon, England: Routledge.

Lingard, B., Martino, W., & Rezai-Rashti, G. (2013). Testing regimes, accountabilities, and education policy: Commensurate global and national developments. *Journal of Education Policy, 28*(5), 539–556. doi:10.1080/02680939.2013.820042

López Boo, F., Caridad Araujo, M., & Tomé, R. (2016). *How is child care quality measured?* Washington, DC: Inter-American Development Bank. Retrieved from https://publications.iadb.org/bitstream/handle/11319/7432/How-is-child-care-quality-measured.pdf

Malone, A., & Smith, G. (2010). Developing schools as professional learning communities: The TL21 experience. *Online Submission, 7*(9), 106–114. Retrieved from https://eric.ed.gov/?id=ED514798

Mayhew, K., & Edwards, A. (1936). *The Dewey School. The laboratory school of the University of Chicago 1896–1903.* New York, NY: D. Appleton-Century.

McClelland, M. M., Acock, A. C., Piccinin, A., Rhea, S. A., & Stallings, M. C. (2013). Relations between preschool attention span-persistence and age 25 educational outcomes. *Early Childhood Research Quarterly, 28*(2), 314–324. doi:10.1016/j.ecresq.2012.07.008

McGann, M., Ryan, M. C., McMahon, J., & Hall, T. (2018). *REX: The Research expertise exchange. Cultivation of an online community of practice for educational researchers.* (Manuscript in preparation). www.researchexpertiseexchange.com

McLaughlin, C., & Black-Hawkins, K. (2007). School-university partnerships for educational research—distinctions, dilemmas and challenges. *The Curriculum Journal, 18*, 327–341. doi:10.1080/09585170701589967

Melhuish, E. (2014). The impact of early childhood education and care on improved wellbeing. In *"If you could do one thing" Nine local actions to reduce health inequalities* (pp. 33–43). London, England: British Academy. Retrieved from http://ro.uow.edu.au/cgi/viewcontent.cgi?article=2641&context=sspapers

Melhuish, E., Ereky-Stevens, K., Petrogiannis, K., Ariescu, A., Penderi, E., Rentzou, K.,...Leseman, P. (2015). A review of research on the effects of early childhood Education and Care (ECEC) upon child development. CARE project; Curriculum Quality Analysis and Impact Review of European Early Childhood Education and Care (ECEC).

Mistry, J., Rogoff, B., & Herman, H. (2009). What is the meaning of meaningful purpose in children's remembering? Istomina revisited. *Mind, Culture, and Society, 8*, 28–41. doi:10.1207/S15327884MCA0801_03

Morris, P. (2016). *Education policy, cross-national tests of pupil achievement, and the pursuit of world-class schooling.* London, England: UCL Institute of Education Press.

Moss, P. (2016). Structures, understandings and discourses: Possibilities for re-envisioning the early childhood worker. *Contemporary Issues in Early Childhood, 17*(3), 343–351. Retrieved from https://doi.org/10.2304/ciec.2006.7.1.30

Moss, P., Dahlberg, G., Grieshaber, S., Mantovani, S., May, H., Pence, A., ... Vandenbroeck, M. (2016). The organisation for economic co-operation and development's international early learning study: Opening for debate and contestation. *Contemporary Issues in Early Childhood, 17,* 343–351. doi:10.1177/1463949116661126

Organisation for Economic Co-Operation and Development. (2017a). *Starting strong 2017: Key OECD indicators on early childhood education and care.* Paris, France: Author. Retrieved from https://read.oecd-ilibrary.org/education/starting-strong-2017_9789264276116-en#page3

Organisation for Economic Co-operation and Development. (2017b). *International early learning and child well-being study* (IELS). Retrieved from http://www.oecd.org/education/school/international-early-learning-and-child-well-being-study.htm

O'Sullivan, L. (2016). Social pretend play and self-regulation. *Early Education Journal, 80,* 12–15.

O'Sullivan, L., & Ring, E. (2016). Supporting a playful approach to learning in the early years: Early years education-focused inspections: A license to play. *Childlinks, 1,* 2–7.

Piaget, J. (1962). *Play Dreams and Imitation in Childhood* (C. Gattegno, Trans.). New York, NY: WW Norton.

Pring, R. (2014). *John Dewey,* New York, NY: Bloomsbury Academic.

Pring, R. (2015). *Philosophy of educational research* (3rd ed.). New York, NY: Bloomsbury Academic.

Ring, E., & O'Sullivan, L. (2018). Dewey: A panacea for the schoolification epidemic. *Education, 4*(4), 402–412. doi:10.1080/03004279.2018.1445474

Ring, E., Mhic Mhathúna, M., Moloney, M., Hayes, N., Breatnach, D., Stafford, P., ... Ozonyia, M. (2016). An examination of concepts of school-readiness among parents *and educators in Ireland.* Dublin, Ireland: Department of Children and Youth Affairs. Retrieved from https://www.dcya.gov.ie/documents/early years/20170118AnExaminationOfConceptsOfSchoolReadinessAmongParents EducatorsIreland.PDF

Research Expertise Exchange Consortium. (2016). *Research expertise exchange.* Retrieved from https://www.researchexpertiseexchange.com/

Roberts-Holmes, G. (2015). The "datafication" of early years pedagogy: "If the teaching is good, the data should be good and if there's bad teaching, there is bad data." *Journal of Education Policy, 30*(3), 302–315. doi:10.1080/02680939.2014.924561

Robson, S. (2016). Self-regulation, metacognition and child- and adult-initiated activity: Does it matter who initiates the task? *Early Child Development and Care, 186,* 764–784. doi:10.1080/03004430.2015.1057581

Sahlberg, P. (2010). Rethinking accountability in a knowledge society. *Journal of Educational Change, 11*(1), 45–61. Retrieved from https://pasisahlberg.com/wp-content/uploads/2013/01/Rethinking-accountability-JEC-20101.pdf

Sexton, M. (2007) Evaluating teaching as a profession: Implementation of a research study for the work of the Teaching Council. *Irish Educational Studies, 26*(1), 79–105.

Shirley, D., & Hargreaves, A. (2006). Data-driven to distraction. *Education Week, 26*(6), 32–33. Retrieved from https://www.edweek.org/ew/articles/2006/10/04/06hargreaves.h26.html

Stenhouse, L. (1975). *An introduction to curriculum research and development.* London, England: Heinemann.

Sylva, K., Bruner, J., & Genova, P. (1976). The role of play in the problem-solving of children 3–5 years old. In J. Bruner, A. Jolly, & K. Sylva (Eds.), *Play: Its role in development and evolution* (pp. 25–42). New York, NY: Basic Books.

Thomas, L., Howard, J., & Miles, G. (2006). The effectiveness of playful practice for learning in the early years. *The Psychology of Education Review, 30,* 52–58.

Urban, M., Robson, S., & Scacchi, V. (2017). *Review of occupational role profiles in Ireland in early childhood education and care.* Dublin, Ireland: Department of Education and Skills. Retrieved from http://www.education.ie/en/publications/education-reports/final-review-of-occupational-role-profiles-in-early-childhood-education-and-care.pdf

Weisberg, D. S., Kittredge, A. K., Hirsh-Pasek, K., Golinkoff, R. M., & Klahr, D. (2015). Making play work for education. *Phi Delta Kappan, 96*(8), 8–13. doi:10.1177/0031721715583955

Whitebread, D. (2015). Young children learning and early years teaching. In D. Whitebread & P. Coltman (Eds.), *Teaching and learning in the early years* (4th ed., pp. 1–21). London, England: Routledge.

Whitebread, D., Coltman, P., Jameson, H., & Lander, R. (2009). Play, cognition and self-regulation: What exactly are children learning when they learn through play? *Educational and Child Psychology, 26*(2), 40–52.

Whitebread, D., Jameson, H., & Basilio, M. (2015a). Play beyond the foundation stage. In J. Moyles (Ed.), *The excellence of play* (3rd ed., pp. 84–93). Buckinghamshire, England: Open University Press.

Whitebread, D., Kuvalja, M., & O'Connor, A. (2015b). *Quality in early childhood education: An international review and guide for policy makers.* Report for the World Summit for Education. Dohar, Qatar: WISE. Retrieved from https://www.wise-qatar.org/sites/default/files/asset/document/wise-research-7-cambridge-11_17.pdf

Whitebread, D., & O'Sullivan, L. (2012). Preschool children's social-pretend play: Supporting the development of metacommunication, metacognition and self-regulation. *International Journal of Play, 1*(2), 197–213. doi:10.1080/21594937.2012.693384

Wien, C. A. (2008). *Emergent curriculum in the primary school: Interpreting the Reggio Emilia approach in schools.* New York, NY: Teachers' College Press.

Wilhelmsen, G. B. (2016). School starters' vision: An educational approach. *Improving Schools, 19,* 141–153. doi:10.1177/1365480216651523

Wirth, A. G. (1964) *John Dewey as educator: His design for work in education (1894–1904).* New York, NY: Wiley.

World Health Organization and United Nations Children's Fund. (2012). *Early childhood development and disability: A discussion paper.* Geneva, Switzerland: World Health Organization. Retrieved from http://apps.who.int/iris/bitstream/

handle/10665/75355/9789241504065_eng.pdf;jsessionid=CB1317D2801C4 55DB4D956FF91B4B5C6?sequence=1

Zingoni, S. (2014). Protagoinists from the outset. In A. Fortunati (Ed.), *San miniato's approach to the education of children* (pp. 37–76), Pisa, Italy: EdizioniETs.

PART IV

CONCLUSION

CHAPTER 11

CHILD DEVELOPMENT LABORATORY SCHOOLS

Contemporary Research and Future Directions

Olivia N. Saracho

Throughout the previous century, college and university institutions have established child development laboratory schools. In the early 1900s, they were initially considered to be sites for the recent discipline of child study but their purposes have progressed gradually. They also have assumed a fundamental function in promoting teaching, research, and service (such as outreach/engagement practice) in child development and early childhood education. However, a lot of them had to struggle for their survival when economic periods turned out to be problematic. Several extended operating programs were discontinued (Barbour & McBride, 2017).

Child development laboratory schools differ from preschool programs. They are in small colleges and major universities but have an indefinite future. Initially, the child development laboratory schools were models to prepare preservice teachers and their role extended toward the end of the century. In 1883, Colonel Frances W. Parker, who headed the Cook County

Contemporary Perspectives on Research on Child Development Laboratory Schools in Early Childhood Education,
pages 197–212
Copyright © 2019 by Information Age Publishing
197

Normal School of Chicago, stressed research and the study of teaching. Before long the Horace Mann School at Teachers College in New York City was established for the same purpose (Page & Page, 1981). In 1896, John Dewey initiated an experimental school at the University of Chicago to test concepts and educate children. His innovative philosophical work on pragmatism gave birth to the laboratory school, where Dewey and his colleagues founded a "community of inquiry" (Durst, 2010). Dewey considered the laboratory school a perfect environment to conduct educational research. His purpose for the laboratory school was to examine theory and increase the knowledge of teaching and learning. Since his interest did not include a practice school for preparing teachers, he focused his laboratory school in generating innovative educational philosophies that could be tested and replicated in several natural situations in the public schools (Provenzo, 1979) as part of the teachers' professional development. Professional development was rooted within teacher research that was intertwined with children's studies. Dewey and others formed communities of practice, cooperatively investigating each other's teacher inquiries, and implementing a sequence of procedures as their guide (Given et al., 2009; Goldhaber, 2007).

When young children are part of the academic world that focuses on higher learning, they need to be provided with the best conceivable education, which should be based on current researched instructional practices and preeminent innovative educational methodologies. The child development laboratory schools would have master teachers model their instructional abilities supporting research and inquiry with children and skillfully introducing observers, partakers, and preservice teachers to the well-known conceivable educational theory and practice.

THE PREPARATION OF TEACHERS IN THE CHILD DEVELOPMENT LABORATORY SCHOOLS

The university child development laboratory schools developed a well-defined educational mission to prepare early childhood teachers and to enhance their teaching. They have the best facilities for students and faculty to observe and conduct research. Academic departments can make it convenient for faculty and other experienced early childhood professionals to cooperate; to enhance their knowledge about young children's experiences in initial education; to examine philosophical teaching and learning procedures; and to tryout innovative methods of teaching, learning, and working with families.

Since the purpose of colleges of education in preparing the country's teachers continues to be disputed, the existence of child development laboratory schools is challenged. The latest issues in teacher education can affect the future of laboratory schools. For example, colleges of education are being confronted about their requirement of a huge number of hours of clinical and field experiences for preservice teachers. Such field experiences require them to devote approximately 300 hours observing teachers in the classroom and learning instructional techniques before student teaching. There have been plenty of debates about such "early field experiences." Typically, the value of the field experiences is based on any concerns pertaining to the convenience of the child development laboratory schools to the location to the university grounds, the requirements for the college students' field experiences, supervision of these field experiences, and the absence of well-prepared teachers in the field (Applegate & Lasley, 1982; Erdman, 1983). The solutions for these field experiences depend on the students' convenience to their assigned classrooms (Ross, Raines, Cervetti, & Dillow, 1980) in the schools. The type of environment and the circumstances determine the quality of the field experiences instead of some arranged effort between the university and the host school (Bonar, 1992).

The child development laboratory schools are in the exclusive position to meet the required number of hours of early field experiences. The specified excess of field experiences that are mandatory in many states for teacher education challenge the universities' capability to control the value and efficiency of the field placements. The university faculty can assume the responsibility for managing the college students' field experiences in the teacher preparation program in the child development laboratory schools, which is one of their major responsibilities (Bonar, 1992).

The concern to improve the quality of the field experiences has reintroduced a concern in the child development laboratory schools. This issue affects their structure or disposition. Haberman (1985) predicted that laboratory schools would become unique mission schools mainly to present information of applied research on the day to day complications of teachers and education. Nielsen (1986) perceived that the child development laboratory schools would be the forerunner in improving the quality of the field experiences that was missing in the majority of the college programs. Goodlad (1980) thought that nearly all child development laboratory schools (a) were in a stationary position and (b) required a restructure of some energetic, avant-garde child development laboratory schools to lead transformation. A professional organization can provide some guidance.

CHILD DEVELOPMENT LABORATORY SCHOOLS: PROFESSIONAL ORGANIZATION

A professional organization can assist in promoting research, the preparation of teachers, and young children's education. The National Association of Laboratory Schools (NALS) is an organization for child development laboratory schools that are housed in colleges and universities throughout the country. The NALS members are faculty (university professors and practitioners) working in campus based schools. Most member schools in NALS are comparable because they have a higher education orientation and are campus based. However, they differ in the way they function based on the needs and orientation of their parent institution. Several schools are entirely run by (a) higher education faculty, (b) certified public school teachers who have special agreements, and (c) both certified public school personnel and university faculty working jointly under an agreed leadership plan (Ulm, Buck, Creek, Tobin, & Miller, 1989).

All NALS schools are responsible for preparing teachers in a higher education environment. The university professors and practitioners in child development laboratory schools offer preservice clinical teaching for the effective training of future teachers. The NALS schools are responsible for clinical teaching experiences, research, curriculum development, and staff training. Therefore, they educate both children and prospective teachers, which provide the children enrolled in these schools with an outstanding education (Ulm et al., 1989).

Modification of NALS

After more than 5 decades, NALS became an international organization. Therefore, the National Association of Laboratory Schools changed its name to the International Association of Laboratory Schools (IALS). The name IALS broadly offers an all-encompassing definition of child development laboratory schools to meet all of their extensive different configurations. Certainly, these are modified considerably to adapt to all the situations in which the schools are established. Thus,

> A lab school may be an institution formally integrated into a university department, such as the one founded by John Dewey. This is the case for the majority of North American and Japanese laboratory schools, such as the Shinwa Kindergarten School of Kobe Shinwa Women's University, recently affiliated with the IALS. (The Conversation, 2017, n.p.)

This term IALS includes their current global membership and goals for future development as well as their extremely far-reaching definition of "laboratory schools" that includes both campus-based schools and those that have various university associations, such as charter schools, professional development schools, child study institutes, research and development schools, and so forth (IALS, 2018). Its global membership places IALS in a position to develop international partnerships.

International Partnerships

Establishing successful, important international partnerships is a primary responsibility of a wide-ranging education for schoolchildren. Learning about different cultures and beliefs offers a more affluent and full meaning of educational knowledge for school children growing up in a different part of the world (Brinson, 2012). All over the world, child development laboratory schools have launched contacts with each other. Most of them are members of the International Association of Laboratory and University Affiliated Schools (IALS). All are involved in practices of research, teacher preparation, curriculum development, professional development, and educational enquiry that (a) support the members' schools and (b) advocate the promotion of all of the children's learning. Throughout the years, the laboratory schools have transformed to include the distinctive needs of the teaching professionals and have frequently contributed to the enhancement of teaching (IALS, 2018) through the following:

- *Research.* School conducts or collaborates in research that upholds a lab school's important role in education.
- *Educational Experimentation.* The school has a solid background allowing teachers to carry out innovative projects.
- *Teacher Training.* The school solidly provides mentorship and assists student teachers during their field experience.
- *Professional Development.* There is a solid institutional plan regarding professional development for teachers and staff.
- *Curriculum Development.* School designs and publishes its own curriculum for teaching and learning (IALS, 2018)

Typically, IALS laboratory schools' allegiance has been to support the preparation of teachers in order that they can provide excellent educational programs to young children. These child development laboratory schools are associated with a college or university for explicit reasons that go beyond the range of established public and private schools. When examining the mandate for international education, internationalization, and intercultural competence, Emmert and Pearson (2007) support the efforts of IALs with this statement: "International Education comprises educational efforts that infuse globally oriented content, perspectives, and experiences into all levels of education as a means to increase awareness and understanding of the diverse world in which we live" (p. 68). This international collaboration by IALS is aimed to achieve this undertaking. IALS continues to be an organization that combines the researchers' skills to recommend an "evidence-based" pedagogy (The Conversation, 2017).

CHILD DEVELOPMENT LABORATORY SCHOOLS:
A BLUEPRINT FOR THE FUTURE

Future child development laboratory schools need to focus on increasing their research productivity. Goodlad (1980) proposes that they provide research and development support for the college of education. Keislar (1980) considers that they are in a unique position to support high quality research. Nielsen (1986) views them to be involved in carrying out action research that can be freely distributed to the education community and to offer an ideal way to form collegiality between the child development laboratory schools and college of education faculties.

The child development laboratory schools faculty encountered unique situations. Nielsen (1986) insisted that child development laboratory schools' teachers should have the equivalent rank at the university as their college of education contemporaries, which should include sufficient paraprofessional and equitable assistance. In return, they must be outstanding teachers who are willing to demonstrate effective methods and move forward the boundaries of knowledge (Bonar, 1992). Master teachers, college, and university professors would be comparable colleagues at the child development laboratory school. The professors would expertly combine their classroom teaching with the preservice teachers' all-embracing observation and participation at the laboratory school. In addition, the professors would communicate the contemporary and important research with the research faculty (VanTil, 1969).

Future child development laboratory schools need to make numerous changes in configuration (Bonar, 1992; Goodlad, 1980; Hendrick, 1980; Nielsen, 1986). Hendrick (1980) indicated that child development laboratory schools must rationalize their presence by offering services that were usually lacking in the public schools. Goodlad (1980) reviewed the purposes of laboratory schools, which included to (a) educate the school children, (b) create fresh and groundbreaking practices, (c) conduct research to develop educational theory, (d) prepare teachers, and (e) provide inservice education to experienced teachers. Nielsen (1986) added that an effective instructional program should consider multicultural students and settings to be all-inclusive and deliver a widespread variety of programs. It needs to offer excellent amenities, configurations, and perspectives. Keislar (1980) determined that for the most part child development laboratory schools have fallen short in engaging in methodical research or frequently the studies resemble the present trend in education. Nearly all of the child development laboratory schools seem to lack research on longitudinal studies about the disposition of teaching and learning similar to Dewey's classical paradigm, even if this has been integrated in their three-part mission statement.

MISSION STATEMENTS IN CONTEMPORARY UNIVERSITIES

The future of the child development laboratory school in the United States depends on the institutions' goals and missions. It is important for institutions to determine the purpose of the child development laboratory school in teacher education. According to Carnahan and Doyle (2012), it is reasonable to associate the mission and activities of the laboratory schools with "the overall aims of the sponsoring college" (p. 1). Bonar (1992) suggests the following considerations:

- Is the child development laboratory school expected to be a research center? If so, what type of research should be conducted?
- Is the child development laboratory school expected to be a model of excellent practice or an initiator of innovative practices?
- Is the child development laboratory school expected to prepare better teachers with advanced clinical practices?
- Is the child development laboratory school expected to offer staff development for other schools? If so, will it be an example for others to pursue?

The child development laboratory school is in an excellent position to accomplish its mission in the 21st century. These are institutions that are energetically involved in solving the families and educators' frequent problems and dedicated to contributing to the world. In addition, they can establish a situation for global citizenship, leadership, meaningful service, and an introduction to diversity (Carnahan & Doyle, 2012).

The mission statements for most child development laboratory schools usually resemble each other. They usually require their students to: (a) experience and obtain a liberal education, (b) influence the world, (c) become socially responsible, and (d) become dependable citizens (Meacham, 2008). They emphasize the significance of progressing based on a mission statement as it assists the laboratory schools to be "focused, productive, and energized" (Carnahan & Doyle, 2012, p. 2). McDonald (2007) states that

> ...a clear, motivating organizational mission helps an organization to focus its attention on those innovations that will most likely support the accomplishment of that mission. Such a mission also creates a climate in which innovations are given a fair chance to succeed. As a result, (organizations) with clear, motivating missions tend to be more innovative. (p. 256)

However, Taylor and Morphew (2010) found that most colleges and universities have more than one published mission statement, which can lead to confusion. For instance, Wang, Gibson, Salinasm, Solis, and Slate (2007) compared the thematic differences in mission statements between 4-year public institutions and 2-year colleges. Mission statements of 34 four-year and 68 two-year colleges in the State of Texas were examined. They identified and compared themes in their mission statements to establish their similarities and differences. They found 15 themes: leadership, citizenship, cultural diversity, life-long learning, excellence in teaching and research, creativity, critical thinking, academic achievement, collaboration and partnership, vocational and technical skills, access to higher education, academic readiness and skill development, student services, community focus, and technology. Themes differed between the two levels of Texas higher education institutions. Four-year institutions focused on (a) excellence in teaching, (b) research, and (c) leadership, whereas 2-year colleges focused on open-access and vocational training.

Three-Part Mission Statement

After more than nine decades since their beginning, the majority of the child development laboratory schools at colleges and universities continue to flourish and achieve

> a three-part mission: research (generating knowledge about child development), education (preparing teachers, therapists, and other child and family clinicians), and service (disseminating evidence-based information about child development and childrearing to parents and the general public). (Elicker & Barbour, 2012, p. 139)

Demonstration programs associated with teacher education normal schools have historically modified their mission (Buck, Hymel, McDonald, Martin, & Rodgers, 1991), whereas many child development laboratory schools have continuously retained an equal value on all three parts of their mission (Osborn, 1991).

Currently, these child development laboratory schools have the same mission but differ in their emphasis on research, teaching, and service (McBride et al., 2012). They have placed a different level of emphasis for training and research. Such three-part mission functions as the basis for child development laboratory programs, and guides all phases of their services and activities. In this mission, child development programs have assumed the responsibility to function as a: (a) setting to prepare prospective teachers in child development and early childhood education; (b) setting to conduct research on several facets of child development and early childhood education; and (c) model program/leadership program for the local, state, and national early childhood communities. The concentration on this three part mission has assisted child development laboratory programs' staff members to assume important responsibilities in communicating the interconnections between theory, research, and practice in child development and early childhood education.

In 1983 the Steering Committee of the National Organization of Child Development Laboratory Schools (NOCDLS) developed a nationwide report to help administrators and staff in child development laboratory schools to be kept up-to-date about theory and practice. It surveyed administrators in child development laboratory schools nationwide (Anderson, 1992; Ulm et al., 1989). The 1993 *Membership Directory of the National Organization of Child Development Laboratory Schools* (NOCDLS, 1993) indicated that most of its programs stated that they adopted all three parts of this mission. It was unclear if the programs actually included all three parts of this mission, which has caused doubt among their sponsors (McBride, 1996; Townley & Zeece, 1991). At the international level there are endorsements to strengthen the relationship between research and teaching.

According to Carnahan and Doyle (2012), earlier the National Association of Laboratory Schools (NALS) established a set of criteria for the mission of laboratory schools on improving education through research and experimentation, excellence in clinical and teaching practices, staff development, and student teaching. Since the NALS website is now IALS, the information about NALS is presently inaccessible; however, IALS identifies the essential components of the child development laboratory schools to include curriculum development, educational experimentation, professional development, research, and teacher training (Dillon & Pinedo-Burns, 2017).

VanTil (1969) provided the most positive projection for the contemporary child development laboratory school:

> To this center of educational enlightenment would journey educators from near and far to observe the best in education. They would then return to their schools to put new ideas into practice, thus raising the level of American education. The laboratory school would be the pride of the college and university administration, the joy of parents fortunate enough to have young people enrolled therein, and the darling of state legislators, boards of trustees, and philanthropists. (Van Til, 1969, p. 1)

Although this proposed model is approximately 50 years old, a limited number of child development laboratory schools have fulfilled Van Til's view of the perfect representation. A report of the NALS (Ulm et al., 1989) states that the benefit of the laboratory school is its structured setting for research and clinical teacher preparation. Reaching these ends will establish the value of the child development laboratory schools in the improvement of teacher education in America. In addition, since VanTil's (1969) concept has not been observed in these schools, this expectation would be appropriate for the future. In the future, child development laboratory schools can continuously reexamine their three-part mission statement to confirm that they meet their purposes. Carnahan and Doyle (2012) believe that this process will keep them stimulated, concentrated, inventive, constructive, and invigorated. Cucchiara (2010) points out that laboratory schools have their own purpose and are unique to their mission rather than "be everything to everyone" (Jozwiak & Vera, 2016, p. 15). Jozwiak and Vera (2016) discovered that "there is no single formula for what makes a university laboratory school sustainable" (p. 16). There is not a particular mission statement that can guarantee a child development laboratory school's stability in the future.

THEORETICAL FRAMEWORK AND RECOMMENDATIONS FOR STABILITY

Elicker and Barbour (2012) raise the question, "What is the future of university laboratory schools in the twenty-first century?" (p. 140). They searched for an answer to this question in a special issue that they edited for the *Early Education and Development* journal. They concentrated on the child development laboratory schools' research mission through (a) generally analyzing their fluctuating roles in recent higher education institutions and (b) describing up-to-date groundbreaking research. Several researchers proposed some recommendations. For example, File (2012) and McBride and colleagues (2012) provided recommendations on how research on child development laboratory schools can be pertinent now. They proposed different but compatible suggestions. File (2012) claimed that the child development laboratory schools are exclusively well-matched for research relating to using the setting for careful inquiry about teaching and learning as well as young children's experiences and learning. In addition, studies can be combined with the teaching and service missions. She indicated that their supportive settings offer researchers the opportunity to conduct in-depth studies through qualitative research methodologies and teacher–researcher partnerships.

Applied Developmental Science Framework

McBride and colleagues (2012) use applied developmental science (Learner, Wertlieb, & Jacobs, 2005) as a framework to synthesize research and its practical uses in early childhood education. They contend that this method consists of meticulous research but still incorporates the conventional teaching and service missions of the child development laboratory schools. For instance, faculty-guided research may engage college students in an early childhood class to investigate questions of importance to early childhood teachers and children in the child development laboratory schools. Furthermore, McBride and colleagues (2012) encourage that future research be conducted in cooperation with several child development laboratory schools. They can combine their data to increase the studies' statistical power, diversity in their samples, and meticulous differences in practice.

Barbour and McBride (2017) recommend that in the future, child development laboratory schools need to include an applied developmental science framework. "Applied developmental science (ADS) is scholarship that seeks to advance the integration of developmental research with actions—policies and programs—that promote positive development and/or enhance the life chances of vulnerable children and families" (Learner, Fisher, & Weinberg, 2000, p. 11). The integration of ADS may be the a most important way to promote "a science for and of the people" (Learner, et al., 2000, p. 11). It may provide a model for scholarship and community collaboration that influences social justice to transfer the model of amelioration, prevention, or expansion of research from representing efficiency to fostering outreach. Such provision in the setting of university–community collaborations can be used as an ADS model on the way higher education can involve policy makers, influence community ability to maintain esteemed programs, and preserve civil society using knowledge-based, interinstitutional systems modification (Learner, Fisher, & Weinberg, 1997, 2000; Learner et al., 2005). ADS can be an influential supporter of the child development laboratory schools in their pursuit to continue their critical function in the conventional three-part mission statement of research, service, and professional preparation. In addition, ADS can provide understandings that can guide and reform activities in the child development laboratory schools. Lastly, engaging policy associates as partners can affect social policy in the child development laboratory schools. ADS is primary all applied work, which particularly affects children, families, policymakers, and practitioners (Learner et al., 2000, 2005). Barbour and McBride (2017) highlight certain characteristics of ADS as defined by Lerner and his associates (1997, 2000, 2005):

- It's *applied in* nature.
- The *developmental* component speaks to the assessment of development across the lifespan and across contexts.
- *Science* implies the need to consider a variety of methodologies for systematic, intentional inquiry that leads to putting theory into practice (Barbour & McBride, 2017, p. 2).

The child development laboratory schools have been self-sufficient, which restricts their authority to affect policy and practice on a far-reaching extent. Therefore, Learner and his colleagues (2005) proposed that the different child development laboratory schools unite to conduct research on real-world problems in a multiplicity of community settings, concentrating on the critical analyses of research with practical functions in a high quality early childhood education environment. According to McBride and his colleagues (2012) contend that this method should conduct meticulous studies but also incorporate the conventional teaching and service missions of the child development laboratory schools. These high quality components indicate the following:

- It is critical to have a clearly defined mission, a plan for addressing the mission, and a means for documenting accomplishments.
- At least some funding should be secure; reliance on "soft" money may rob a site of energy and control.
- Collaboration across disciplines is not easy, but it expands the potential for diverse endeavors.
- Strong personalities can be both helpful in defining the work of the site, but they can also limit the work.
- The strength of a site is in its ability to balance the three-part mission of research, training, and service.
- Laboratory settings must be sensitive and responsive to the surrounding communities (local, national, intellectual). (Barbour, 2003, p. 28)

Advanced research paradigms and theoretical frameworks have emerged to conduct studies in these settings. Frameworks, like ADS, can be used as a foundation to think through this period of exploration and the setting can indicate ways to stimulate a theoretical development, enhancement, and sustained rigor in examining different types and issues of research in the child development laboratory schools. It is important to keep in mind that their progress is an incomplete task. Researchers need to evaluate their area of interest to determine the next steps.

Research Modifications

Nevertheless, modifications throughout the years in child development research methodologies, the measure of contemporary child studies, demographic variations in the United States, and main financial burdens have united to test the applicability of conventional child development laboratory schools. For instance, presently child development research frequently has bigger, more varied samples of subjects. The important clinical features of early childhood teacher preparation may be improved in the representative community location that includes a variety of individuals. In addition, the essential mission of the child development laboratory schools can propose high-quality early childhood education and family assistance to children of the university faculty, staff, and students, which may be delegated to those early childhood programs that are currently well-known in nearby communities. Thus, programs at the university child development laboratory schools may be seldom used as the single source of high-quality child care, early education, and parent education (Elicker & Barbour, 2012).

CONCLUSION

Although the volume has a wide representation of topics on child development laboratory schools, there continues to be a void in the research literature. A wide-ranging scale of studies needs to be conducted to fill the gaps and offer insights about the children's child development laboratory schools. However, the chapters in this volume can provide knowledge and a better understanding in some areas on child development laboratory schools.

REFERENCES

Anderson, O. A. (1992). A national profile of child development laboratory schools (Master's thesis). Utah State University. Retrieved from All Graduate Theses and Dissertations. (Paper 2355).

Applegate, J. H., & Lasley, T. J. (1982). Cooperating teachers' problems with preservice field experience students. *Journal of Teacher Education, 33*(2), 15–18. doi:10.1177/002248718203300203

Barbour, N. (2003). The early history of child development laboratory programs. In B. McBride & N. Barbour (Eds.), *Bridging the gap between theory, research and practice: The role of child development laboratory programs in early childhood education* (pp. 9–29). Kidlington, Oxford: Elsevier.

Barbour, N. E., & McBride, B. A. (2017). An introduction to the future of child development laboratory settings: A consortium for applied. In N. E. Barbour & B. A. McBride (Eds.), *The future of child development lab schools: Applied developmental science in action* (pp. 1–3). New York, NY: Taylor and Francis.

Bonar, B. D. (1992). The role of laboratory schools in American education. *National Association of Laboratory Schools Journal, 17*(1), 42–53.

Brinson, D. (2012). Building international partnerships: Country to country, school to school. *The International Association of Laboratory Schools Journal, 2*(2), Article 1. Retrieved from https://digitalcommons.ric.edu/nals/vol2/iss2/1/

Buck, C. L., Hymel, R., McDonald,G., Martin,J. J., & Rodgers, T. S. (1991). Functions in laboratory schools. In National Association of Laboratory Schools (Eds.), *Laboratory schools: An educational resource* (pp. 23–34). Honolulu, HI: Curriculum Research and Development Group.

Carnahan, S., & Doyle, D. T. (2012). College mission alignment: Lessons for laboratory schools. *National Association of Laboratory Schools Journal, 4*(1), article 2. Retrieved from http://digitalcommons.ric.edu/nals/vol4/iss1/2

Cucchiara, M. (2010). New goals, familiar challenges?: A brief history of university-run schools. *Penn GSE Perspectives on Urban Education, 7*(1), 96–108.

Dillon, A., & Pinedo-Burns, H. (2017). Intercultural reflective conversations: Fulfilling the mission of laboratory schools in the United Arab Emirates and United States. *International Association of Laboratory Schools Journal, 7*(1), 14–23.

Durst, A. (2010). John Dewey and the beginnings of the laboratory school. In A. Durst (Ed.), *Women educators in the progressive era* (pp. 9–24). New York, NY: Palgrave Macmillan.

Elicker, J., & Barbour, N. (2012). Introduction to the special issue on university laboratory preschools in the 21st century. *Early Education & Development, 23*(2), 139–142. doi:10.1080/10409289.2012.649665

Emmert, H. A., & Pearson, D. L. (2007). Expanding the vision of international education: Collaboration, assessment and intercultural development. *New Directions for Community Colleges, 138*(9), 67–75. doi:10.1002/cc.283

Erdman, J. I. (1983). Assessing the purposes of early field experience programs. *Journal of Teacher Education, 34*(4), 27–31.

European Commission/EACEA/ Eurydice. (2017). *The structure of the European education systems 2017/18: Schematic diagrams: Eurydice facts and figures*. Luxembourg: Publications Office of the European Union.

File, N. (2012). Identifying and addressing challenges to research in university laboratory preschools. *Early Education & Development, 23*(2), 143–152. doi:10.108 0/10409289.2012.619136

Given, H., Juh, L., LeeKeenan, D., Mardell, B., Redditt, S., & Twombly, S. (2009). Changing school culture: Using documentation to support collaborative inquiry. *Theory into Practice, 49*(1), 36–46. doi:10.1080/00405840903435733

Goldhaber, J. (2007). The development of an early childhood teacher research collaborative. *Theory into Practice, 46*(1), 74–80. doi:10.1080/00405840709336551

Goodlad, J. I. (1980). How laboratory schools go awry. *UCLA Educator, 21*(2), 46–33.

Haberman, M. (1985). Fifty-one predictions regarding teacher education. *Teacher Education and Practice, 2*(1), 52–60.

Hendrick, I. G. (1980). University controlled laboratory schools in historical perspective. *UCLA Educator, 21*(2), 55–59.

International Association of Laboratory Schools. (2018). About Us. Retrieved from http://laboratoryschools.org/about-us/16-about-us

Jozwiak, M., & Vera, D. (2016). Unraveling the threads that have preserved university laboratory schools: A qualitative study on sustainability. *The International Association of Laboratory Schools Journal, 6*(1), 13–19.

Keislar, E. R. (1980). The inquiry-oriented laboratory school. *UCLA Educator, 21*(2), 26–31.

Learner, R. M., Fisher, C. B., & Weinberg, R. A. (1997). Applied developmental science: Scholarship for our times. *Applied Developmental Science, 1*(1), 2–3.

Learner, R. M., Fisher, C. B., & Weinberg, R. A. (2000). Toward a science for and of the people: Promoting civil society through the application of developmental science. *Child Development, 71*(1), 11–20. doi:10.1111/1467-8624.00113

Learner, R. M., Wertlieb, D., & Jacobs, F. (2005). Historical and theoretical bases of applied developmental science. In R. M. Learner, F. Jacob, & D. Wertlieb (Eds.), *Applied developmental science: An advanced textbook* (pp. 1–29). Thousand Oaks, CA: SAGE. doi:10.4135/9781452233512.n1

McBride , B., Groves, M., Barbour, N., Horm, D., Stremmel, A., Lash, M.,... Toussaint, S. (2012). Child development laboratory schools as generators of knowledge in early childhood education: New models and approaches. *Early Education & Development, 23*(2), 153–164. doi:10.1080/10409289.2012.651068

McBride, B. (1996). University-based child development laboratory programs: Emerging issues and challenges. *Early Childhood Education Journal, 24*(1), 17–21.

McDonald, R. E. (2007). An Investigation of innovation in nonprofit organizations: The role of organizational mission. *Nonprofit and Voluntary Sector Quarterly, 36*(2), 256–281. doi:10.1177/0899764006295996

Meacham, J. (2008). What's the use of a mission statement? *Academe, 94*(1), 21–24.

National Organization of Child Development Laboratory Schools. (1993). *The national organization of child development laboratory schools 1989 directory.* Salt Lake City, UT: Author.

Nielsen, R. A. (1986, February). *Laboratory schools: Blueprint for success.* Paper presented at the meeting of the Annual Convention of the National Association of Laboratory Schools, Chicago, IL. Retrieved from ERIC database. (ED273626)

Osborn, D. K. (1991). Early childhood education in historical perspective (3rd ed.). Athens, GA: Education Associates.

Page, F., & Page, J. A. (1981). Laboratory schools: Updated or Outdated? Retrieved from ERIC database. (ED213672)

Provenzo, E. F. (1979). History as experiment: The role of the laboratory school in the development of John Dewey's philosophy of history. *History Teacher, 12*(3), 373–382.

Ross, S. M., Raines, F. B., Cervetti, M. J., & Dellow, D. A. (1980). Field experiences for teacher candidates: A comparison between tutorial and apprenticeship programs on student activities and attitudes. *Journal of Teacher Education, 31*(6), 57–61. doi:10.1177/002248718003100621

Taylor, B. J., & Morphew, C. C. (2010). An analysis of baccalaureate college mission statements. *Research in Higher Education, 51*(5), 483–503. doi:10.1007/s11162-010-9162-7

The Conversation. (2017, June 12, June 12). *Laboratory schools: A new educational phenomenon.* Retrieved from https://theconversation.com/laboratory-schools-a-new-educational-phenomenon-79071

Townley, K. E., & Zeece, E. D. (1991). Managing the mission: The primary challenge to campus child care. *Early Childhood Research Quarterly, 6*(1), 19–27. doi:10.1016/0885-2006(91)90019-H

Ulm, G., Buck, C., Creek, R., Tobin, W., & Miller, K. (1989). The various education reform reports on teacher education in the U.S. from 1983 to present day. Cambridge, OH: National Association of Laboratory Schools Salt Fork Task Force. Retrieved from https://www.laboratoryschools.org/attachments/article/99/NALS-Salt-Fork-Task-Force-Report.pdf

Van Til, W. (1969). *The laboratory school: Its rise and fall?* Laboratory School Administrators Association. Terre Haute, IN: Indiana State University. Retrieved from ERIC database. (ED034703)

Wang, J., Gibson, A. M., Salinas, L., Solis, F., & Slate, J. R. (2007). Thematic Differences in Mission Statements between Four-Year Public Institutions and Two-Year Colleges in Texas. *International Electronic Journal for Leadership in Learning, 11,* Article 1. Retrieved from https://files.eric.ed.gov/fulltext/EJ987299.pdf

ABOUT THE CONTRIBUTORS

Nancy Barbour is professor emeritus in the College of Education, Health, and Human Services at Kent State University. Her research has focused on the preparation of the early childhood workforce, particularly within child development laboratory schools in university settings. She is on the editorial board of *Child and Youth Care Forum, European Early Childhood Education Research Journal,* and *Early Education and Development.* She is a book series editor for the European Early Childhood Education Research Association series, *Towards an Ethical Praxis in Early Childhood: Research Into Practice.* She has recently coedited an international book on early childhood policy for SAGE.

Sharon Carnahan is professor of psychology, Cornell Professor of Service, and executive director of the Hume House Child Development and Student Research Center at Rollins College (since 1991). She is a prevention scientist whose primary areas of interest are program evaluation, community engagement, developmental screening and early identification, preschool inclusion, and child development laboratory schools. She has authored more than 50 publications and presentations, and also writes about mental health, women in the Academy, and religion in blogs and informal sources. She is the author of the *Ages and Stages Manager* and *Six Steps to Screening Success* (Paul H. Brookes).

Meghan Fisher is currently a doctoral candidate at the University of Illinois at Urbana–Champaign (UIUC) in the Department of Human Development and Family Studies (HDFS). She has spent the past 5 years involved with coordinating and executing research projects at the university's Child

Contemporary Perspectives on Research on Child Development Laboratory Schools in Early Childhood Education, pages 213–216

Development Laboratory (CDL). Her research focuses on early childhood educators' professional development, specifically, on nutrition and feeding practices.

Rochelle Hostler is the International Baccalaureate Primary Years Program coordinator at the Kent State University Child Development Center and a lecturer for the School of Teaching, Learning, and Curriculum Studies. Rochelle facilitates the Primary Years Program at the Child Development Center through the study of teacher's inquiries with children, the engagement of faculty in reflective practices, and the implementation of authentic assessment. The majority of her career has focused on the planning and facilitation of social constructivist curriculum in early years contexts. Rochelle holds a Master of Arts in human development from Pacific Oaks College.

Pam Hutchins currently serves as the coordinator of the children's program–admissions at the Kent State University Child Development Center and a lecturer for the School of Teaching, Learning, and Curriculum Studies. She has been a preschool teacher in community child care and parent cooperative programs in northeastern Ohio. She holds degrees in individual and family studies and early childhood education, both from Kent State University.

Jennifer Kampmann is an assistant professor in the Department of Teaching, Learning, and Leadership at South Dakota State University. She also serves as assessment and accreditation coordinator in the College of Education and Human Science. Her scholarship is focused on the impact of socio-emotional development on academic achievement in at risk youth and benefits of inquiry based learning. Dr. Kampmann teaches undergraduate teacher education students in early childhood education and has been a teacher in the Fishback Center for Early Childhood Education.

Rachel Langford is an associate professor in the School of Early Childhood Studies at Ryerson University, Toronto, Canada. From 2006 to 2016 she served as the director of the school. She is a co-editor of the volume, *Caring for Children: Social Movements and Public Policy in Canada* (2017, UBC Press) and editor of a forthcoming volume, *Theorizing Feminist Ethics of Care in Early Childhood Practice: Possibilities and Dangers* (Bloomsbury Academic Press). Her current research project, *Caring About Care: An Examination of Care in Canadian Childcare*, is funded by the Social Sciences and Humanities Research Council of Canada.

Martha Lash is an associate professor of early childhood education and coordinator of the International Baccalaureate Primary Years Program certificate program at Kent State University. Early childhood education research interests include professional development, curriculum, and cultural understandings of early childhood issues.

Monica Miller Marsh is associate professor and director of the Kent State University Child Development Center. Her areas of interest include family diversity, early childhood, and curriculum. She is cofounder of the Family Diversity Education Council and the *Journal of Family Diversity in Education*.

Brent A. McBride is a professor in the Department of Human Development and Family Studies (HDFS) at the University of Illinois at Urbana–Champaign (UIUC), where he also serves as the director of the Child Development Laboratory (CDL) program, and as a professor of nutritional sciences. As director of the CDL for the past 29 years, Dr. McBride has been actively engaged in working with investigators from a variety of disciplines on the UIUC campus as they explore protocols and approaches for studying young children's development in the context of classroom environments as well as in laboratory settings.

Lisha O'Sullivan is currently acting head of the Department of Reflective Pedagogy and Early Childhood Studies at Mary Immaculate College (MIC), Limerick. Lisha lectures on the Bachelor of Arts in Early Childhood Care and Education (BAECCE) program, the Bachelor of Education (BEd) program at MIC, and also supervises students' research at undergraduate, master's, and PhD levels. A qualified play therapist, Lisha has extensive experience in the area of early childhood education and her research interests include developmentally appropriate pedagogy and curricula in the early years; self-regulation and play. Lisha has published widely in these areas.

Megan Purcell is clinical faculty for the Early Childhood Education and Exceptional Needs program at Purdue University. Her main priority is the development and mentoring of preservice teacher education candidates preparing them for working with children ages birth through third grade, with and without disabilities. Having been in teacher education for over 15 years, Dr. Purcell works hard to ensure candidates have access to best practices and innovative approaches in early childhood education in order to continue to move the field forward ensuring high quality early education and care for all young children.

Emer Ring is professor and dean of Early Childhood and Teacher Education at Mary Immaculate College (MIC), Limerick. Emer lectures on early childhood and teacher education programmes in addition to supervising research at undergraduate, master's and PhD levels. Emer is consultant supervisor for students during practicum experiences. Emer has been principal investigator on a range of national research projects and her research interests include policy and practice in early childhood and elementary education, inclusion, autism and the work of John Dewey. Emer has published and presented widely in these areas.

Marie Ryan is an educational psychologist and lectures on developmental and educational psychology at Mary Immaculate College (MIC), Limerick. Marie is a member of the Department of Reflective Pedagogy and Early Childhood Studies. Marie lectures on the Bachelor of Arts in early childhood care and education (BAECCE) program and the Bachelor of Education (BEd) programs at MIC. Marie has extensive experience in the area of early childhood and primary education. Marie's research interests include developmental and educational psychology, assessment, inclusion, and the concept of the teacher as researcher. Marie has published widely in these areas.

Elizabeth Schlesinger-Devlin is the director of the Miller Child Development Laboratory School at Purdue University. Her focus is in fostering research within the context of early childhood programs and applying research findings, particularly in the area of curriculum and instruction, in the early childhood setting.

Andrew Stremmel is professor in the Department of Teaching, Learning, and Leadership at South Dakota State University. His research interests are in the area of early childhood teacher education, in particular teacher action research and inquiry-based practices. He is former director of the laboratory school at Virginia Tech.

Rebecca Anne Swartz serves as an early learning specialist in the Department of Special Education at the University of Illinois at Urbana Champaign (UIUC). In this role, she serves as a content specialist for training and technical assistance projects in early care and education, and early intervention. Swartz completed her doctorate in human development and family studies at the UIUC. She has served in a variety of roles in early care and education settings since 1996, beginning as an assistant teacher in a community childcare program and has since served in a variety of roles in the early childhood field in the realms of research, outreach, special education, and child care. Her research and outreach work focuses on infant-toddler care, home-based child care, and the social-emotional development of young children.

D. Reece Wilson is an assistant professor in the Department of Early, Elementary, and Reading Education in the College of Education at James Madison University where he teaches elementary education courses. He was the director of the Young Children's Program at James Madison University for 3 years. His research interests are in early literacy and early childhood workforce development. He provides leadership for the local National Association for the Education of Young Children (NAEYC) chapter.